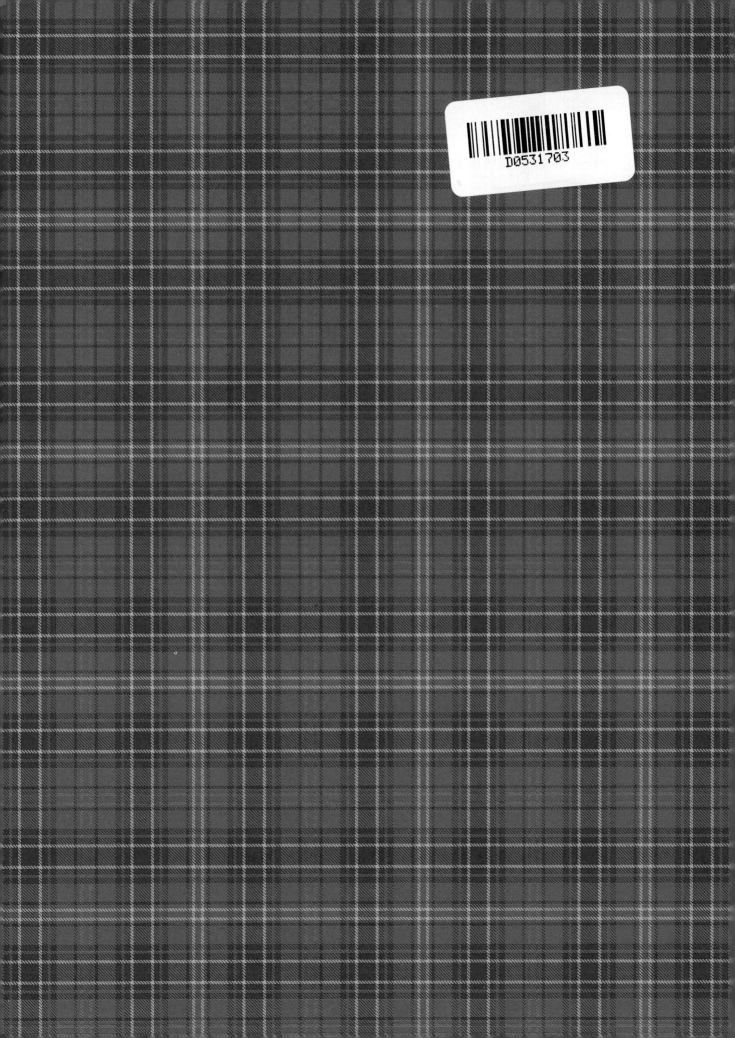

Christmas

RDA ENTHUSIAST BRANDS, LLC
MILWAUKEE, WI

Taste of Home

EDITORIAL

Editor-in-Chief **CATHERINE CASSIDY**
Creative Director **HOWARD GREENBERG**
Editorial Operations Director **KERRI BALLIET**

Managing Editor/Print & Digital Books **MARK HAGEN**
Associate Creative Director **EDWIN ROBLES JR.**

Editor **MICHELLE ROZUMALSKI**
Associate Editor **MOLLY JASINSKI**
Art Director **JESSIE SHARON**
Layout Designer **NANCY NOVAK**
Editorial Production Manager **DENA AHLERS**
Copy Chief **DEB WARLAUMONT MULVEY**
Copy Editors **DULCIE SHOENER, MARY-LIZ SHAW**
Contributing Copy Editor **STEPH KILEN**
Editorial Intern **MICHAEL WELCH**

Food Editors **JAMES SCHEND; PEGGY WOODWARD, RD**
Recipe Editors **MARY KING; JENNI SHARP, RD; IRENE YEH**
Content Operations Assistant **SHANNON STROUD**
Editorial Services Administrator **MARIE BRANNON**

Test Kitchen & Food Styling Manager **SARAH THOMPSON**
Test Cooks **NICHOLAS IVERSON (LEAD), MATTHEW HASS, LAUREN KNOELKE**
Food Stylists **KATHRYN CONRAD (LEAD), SHANNON ROUM, LEAH REKAU**
Prep Cooks **BETHANY VAN JACOBSON (LEAD), MEGUMI GARCIA, MELISSA FRANCO, SARA WIRTZ**

Photography Director **STEPHANIE MARCHESE**
Photographers **DAN ROBERTS, JIM WIELAND**
Photographer/Set Stylist **GRACE NATOLI SHELDON**
Set Stylist **STACEY GENAW, MELISSA HABERMAN, DEE DEE JACQ**
Photo Studio Assistant **ESTER ROBARDS**
Creative Contributors **MARK DERSE (PHOTOGRAPHER), PAM STASNEY (SET STYLIST & CRAFTS), NANCY SEAMAN (SET STYLIST)**

Editorial Business Manager **KRISTY MARTIN**
Editorial Business Associate **SAMANTHA LEA STOEGER**

Editor, *Taste of Home* **JEANNE AMBROSE**
Associate Creative Director, *Taste of Home* **ERIN BURNS**
Art Director, *Taste of Home* **KRISTIN BOWKER**

BUSINESS

Vice President, Group Publisher **KIRSTEN MARCHIOLI**
Publisher, *Taste of Home* **DONNA LINDSKOG**
General Manager, Taste of Home Cooking School **ERIN PUARIEA**
Executive Producer, Taste of Home Online Cooking School **KAREN BERNER**

THE READER'S DIGEST ASSOCIATION, INC.

President and Chief Executive Officer **BONNIE KINTZER**
Chief Financial Officer **TOM CALLAHAN**
Vice President, Chief Operating Officer, North America **HOWARD HALLIGAN**
Chief Revenue Officer **RICHARD SUTTON**
Chief Marketing Officer **LESLIE DUKKER DOTY**
Vice President, Content Marketing & Operations **DIANE DRAGAN**
Senior Vice President, Global HR & Communications **PHYLLIS E. GEBHARDT, SPHR**
Vice President, Brand Marketing **BETH GORRY**
Vice President, Chief Technology Officer **ANEEL TEJWANEY**
Vice President, Consumer Marketing Planning **JIM WOODS**

COVER PHOTOGRAPHY

Photographer **JIM WIELAND**
Food Stylist **SUE DRAHEIM**
Set Stylist **DEE DEE JACQ**

© 2015 RDA Enthusiast Brands, LLC
1610 N. 2nd St., Suite 102, Milwaukee WI 53212-3906

International Standard Book Number: 978-1-61765-451-0
International Standard Serial Number: 1948-8386
Component Number: 119600026H

PICTURED ON THE BACK COVER: Holiday Crown Roast Pork (p. 47), Holiday Chicken & Sausage Wreath (p. 8), Favorite Hazelnut-Mocha Torte (p. 130), Festive Holiday Punch (p. 88).

ADDITIONAL PHOTOGRAPHY USED: Nattle/Shutterstock.com (endpapers); S-F/Shutterstock.com (p. 1); kitty/Shutterstock.com (p. 3); Subbotina Anna/Shutterstock.com (p. 4).

Taste of Home Christmas

- HOLLY BUTTER MINTS, P. 123
- GINGER & MAPLE MACADAMIA NUT COOKIES, P. 150
- SUGAR DOVES, P. 121
- CHOCOLATE REINDEER, P. 115
- SWEETHEART COCONUT COOKIES, P. 122
- GINGERBREAD PEPPERMINT PINWHEELS, P. 73
- SANTA CLAUS SUGAR COOKIES, P. 120

Taste of Home ✳ CHRISTMAS

Contents

Christmas Eve Appetizers 5

Sparkling Brunch 21

Holiday Dinners 39

Jolly Gingerbread 65

Seasonal Get-Togethers 77

Entertaining Shortcuts 95

Cute Confections 113

Elegant Desserts 129

Stocking Stuffer Gifts 147

After-Holiday Feasts 161

Deck the Halls 179

Gifts to Give 205

Recipe and Craft Indexes 230

Spread cheer all season long with
TASTE OF HOME CHRISTMAS

In this exciting holiday treasury, you'll discover hundreds of brand-new ideas for making Christmas get-togethers unforgettable. Share scrumptious food, heartwarming gifts, sparkling decorations and much more, all in these convenient chapters:

CHRISTMAS EVE APPETIZERS. On that magical night before Christmas, tide over your family and friends with a spread featuring the merriest of munchies.

SPARKLING BRUNCH. The holiday season will shine even brighter with a Christmas-morning buffet full of dazzling treats, from gooey caramel rolls to bubbly mimosas.

HOLIDAY DINNERS. Starring main courses of pork roast, chicken and lobster, these three complete menus give you sensational choices. Enjoy bonus recipes, too!

JOLLY GINGERBREAD. Love that Christmastime treat? These sugar-and-spice recipes put a gingerbread twist on scones, muffins, cupcakes and more.

SEASONAL GET-TOGETHERS. Celebrate with a festive themed party! Host a coffee get-together, Christmas tree-trimming event or New Year's Eve bash.

ENTERTAINING SHORTCUTS. Thanks to convenience products and quick ideas, these favorites will impress yuletide guests without keeping you in the kitchen.

CUTE CONFECTIONS. How adorable! Make your holiday platter even harder to resist with an array of the most whimsical cookies and candies imaginable.

ELEGANT DESSERTS. Frosted layer cakes, golden fruit pies, luscious cheesecakes...any of the Christmasy delights here will put the crowning touch on your meal.

STOCKING STUFFER GIFTS. These popular homemade goodies from the kitchen are perfect to tuck into a loved one's stocking—or a tin, bag or basket!

AFTER-HOLIDAY FEASTS. Transform that turkey, ham and other leftover food from your special dinner into new dishes your family will request time and again.

DECK THE HALLS. With the do-it-yourself decorations in this crafty chapter, you'll dazzle guests with gorgeous holiday decor throughout your home.

GIFTS TO GIVE. Handmade Christmas presents are the most heartwarming. Choose from beautiful gifts you can easily create for everyone on your list.

With the merry yuletide ideas packed inside Taste of Home Christmas, you'll make this holiday season your family's most memorable ever!

CHRISTMAS EVE
APPETIZERS

Crab Crescent Triangles

PREP: 30 MIN. • **BAKE:** 10 MIN.
MAKES: 40 APPETIZERS

- **1 package (8 ounces) cream cheese, softened**
- **2 teaspoons mayonnaise**
- **1½ teaspoons Dijon mustard**
- **1½ cups (6 ounces) shredded Colby-Monterey Jack cheese**
- **¾ cup shredded carrot (about 1 medium)**
- **¼ cup finely chopped celery**
- **2 green onions, chopped**
- **1 garlic clove, minced**
- **1 can (6 ounces) lump crabmeat, drained**
- **2 tubes (8 ounces each) refrigerated seamless crescent dough sheet**

1. Preheat oven to 375°. In a large bowl, beat cream cheese, mayonnaise and mustard until blended. Stir in the shredded cheese, carrot, celery, green onions and garlic. Gently fold in crab.

2. Unroll crescent dough and roll into a 12½x10-in. rectangle. Cut each sheet into twenty 2½-in. squares.

3. Spoon a heaping teaspoonful of crab mixture diagonally over half of each square to within ½ in. of edges. Fold one corner of dough over filling to opposite corner, forming a triangle. Pinch seams to seal; press edges with a fork. Place on ungreased baking sheets. Bake 8-10 minutes or until golden brown.

Roasted Cheddar Herb Almonds

I prepared these almonds one Christmas for my son, who was on a low-carb diet. I was afraid he'd be disappointed because he couldn't eat holiday cookies, but these made up for it—he loved them!

—**MARY BILYEU** ANN ARBOR, MI

PREP: 10 MIN. • **BAKE:** 20 MIN. + COOLING
MAKES: 2 CUPS

- 1 egg yolk
- 2 cups unblanched almonds
- ¾ cup finely shredded sharp cheddar cheese
- 1 teaspoon salt-free herb seasoning blend
- ¾ teaspoon salt
- ½ teaspoon garlic powder

1. Preheat oven to 325°. In a large bowl, whisk the egg yolk; stir in the almonds. In a small bowl, toss sharp cheddar cheese with seasonings. Add to almond mixture; toss to combine. Transfer to a greased 15x10x1-in. baking pan.

2. Bake 20-25 minutes or until cheese is golden brown, stirring occasionally. Cool completely.

Buffalo Chicken Cheese Ball

Cheese and Buffalo wings are so popular on appetizer buffets, I decided to combine the two. Now we enjoy those flavors together on our favorite crackers.

—**REBECCA CLARK** WARRIOR, AL

PREP: 10 MIN. + CHILLING
MAKES: 2 CUPS

- 1 package (8 ounces) cream cheese, softened
- 3 tablespoons Buffalo wing sauce
- 1 envelope ranch salad dressing mix
- 1 cup shredded cooked chicken
- 1 tablespoon finely chopped seeded jalapeno pepper
- ⅓ cup crumbled blue cheese, optional
- ½ cup finely shredded cheddar cheese
  Celery sticks
  Additional crumbled blue cheese and Buffalo wing sauce

1. In a large bowl, beat cream cheese, Buffalo wing sauce and dressing mix until smooth. Add chicken, jalapeno and, if desired, blue cheese; beat until combined. Refrigerate, covered, at least 1 hour.

2. Spread the shredded cheddar cheese on a large piece of plastic wrap. Shape the cream cheese mixture into a ball; roll in the shredded cheddar cheese to coat evenly. Wrap ball in plastic wrap; refrigerate at least 1 hour. Serve with celery and additional blue cheese and Buffalo wing sauce.

NOTE *Wear disposable gloves when cutting hot peppers; the oils can burn skin. Avoid touching your face.*

Holiday Helper

Roasted Cheddar Herb Almonds require just 10 minutes of prep time. Consider making an extra batch to give as a holiday gift or to keep on hand to dress up dinner dishes. For example, you could sprinkle the flavorful nuts over a green salad or mix them into your favorite pasta.

Holiday Chicken & Sausage Wreath

Hearty enough to cut into larger slices as a main dish, this golden wreath brims with a delicious, ooey-gooey filling.

—**JANE WHITTAKER** PENSACOLA, FL

PREP: 30 MIN. • **BAKE:** 25 MIN. + STANDING
MAKES: 16 SERVINGS

- 2 **tubes (8 ounces each) refrigerated crescent rolls**
- ½ **pound bulk pork sausage**
- 1 **carton (8 ounces) spreadable chive and onion cream cheese**
- 1 **can (8 ounces) sliced water chestnuts, drained and finely chopped**
- 1¼ **cups (5 ounces) shredded Swiss cheese**
- 1¼ **cups (5 ounces) shredded part-skim mozzarella cheese**
- 1¼ **cups cubed cooked chicken**
- 3 **green onions, chopped**
- 2 **jalapeno peppers, seeded and minced**
- ¼ **cup finely chopped sweet red pepper**
- ¼ **cup finely chopped green pepper**
- 3 **tablespoons coleslaw salad dressing**
- 2 **teaspoons Worcestershire sauce**
- 1 **teaspoon hot pepper sauce**
- ¼ **teaspoon pepper**

1. Preheat oven to 375°. Unroll the dough and separate into triangles. On an ungreased 12-in. pizza pan, arrange the triangles in a ring with the points toward the outside and the wide ends overlapping, leaving a 3-in. circle open in the center. Press overlapping edges of dough to seal.

2. In a large skillet, cook sausage over medium heat 4-6 minutes or until no longer pink, breaking into crumbles; drain and transfer to a large bowl. Stir in remaining ingredients.

3. Spoon mixture across wide end of triangles. Fold pointed end of triangles over filling, tucking the points under to form a ring (filling will be visible). Bake 25-30 minutes or until golden brown. Let stand 15 minutes before slicing.

NOTE *Wear disposable gloves when cutting hot peppers; the oils can burn skin. Avoid touching your face.*

Holiday Chicken & Sausage Wreath Assembly

1. Arrange the triangles of dough in a ring on the pizza pan, leaving a 3-inch circle open in the center to form the wreath shape. Overlap only about half of the wide end of each dough triangle.

2. Spoon the filling onto the ring and fold the pointed ends of the triangles over the filling. Be sure to tuck the pointed ends underneath the ring so the dough will not bake into the center of the ring.

Shrimp-Stuffed Mushrooms

We indulge in these yummy mushrooms every Christmas and whenever we have company for dinner. With the chopped shrimp in the stuffing, they really stand out from other recipes. Specks of pepper and a sprinkling of fresh parsley add festive touches of red and green for the holidays.
—JACQUI BEAL DALLAS, OR

PREP: 35 MIN. • **BAKE:** 25 MIN.
MAKES: 2 DOZEN

- 24 large fresh mushrooms
- 2 tablespoons butter
- ¼ cup chopped sweet red pepper
- 2 tablespoons finely chopped onion
- 1 garlic clove, minced
- 1 teaspoon Italian seasoning
- ½ teaspoon salt
- 3 tablespoons cream cheese
- 1 cup chopped cooked shrimp
- ½ cup seasoned bread crumbs
- ¼ cup grated Parmesan cheese
  Minced fresh parsley, optional

1. Preheat oven to 350°. Remove the stems from mushrooms; chop enough stems to measure ¾ cup. Discard the remaining stems. Place the mushroom caps in a foil-lined 15x10x1-in. baking pan, stem side up. Bake 10 minutes.
2. Meanwhile, in a large skillet, heat butter over medium-high heat. Add red pepper, onion, garlic, Italian seasoning, salt and chopped stems; cook and stir 2-3 minutes or until tender. Add cream cheese; cook and stir until melted. Stir in shrimp and bread crumbs.
3. Drain the liquid from the caps; fill with the shrimp mixture. Sprinkle with Parmesan cheese. Bake 15-20 minutes longer or until mushrooms are tender and filling is heated through. If desired, sprinkle with parsley.

Zesty Pepperoni Dip

Here's a special snack we all look forward to at Christmastime. I combined one of my mom's cheese ball recipes with a dip from my husband's aunt. For a lighter option, use reduced-fat cream cheese and either reduced-fat or turkey pepperoni.

—HEATHER CHURCH GAFFNEY, SC

START TO FINISH: 15 MIN.
MAKES: 2 CUPS

- 6 ounces sliced pepperoni, chopped (1½ cups)
- 1 package (8 ounces) cream cheese, softened
- 6 tablespoons 2% milk
- 1½ packages Italian salad dressing mix
- 1 tablespoon olive oil
  Dash hot pepper sauce
  Dash Worcestershire sauce
- ½ cup shredded Italian cheese blend
- 2 tablespoons chopped green pepper
- 2 tablespoons finely chopped onion
  Assorted crackers

1. Place the chopped pepperoni on a paper towel-lined microwave-safe plate; microwave, covered, on high for 1-2 minutes or until fat is rendered.
2. In a large bowl, beat cream cheese, milk, salad dressing mix, oil, pepper sauce and Worcestershire sauce until blended. Stir in pepperoni, cheese, green pepper and onion. Serve at room temperature with crackers.

Cocktail Mushroom Meatballs

Tide over even the biggest appetites with beef-and-sausage meatballs in a chunky mushroom sauce. Larger portions served over a bed of hot egg noodles or rice can make a terrific dinner, too.

—DIANE KELLEY MADISON, WI

PREP: 40 MIN. • **COOK:** 25 MIN.
MAKES: ABOUT 4½ DOZEN

- 1 egg
- 1 envelope onion soup mix
- ¼ cup dry bread crumbs
- 1½ teaspoons Worcestershire sauce
- 1½ pounds ground beef
- ½ pound bulk pork sausage

SAUCE
- 1 tablespoon olive oil
- 1 tablespoon butter
- ½ pound sliced baby portobello mushrooms
- ½ pound sliced fresh mushrooms
- 1 small onion, halved and sliced
- 1 garlic clove, minced
- 1 envelope brown gravy mix
- 1 teaspoon minced fresh thyme
- 1 cup water
- ¼ cup white wine
- 1 can (10¾ ounces) condensed cream of mushroom soup, undiluted
- ¼ teaspoon coarsely ground pepper

1. Preheat oven to 400°. In a large bowl, whisk the egg, onion soup mix, dry bread crumbs and Worcestershire sauce. Add the beef and sausage; mix lightly but thoroughly. Shape into 1-in. meatballs. Place meatballs on a greased rack in a 15x10x1-in. baking pan. Bake 12-15 minutes or until browned.
2. Meanwhile, in a 6-qt. stockpot, heat oil and butter over medium-high heat. Add mushrooms and onion; cook and stir 6-8 minutes or until tender. Add garlic; cook 1 minute longer. Stir in the brown gravy mix and thyme. Add water and white wine; bring to a boil, stirring constantly. Cook and stir 1-2 minutes or until thickened.
3. Stir in the cream of mushroom soup, pepper and meatballs; return to a boil. Reduce the heat; simmer, covered, 15-20 minutes or until the meatballs are cooked through.

Bacon, Cheddar and Swiss Cheese Ball

When it's time for a party, nearly everyone I know requests this impressive appetizer. It's great spread on crackers, and it makes a fabulous hostess gift, too.

—SUE FRANKLIN LAKE ST. LOUIS, MO

PREP: 20 MIN. + CHILLING
MAKES: 4 CUPS

- 1 package (8 ounces) cream cheese, softened
- ½ cup sour cream
- 2 cups (8 ounces) shredded Swiss cheese
- 2 cups (8 ounces) shredded sharp cheddar cheese
- 1 cup crumbled cooked bacon (about 12 strips), divided
- ½ cup chopped pecans, toasted, divided
- ½ cup finely chopped onion
- 1 jar (2 ounces) diced pimientos, drained
- 2 tablespoons sweet pickle relish
- ¼ teaspoon salt
- ¼ teaspoon pepper
- ¼ cup minced fresh parsley
- 1 tablespoon poppy seeds
  Assorted crackers

1. In a large bowl, beat the cream cheese and sour cream until smooth. Stir in Swiss cheese, sharp cheddar cheese, ½ cup bacon, ¼ cup pecans, onion, pimientos, sweet pickle relish, salt and pepper. Refrigerate, covered, at least 1 hour.

2. In a small bowl, mix fresh parsley, poppy seeds and remaining bacon and pecans. Spread half of the parsley mixture on a large piece of plastic wrap. Shape half of the cheese mixture into a ball; roll in the parsley mixture to coat evenly. Wrap in plastic wrap. Repeat. Refrigerate at least 1 hour. Serve with assorted crackers.

NOTE *To toast nuts, bake in a shallow pan in a 350° oven for 5-10 minutes or cook in a skillet over low heat until lightly browned, stirring occasionally.*

Maryland Deviled Eggs

Perk up the usual deviled eggs with a dash of seafood seasoning in the filling. Guests will be trying to guess your secret!

—SHANA MOE SHARPTOWN, MD

START TO FINISH: 30 MIN.
MAKES: 4 DOZEN

- 24 **hard-cooked eggs, peeled**
- ½ **cup mayonnaise**
- ¼ **cup honey mustard**
- 3 **tablespoons dill pickle juice**
- 1 **tablespoon seafood seasoning**
  Additional seafood seasoning

1. Cut eggs lengthwise in half. Remove yolks, reserving whites. In a small bowl, mash yolks.
2. Stir in mayonnaise, honey mustard, dill pickle juice and seafood seasoning. Spoon or pipe into egg whites. Sprinkle with additional seafood seasoning. Refrigerate, covered, until serving.

Broccoli-Carrot Vegetable Dip

When you want a lighter option, look here! Reduced-fat ingredients keep things on the healthier side while Worcestershire sauce and a veggie dip mix lend plenty of zip.

—CONNIE BRYANT FARMERS BRANCH, TX

PREP: 15 MIN. + CHILLING
MAKES: 14 SERVINGS (¼ CUP EACH)

- 1 **can (8 ounces) sliced water chestnuts, drained**
- ½ **cup sliced fresh carrots**
- ½ **cup small fresh broccoli florets**
- 1½ **cups (12 ounces) reduced-fat plain yogurt**
- 1 **cup reduced-fat mayonnaise**
- 1 **envelope (1.4 ounces) vegetable recipe mix (Knorr)**
- 1 **teaspoon Worcestershire sauce**
  Assorted fresh vegetables and crackers

1. Place the water chestnuts, carrots and broccoli in a food processor; pulse until finely chopped.
2. Transfer to a small bowl; stir in the plain yogurt, mayonnaise, vegetable recipe mix and Worcestershire sauce. Refrigerate, covered, at least 4 hours to allow the flavors to blend. Serve with vegetables and crackers.

Cranberry Bacon Galette

Sweet, smoky, tangy, fresh...the flavors in this distinctive appetizer are sure to get taste buds ready for dinner. I sprinkle the baked squares with basil and dollop on a Mascarpone cheese topping.

—MERRY GRAHAM NEWHALL, CA

PREP: 25 MIN. • **BAKE:** 20 MIN. + COOLING
MAKES: 12 SERVINGS

- 1 **carton (8 ounces) Mascarpone cheese**
- 1 **tablespoon orange marmalade**
- 1 **tablespoon jellied cranberry sauce**
- 2 **tablespoons sugar**
- 1 **cup chopped red onion**
- 1 **cup dried cranberries**
- ¾ **cup chopped fresh mushrooms**
- 1 **tablespoon olive oil**
- ½ **teaspoon lemon-pepper seasoning**
- ¼ **teaspoon salt**
- ¼ **teaspoon smoked paprika**
- 3 **tablespoons cranberry-tangerine juice**
- 1 **sheet frozen puff pastry, thawed**
- 5 **cooked bacon strips, crumbled**
- ¼ **cup minced fresh basil**

1. Preheat oven to 400°. For topping, in a small bowl, combine Mascarpone cheese, marmalade and cranberry sauce. Refrigerate until serving.
2. In a large skillet, cook the sugar over medium-high heat 1-2 minutes or until it just begins to melt. Add onion; cook and stir 2 minutes longer.
3. Stir in cranberries, mushrooms, oil, lemon pepper, salt and paprika; cook and stir 2 minutes. Reduce heat. Stir in juice; cook and stir until mushrooms are tender, about 4 minutes.
4. Unfold puff pastry onto a greased baking sheet. Spread the cranberry mixture to within 1½ in. of edges; sprinkle with crumbled bacon. Bake 18-22 minutes or until pastry is golden brown. Cool 10 minutes. Sprinkle with basil. Serve warm with topping.

Tuscan Chicken Tenders with Pesto Sauce

Golden bites of breaded chicken? How can you go wrong? Children and adults alike will dig in to these satisfying appetizers. A red and green sauce for dipping adds an Italian accent and festive Christmas color. Serve the tasty little tenders warm or at room temperature, whichever you prefer.
—**MARY LOU COOK** WELCHES, OR

PREP: 20 MIN. • **BAKE:** 25 MIN.
MAKES: 2 DOZEN

- 1¼ **cups cornflake crumbs**
- ½ **cup grated Parmesan cheese, divided**
- ½ **teaspoon salt**
- ½ **cup 2% milk, divided**
- 24 **chicken tenderloins**
- 1 **cup mayonnaise**
- ¼ **cup prepared pesto**
- ½ **teaspoon garlic powder**
- ⅛ **teaspoon pepper**
- 1 **plum tomato, seeded and chopped**
- 1 **tablespoon minced fresh basil**

1. Preheat oven to 350°. In a shallow bowl, mix the cornflake crumbs, ¼ cup Parmesan cheese and salt. Place ¼ cup milk in a separate shallow bowl. Dip the chicken tenderloins in the milk, then in the crumb mixture, patting to help the coating adhere. Place on greased racks in two foil-lined 15x10x1-in. baking pans. Bake 25-30 minutes or until a thermometer reads 165°.
2. Meanwhile, in a small bowl, mix mayonnaise, prepared pesto, garlic powder, pepper and remaining milk and cheese; top with tomato and basil. Serve with chicken.

Holiday Helper

If you'd like to have an appetizer buffet that serves as your meal, plan on setting out five or six different appetizers (including some substantial selections) and providing eight to nine pieces per person. If you'll be serving a meal as well as appetizers, two to three pieces per person is sufficient.

Avocado Goat Cheese Truffles

Give Christmas guests the VIP treatment with change-of-pace avocado truffles you can prepare in your own kitchen.

—ROXANNE CHAN ALBANY, CA

PREP: 45 MIN. + CHILLING
MAKES: 4 DOZEN

- 1 **package (8 ounces) cream cheese, softened**
- ½ **cup shredded pepper jack cheese**
- ¼ **cup fresh goat cheese**
- 1 **garlic clove, minced**
- 1 **teaspoon grated lime peel**
- 1 **teaspoon olive oil**
- ½ **teaspoon chili powder**
- ¼ **teaspoon crushed red pepper flakes**
- 1 **green onion, minced**
- 1 **tablespoon minced fresh cilantro**
- 3 **medium ripe avocados, peeled**
- 1 **tablespoon lime juice**
- 2 **cups salted pumpkin seeds or pepitas, finely chopped**
    Pretzel sticks, optional

1. In a small bowl, beat cheeses, garlic, lime peel, oil, chili powder and pepper flakes until blended. Stir in the green onion and cilantro. Refrigerate 1 hour or until firm.

2. With a small melon baller, scoop out avocado balls onto a baking sheet; sprinkle with the lime juice. Shape 1½ teaspoons cheese mixture around each ball, then roll in seeds. Place balls on a waxed paper-lined baking sheet. Refrigerate until serving. If desired, serve with pretzel sticks.

Pacific Northwest Pickled Shrimp

Friends and family rave about this refreshing sweet-and-sour shrimp. For an elegant presentation, serve it in cocktail glasses.

—**KATHY WRIGHT** HIGHLAND, CA

PREP: 40 MIN. • **COOK:** 5 MIN. + CHILLING
MAKES: ABOUT 2½ DOZEN

- 8 cups water
- ½ cup chopped celery leaves
- ¼ cup mixed pickling spices
- 1 tablespoon salt
- 2 pounds uncooked shell-on shrimp (31-40 per pound)

PICKLING MIXTURE

- 2 large onions, sliced
- 8 bay leaves
- 1½ cups olive oil
- ¾ cup white wine vinegar
- 3 tablespoons capers
- 2½ teaspoons celery seed
- 1¼ teaspoons salt
- ¼ teaspoon hot pepper sauce

1. In a large saucepan, combine the water, celery leaves, pickling spices and salt; bring to a boil. Add shrimp. Reduce heat; simmer, uncovered, 4-6 minutes or until shrimp turn pink. Drain; peel and devein shrimp, leaving tails on.

2. Layer shrimp, onions and bay leaves in a 13x9-in. baking dish. In a small bowl, whisk oil, vinegar, capers, celery seed, salt and hot pepper sauce; pour over shrimp. Refrigerate, covered, 24 hours.

3. Just before serving, drain shrimp; discard the marinade and bay leaves.

Bacon-Ranch Spinach Dip

During the hectic holiday season, my slow cooker works overtime. I fill it with a ranch-flavored spinach dip, let it cook for 2 hours and then watch everyone dive in with fresh vegetables or crackers. Keep this recipe in mind for tailgating, too.

—**CRYSTAL SCHLUETER** NORTHGLENN, CO

PREP: 15 MIN. • **COOK:** 2 HOURS
MAKES: 24 SERVINGS (¼ CUP EACH)

- 2 packages (8 ounces each) cream cheese, softened
- 1½ cups bacon ranch salad dressing
- ¼ cup 2% milk
- 2 cups (8 ounces) shredded sharp cheddar cheese
- 1 can (14 ounces) water-packed artichoke hearts, rinsed, drained and chopped
- 1 package (10 ounces) frozen chopped spinach, thawed and squeezed dry
- 2 plum tomatoes, seeded and finely chopped
- ½ cup crumbled cooked bacon
- 4 green onions, thinly sliced
  Assorted crackers and fresh vegetables

1. In a large bowl, beat the cream cheese, bacon ranch salad dressing and milk until blended. Stir in the cheddar cheese, artichokes, spinach, tomatoes, bacon and green onions. Transfer to a 4- or 5-qt. slow cooker.

2. Cook, covered, on low 2-3 hours or until heated through. Serve with crackers and vegetables.

Brie Appetizers with Bacon-Plum Jam

Among my friends, I'm known as the "Pork Master" because I love to cook with just about every cut there is. These appetizers combine slices of soft, mild Brie cheese with a sweet-sour bacon jam that has a splash of Sriracha sauce.

—RICK PASCOCELLO NEW YORK, NY

PREP: 25 MIN. • **COOK:** 1¼ HOURS
MAKES: 2½ DOZEN

- 1 pound bacon strips, chopped
- 1 cup thinly sliced sweet onion
- 1 shallot, finely chopped
- 5 garlic cloves, minced
- 1 cup brewed coffee
- ½ cup water
- ¼ cup cider vinegar
- ¼ cup pitted dried plums, coarsely chopped
- 3 tablespoons brown sugar
- 1 tablespoon maple syrup
- 1 tablespoon Sriracha Asian hot chili sauce
- ½ teaspoon pepper
- 30 slices Brie cheese (¼ inch thick)
- 30 slices French bread baguette (¼ inch thick), toasted

1. In a large skillet, cook the bacon over medium heat until partially cooked but not crisp. Remove the bacon to paper towels with a slotted spoon; drain, reserving 1 tablespoon drippings.
2. Add onion and shallot to drippings; cook and stir 5 minutes. Add the garlic; cook 2 minutes longer.
3. Stir in the brewed coffee, water, cider vinegar, dried plums, brown sugar, maple syrup, chili sauce and pepper. Bring to a boil. Stir in bacon. Reduce the heat; simmer, uncovered, 1¼ to 1½ hours or until the liquid is syrupy, stirring occasionally. Remove from heat. Cool to room temperature.
4. Transfer the mixture to a food processor; pulse until jam reaches desired consistency. Place Brie cheese slices on the toasted baguette slices. Top each with 2 teaspoons jam.

Seven-Layer Mediterranean Dip

I'm a fan of Mediterranean ingredients, so I used them to create a dip. My husband wolfed it down—and he won't even touch hummus or Greek olives on their own!

—BEE ENGELHART
BLOOMFIELD TOWNSHIP, MI

START TO FINISH: 15 MIN.
MAKES: 2½ CUPS

- 1 carton (8 ounces) hummus
- 1 cup (8 ounces) reduced-fat sour cream
- 1 jar (8 ounces) roasted sweet red peppers, drained and chopped
- ¼ cup crumbled feta cheese
- ¼ cup chopped red onion
- 12 Greek olives, pitted and chopped
- 2 tablespoons chopped fresh parsley
  Baked pita chips

Spread the hummus into a 9-in. pie plate. Top with the sour cream, roasted red peppers, feta cheese, red onion and Greek olives. Sprinkle with the parsley. Refrigerate until serving. Serve with baked pita chips.

Cranberry Salsa with Cream Cheese

Always find yourself short on time when expecting company? This spread is a busy host's dream. The day before, stir together the zippy, Christmasy red salsa, then spoon it over blocks of softened cream cheese when guests arrive. Entertaining doesn't get much easier than that!

—LINDA MATTFIELD EUGENE, OR

PREP: 15 MIN. + CHILLING
MAKES: 3 CUPS SALSA
(2 CUPS CREAM CHEESE)

- 1 package (12 ounces) fresh or frozen cranberries, thawed
- ½ cup sugar
- 4 green onions, sliced
- ¼ cup finely chopped fresh cilantro
- 1 jalapeno pepper, seeded and minced
- 2 tablespoons minced fresh gingerroot
- 2 tablespoons lemon juice
- 2 packages (8 ounces each) cream cheese, softened
  Assorted crackers

1. Place the cranberries in a food processor; pulse until finely chopped. Transfer to a small bowl; stir in the sugar, green onions, cilantro, jalapeno pepper, minced ginger and lemon juice. Refrigerate, covered, at least 4 hours or overnight.

2. Place cream cheese on a serving platter; top with cranberry mixture. Serve with crackers.

NOTE *Wear disposable gloves when cutting hot peppers; the oils can burn skin. Avoid touching your face.*

Holiday Helper

I keep fresh lemon juice on hand because it's such an easy way to add refreshing flavor to recipes. After juicing the lemons, I freeze the juice in ice cube trays. Then I just defrost the amount I need for appetizers, iced teas, poultry, desserts and other dishes.

—JUDY M. SOUTH BEND, IN

Brandied Blue Cheese Spread

Pour on the holiday spirit with a splash of brandy. This rich appetizer features a sprinkling of salted pumpkin seeds, too. It's good not only on the usual crackers, but also on fresh apple wedges.

—T.B. ENGLAND SAN ANTONIO, TX

PREP: 15 MIN. + CHILLING
MAKES: ABOUT 2 CUPS

- 1 package (8 ounces) cream cheese, softened
- 1 package (4 ounces) garlic-herb spreadable cheese
- ¾ cup crumbled blue cheese
- 2 tablespoons brandy
- 1 shallot, finely chopped
- 1 tablespoon minced fresh parsley
- 1 tablespoon honey
- ⅛ teaspoon salt
  Dash pepper
- ¼ cup salted pumpkin seeds or pepitas
  Assorted crackers

1. In a small bowl, mix the first nine ingredients until blended. Transfer to a serving dish; sprinkle with salted pumpkin seeds.

2. Refrigerate, covered, 2 hours before serving. Serve with crackers.

Teriyaki Salmon Bundles

If you're looking to shake up your spread of munchies, try my salmon bites. For a festive display, thread each bundle onto the end of a skewer to form a "pop," then stand them together in a small vase filled with table salt.

—DIANE HALFERTY CORPUS CHRISTI, TX

PREP: 30 MIN. • **BAKE:** 20 MIN.
MAKES: 32 APPETIZERS (¾ CUP SAUCE)

- **4 tablespoons reduced-sodium teriyaki sauce, divided**
- **½ teaspoon grated lemon peel**
- **2 tablespoons lemon juice**
- **1¼ pounds salmon fillets, cut into 1-inch cubes**
- **1 package (17.3 ounces) frozen puff pastry, thawed**
- **⅔ cup orange marmalade**

1. Preheat oven to 400°. In a large bowl, whisk 2 tablespoons teriyaki sauce, lemon peel and juice. Add the salmon; toss to coat. Marinate at room temperature 20 minutes.

2. Drain salmon, discarding marinade. Unfold the puff pastry. Cut each sheet lengthwise into ½-in.-wide strips; cut crosswise in half. Overlap two strips of puff pastry, forming an X. Place a salmon cube in the center. Wrap the puff pastry strips over the salmon; pinch the ends to seal. Place on a greased baking sheet, seam side down. Repeat. Bake 18-20 minutes or until golden brown.

3. In a small bowl, mix the orange marmalade and remaining teriyaki sauce. Serve with salmon bundles.

Reuben Rounds

Fans of Reuben sandwiches will devour baked pastry spirals of corned beef, Swiss and sauerkraut. Bottled Thousand Island dressing makes the perfect dipping sauce.

—CHERYL SNAVELY HAGERSTOWN, MD

START TO FINISH: 30 MIN.
MAKES: 16 APPETIZERS

- 1 **sheet frozen puff pastry, thawed**
- 6 **slices Swiss cheese**
- 5 **slices deli corned beef**
- ½ **cup sauerkraut, rinsed and well drained**
- 1 **teaspoon caraway seeds**
- ¼ **cup Thousand Island salad dressing**

1. Preheat oven to 400°. Unfold puff pastry; layer with cheese, corned beef and sauerkraut to within ½ in. of the edges. Roll up jelly-roll style. Trim the ends and cut crosswise into 16 slices. Place on greased baking sheets, cut side down. Sprinkle with seeds.
2. Bake 18-20 minutes or until golden brown. Serve with salad dressing.

Seasoned Spinach Balls

My mom always made her stuffing-filled spinach bites when she needed something for a holiday party or potluck. And they always disappeared in a flash!

—KAREN MOORE JACKSONVILLE, FL

START TO FINISH: 20 MIN.
MAKES: 2 DOZEN

- 2 **eggs**
- 1½ **cups stuffing mix**
- 1 **package (10 ounces) frozen chopped spinach, thawed and squeezed dry**
- 1 **cup grated Parmesan cheese**
- ½ **cup shredded cheddar cheese**
- ¼ **cup butter, melted**
- ⅛ **teaspoon garlic powder**

1. In a large bowl, whisk eggs. Stir in the remaining ingredients. Shape the mixture into 1¼-in. balls. Place in a microwave-safe dish.
2. Microwave, covered, on high for 3-4 minutes or until cooked through.

SPARKLING BRUNCH

Bacon & Eggs Pizza

At a resort buffet, I sampled a delicious breakfast pizza. Back home, I created my own as an alternative to basic egg bakes.

—**NOELLE MYERS** GRAND FORKS, ND

START TO FINISH: 30 MIN.
MAKES: 6 SLICES

- **8** thick-sliced bacon strips, chopped
- **¼** cup finely chopped onion
- **4** eggs
- **¼** cup grated Parmesan cheese
- **1** teaspoon Italian seasoning
- **¼** teaspoon salt
- **¼** teaspoon pepper
- **1** tablespoon butter

- **1** prebaked 12-inch pizza crust
- **½** cup Alfredo sauce
- **½** cup chopped roasted sweet red peppers
- **⅔** cup shredded cheddar cheese
- **½** cup crumbled queso fresco or shredded part-skim mozzarella cheese

1. Preheat oven to 425°. In a large skillet, cook chopped bacon over medium heat until crisp, stirring occasionally. Remove bacon with a slotted spoon; drain on paper towels. Discard bacon drippings, reserving 1 tablespoon in the pan.

2. Add the onion to bacon drippings; cook and stir over medium-high heat until tender. Remove from the pan. Wipe skillet clean if necessary.

3. In a small bowl, whisk the eggs, Parmesan cheese and seasonings until blended. In the same pan, heat butter over medium-high heat. Pour in the egg mixture; cook and stir until the eggs are almost set.

4. Place pizza crust on an ungreased baking sheet. Spread with the Alfredo sauce. Top with red peppers, bacon, onion and scrambled eggs. Sprinkle with the cheeses. Bake 6-8 minutes or until cheese is melted and eggs are set.

Favorite Loaded Breakfast Potatoes

Kids and adults alike go for spuds filled with cheesy eggs, sour cream, bacon and more.
—**MINDY CAMPBELL** RAPID CITY, MI

PREP: 45 MIN. • **BAKE:** 10 MIN.
MAKES: 6 SERVINGS

- 6 medium baking potatoes (about 3 pounds)
- 1 tablespoon butter
- 1 each small sweet red, orange and green pepper, finely chopped
- 1 cup finely chopped fresh mushrooms
- ¼ cup finely chopped red onion
- ½ teaspoon salt
- ¼ teaspoon pepper
- 6 large eggs, beaten
- 1¼ cups (5 ounces) shredded cheddar cheese, divided
- ¼ cup plus 6 tablespoons sour cream, divided
- 6 bacon strips, cooked and crumbled or ⅓ cup bacon bits
- 3 green onions, chopped

1. Preheat oven to 375°. Scrub and pierce potatoes with a fork; place on a microwave-safe plate. Microwave, uncovered, on high 15-18 minutes or until tender, turning once.

2. When cool enough to handle, cut a thin slice off the top of each potato; discard slice. Scoop out pulp, leaving ¼-in.-thick shells.

3. In a large skillet, heat the butter over medium heat. Add the peppers, mushrooms and onion; cook and stir 4-6 minutes or until tender. Stir in salt, pepper and 1 cup pulp (save remaining pulp for another use). Add eggs; cook and stir until eggs are thickened and no liquid egg remains. Stir in ½ cup cheese and ¼ cup sour cream.

4. Spoon egg mixture into potato shells. Place on a 15x10x1-in. baking pan. Sprinkle with remaining ¾ cup cheese. Bake 10-12 minutes or until heated through and cheese is melted. Top with the remaining sour cream; sprinkle with bacon and green onions.
NOTE *This recipe was tested in a 1,100-watt microwave.*

Western Omelet Casserole

We make a Western-style omelet with ham and shredded hash browns using our slow cooker. It's much easier than the traditional method of fixing one at a time in a skillet on the stove—just scoop out a big helping of casserole for everyone and enjoy!
—**KATHLEEN MURPHY** LITTLETON, CO

PREP: 15 MIN. • **COOK:** 6 HOURS + STANDING
MAKES: 8 SERVINGS

- 1 package (30 ounces) frozen shredded hash brown potatoes, thawed
- 1 pound cubed fully cooked ham or ½ pound pork sausage or bacon strips, cooked and crumbled
- 1 medium onion, chopped
- 1 medium green pepper, chopped
- 1½ cups (6 ounces) shredded cheddar cheese
- 12 large eggs
- 1 cup 2% milk
- 1 teaspoon salt
- 1 teaspoon pepper

1. In a greased 5- or 6-qt. slow cooker, layer half of each of the following: hash brown potatoes, ham, onion, green pepper and cheese. Repeat layers.

2. In a large bowl, whisk the eggs, milk, salt and pepper; pour over top. Cook, covered, on low 6-7 hours or until the eggs are set. Turn off the slow cooker. Remove insert; let stand, uncovered, 15-30 minutes before serving.

Hot Spiced Fruit

Combine pears, apples, berries and mandarin oranges for a tangy side salad or topping. With just a touch of sweetness and spice, it's wonderful served over waffles or pancakes.

—LIN KOPPEN ORCHARD PARK, NY

PREP: 25 MIN. • **BAKE:** 30 MIN. + COOLING • **MAKES:** 12 SERVINGS

- ¼ **cup packed brown sugar**
- 2 **tablespoons cornstarch**
- ¼ **teaspoon ground cinnamon**
- ¼ **teaspoon ground ginger**
- ⅛ **teaspoon ground cloves**
- 1 **cup cranberry or white grape juice**
- 3 **medium pears, peeled and sliced**
- 3 **medium apples, peeled and sliced**
- 1 **cup fresh or frozen cranberries, thawed and chopped**
- 1 **can (11 ounces) mandarin oranges, drained**

1. Preheat oven to 375°. In a small bowl, mix the first five ingredients; gradually whisk in cranberry juice.
2. In a greased 13x9-in. baking dish, combine remaining ingredients. Pour cranberry juice mixture over top.
3. Bake, uncovered, 30-35 minutes or until the pears and apples are tender, stirring once. Let stand 10 minutes before serving. Serve warm or cold.

Blueberry Lime Slush

My husband's family always makes a cranberry beverage for the holidays. I changed up the fruit flavors and serve it both in winter and in summer, when blueberries are in season.

—REBECCA BRATSMAN TACOMA, WA

PREP: 5 MIN. • **COOK:** 15 MIN. + FREEZING
MAKES: 20 SERVINGS (1 CUP EACH)

- 2 **cups sugar**
- 4 **cups water**
- 1 **can (12 ounces) frozen limeade concentrate**
- 1 **can (12 ounces) frozen orange juice concentrate**
- 2 **cups blueberry juice or blueberry juice cocktail**
- 2 **liters regular or diet lemon-lime soda, chilled**
  Fresh or frozen blueberries, optional

1. In a large saucepan, combine the sugar and water; bring to a boil, stirring to dissolve sugar. Cool 30 minutes.
2. Stir the juice concentrates and blueberry juice into the syrup; divide the mixture (about 2 cups each) among five 1½-pint freezer containers. Freeze, covered, overnight or until firm.
3. For each batch, place one portion frozen mixture into a blender; add 1⅔ cups soda. Cover and process just until blended. Serve immediately. If desired, serve with berries.

Caramel-Pecan Pumpkin Pull-Aparts

Warm from the oven, ooey-gooey rolls like these will make any morning special—and Christmas morning even more so!

—**CAROLYN KUMPE** EL DORADO, CA

PREP: 40 MIN. + CHILLING • **BAKE:** 25 MIN.
MAKES: 16 SERVINGS

- ¼ **cup butter, cubed**
- 1 **cup chopped pecans**
- ¾ **cup packed brown sugar**
- ½ **cup heavy whipping cream**
- ¼ **cup honey**

DOUGH

- 1 **package (¼ ounce) active dry yeast**
- ¼ **cup warm water (110° to 115°)**
- 2¼ **to 2½ cups all-purpose flour**
- ¼ **cup sugar**
- 1 **teaspoon pumpkin pie spice**
- ¾ **teaspoon salt**
- ½ **teaspoon baking soda**
- ½ **teaspoon baking powder**
- ½ **teaspoon ground cinnamon**
- ¼ **cup cold butter, cubed**
- ½ **cup solid-pack pumpkin**
- ½ **cup buttermilk**
- 1 **teaspoon vanilla extract**

1. In a small saucepan, melt butter over medium heat. Add pecans; cook and stir 2-3 minutes or until pecans are fragrant. Stir in the brown sugar, cream and honey; cook and stir until the sugar is dissolved and the mixture begins to darken. Pour into a greased 9-in.-square baking pan.

2. In a small bowl, dissolve the yeast in warm water. In a large bowl, whisk 2¼ cups flour, sugar, pumpkin pie spice, salt, baking soda, baking powder and cinnamon. Cut in the butter until crumbly. Add pumpkin, buttermilk, vanilla and yeast mixture; mix well.

3. Turn the dough onto a floured surface; knead gently 8-10 times, adding additional flour if needed. Roll dough into a 9-in. square. Cut into 16 squares; arrange over pecan mixture. Cover with plastic wrap; refrigerate overnight.

4. Remove the pan from refrigerator 30 minutes before baking. Preheat oven to 400°. Uncover; bake 24-28 minutes or until golden brown. Carefully invert onto a platter; serve warm.

Shirred Egg Corn Muffins

Shirred (baked) eggs are delicious and fun to eat. We make ours in little cups of corn bread formed in muffin pans, then drizzle on a homemade cheddar cheese sauce.

—**LISA SPEER** PALM BEACH, FL

PREP: 15 MIN. • **BAKE:** 20 MIN.
MAKES: 1 DOZEN

- 1 package (8½ ounces) corn bread/ muffin mix
- ½ cup buttermilk
- 2 tablespoons sour cream
- ½ cup shredded sharp cheddar cheese
- ½ cup crumbled cooked bacon
- 12 eggs
- ¼ teaspoon salt
- ⅛ teaspoon coarsely ground pepper

TOPPING

- 4 teaspoons butter
- 4 teaspoons all-purpose flour
- 1 cup 2% milk
- 1¼ cups shredded sharp cheddar cheese, divided
- ⅛ teaspoon dried thyme
- ¼ teaspoon seasoned salt, divided

1. Preheat oven to 375°. In a small bowl, combine muffin mix, buttermilk and sour cream just until moistened; fold in cheddar cheese and crumbled bacon. Spoon into 12 greased muffin cups. Crack an egg into each cup; sprinkle with salt and pepper.

2. Bake 18-22 minutes or until the egg whites are completely set and the yolks are still soft. Cool 5 minutes before removing from the pan.

3. Meanwhile, in a small saucepan, melt the butter over medium-low heat. Stir in the flour until smooth; gradually whisk in milk. Bring to a boil, stirring constantly; cook and stir 1-2 minutes or until thickened. Remove from heat. Stir in 1 cup cheddar cheese, thyme and ⅛ teaspoon seasoned salt until the cheese is melted.

4. Serve the muffins with the sauce; sprinkle with the remaining cheese and seasoned salt. Serve immediately.

Pumpkin Crepes with Mascarpone Custard

I tweaked my grandmother's wonderful crepe recipe. For even more appeal, stir in bits of chocolate or toffee.

—**KRISTIN WEGLARZ** BREMERTON, WA

PREP: 15 MIN. + CHILLING
COOK: 5 MIN./BATCH
MAKES: 12 SERVINGS (2 CREPES EACH)

- 1 cup all-purpose flour
- 1¾ teaspoons ground cinnamon
- 1 teaspoon ground ginger
- ½ teaspoon salt
- ¼ teaspoon ground cloves
- 3 eggs
- 1½ cups 2% milk
- ⅓ cup solid-pack pumpkin
- 2 tablespoons butter, melted
- 1 teaspoon vanilla extract

FILLING

- 1 carton (8 ounces) mascarpone cheese
- ¼ cup instant French vanilla pudding mix (about 1¼ ounces)
- 1 teaspoon vanilla extract
- 1 cup eggnog
  Toasted chopped pecans

1. In a large bowl, whisk the first five ingredients. In another bowl, whisk the eggs, milk, pumpkin, melted butter and vanilla until blended. Add to the flour mixture; stir just until moistened. Refrigerate, covered, 1 hour.

2. For the filling, in a small bowl, mix mascarpone cheese, pudding mix and vanilla until blended; gradually stir in eggnog. Refrigerate, covered, at least 30 minutes.

3. Heat a lightly greased 8-in. nonstick skillet over medium heat. Stir batter. Fill a ¼-cup measure halfway with batter; pour into the center of the pan. Quickly lift, tilt and rotate the pan to coat the bottom evenly. Cook until the top appears dry; turn crepe over and cook 15-20 seconds longer or until bottom is cooked.

4. Remove to a wire rack. Repeat with the remaining batter, greasing the pan as needed.

5. Spoon about 1 tablespoon filling down center of each crepe; roll up. Sprinkle with pecans.

NOTE *This recipe was tested with commercially prepared eggnog.*

Pecan Bacon

How do you make crispy strips of bacon even better? Coat them with chopped pecans, brown sugar and cinnamon.
—**CATHERINE ANN GOZA** LELAND, NC

PREP: 10 MIN. • **BAKE:** 30 MIN.
MAKES: 6 SERVINGS

- 12 **bacon strips**
- ¼ **cup packed brown sugar**
- ¼ **cup finely chopped pecans**
- ⅛ **teaspoon ground cinnamon**
- ⅛ **teaspoon pepper**

1. Preheat oven to 375°. Place bacon in a single layer in a foil-lined 15x10x1-in. baking pan. Bake 16-18 minutes or until lightly browned.
2. Remove bacon from pan. Discard drippings from pan, wiping pan clean if necessary.
3. In a shallow bowl, mix remaining ingredients. Dip both sides of the bacon in brown sugar mixture, patting to help coating adhere; return to pan.
4. Bake 8-10 minutes longer or until caramelized. Remove immediately from the pan.

Walnut Butter Spread

This not-too-sweet walnut butter is so good slathered on my whole wheat toast. For extra indulgence, spread on apricot preserves and add some Brie.
—**BRYAN KENNEDY** KANEOHE, HI

START TO FINISH: 10 MIN. • **MAKES:** ⅔ CUP

- 2 **cups walnut halves, toasted**
- 2 **teaspoons grated orange peel**
- ½ **teaspoon coarsely ground pepper**
- ⅛ **teaspoon salt**
  Whole wheat bread slices, toasted
  Apricot preserves, optional
  Brie cheese, optional

Place the walnuts, orange peel, pepper and salt in a food processor; cover and process until creamy. Spread on toast, with preserves and Brie if desired.

Sausage Mac & Cheese in a Pumpkin

Made hearty with chunks of Italian sausage and veggies, this mac and cheese can go inside a baked pumpkin. If you don't have one, just use a serving dish.

—ANDRIA GASKINS MATTHEWS, NC

PREP: 1 HOUR 25 MIN. • **COOK:** 20 MIN.
MAKES: 6 SERVINGS

- 1 **large pie pumpkin (5 to 6 pounds)**
- 1 **teaspoon salt**
- ½ **teaspoon pepper**
- 3 **cups uncooked cavatappi or spiral pasta**
- ½ **pound bulk mild or hot Italian sausage**
- 1 **small onion, chopped**
- 3 **tablespoons butter**
- 3 **tablespoons all-purpose flour**
- 1½ **cups half-and-half cream**
- ½ **cup chicken stock**
- 4 **ounces sliced process white American cheese, chopped**
- ¾ **cup shredded Manchego cheese**
- ¾ **cup shredded Monterey Jack cheese**
- 3 **tablespoons grated Parmesan cheese**
- 2 **cups fresh spinach, coarsely chopped**
- ⅓ **cup chopped roasted sweet red peppers**

1. Preheat oven to 350°. Wash the pumpkin; cut a 5-in. circle around stem. Remove top; set aside. Remove loose fibers and seeds from pumpkin; discard the seeds or save for toasting. Sprinkle inside of pumpkin with salt and pepper; replace the top. Place on a wire rack on a baking sheet. Bake 1 to 1¼ hours or until tender. Remove top; let stand on wire rack until ready to fill.

2. Meanwhile, in a large saucepan, cook the cavatappi pasta according to package directions. In a large skillet, cook the Italian sausage and onion over medium heat 4-6 minutes or until the sausage is no longer pink and the onion is tender, breaking up the sausage into crumbles; drain.

3. Drain the pasta, reserving ¼ cup pasta water. In same saucepan, melt the butter over medium heat. Stir in flour until smooth; gradually whisk in half-and-half cream and stock. Bring to a boil, stirring constantly; cook and stir 2-3 minutes or until thickened. Stir in cheeses until melted.

4. Add pasta, sausage mixture, spinach and roasted red peppers; cook and stir until the spinach is wilted. Add enough reserved pasta water to reach desired consistency. Transfer to the baked pumpkin; serve immediately.

Pumpkin Spice Overnight Oatmeal

Warm up your family body and soul on a chilly morning with a hot bowl of oatmeal. My spiced version goes in a slow cooker, and any leftovers store well in the fridge.

—JORDAN MASON BROOKVILLE, PA

PREP: 10 MIN. • **COOK:** 5 HOURS
MAKES: 6 SERVINGS

- 1 **can (15 ounces) solid-pack pumpkin**
- 1 **cup steel-cut oats**
- 3 **tablespoons brown sugar**
- 1½ **teaspoons pumpkin pie spice**
- 1 **teaspoon ground cinnamon**
- ¾ **teaspoon salt**
- 3 **cups water**
- 1½ **cups 2% milk**
    Optional toppings: toasted chopped pecans, ground cinnamon and additional brown sugar and milk

In a large bowl, combine the first six ingredients; stir in the water and milk. Transfer to a greased 3-qt. slow cooker. Cook, covered, on low 5-6 hours or until the oats are tender, stirring once. Serve with toppings as desired.

Holiday Helper

No peeking! Unless your recipe directs you to stir the food or add ingredients, resist the urge to lift the lid while your food is cooking in the slow cooker. The loss of steam can mean an extra 20-30 minutes of cooking time each time you lift the lid. Also, make sure the slow cooker lid is not tilted or askew. The steam during cooking creates a seal.

Pineapple Upside-Down Muffins

If you like traditional upside-down cake, you'll love these little goodies. Crushed pineapple and maraschino cherries give them the same yummy flavor and color. See the note at the end of the recipe if you'd like to make standard-size muffins instead of miniature ones.

—SUZEANNE LONGWILL ORTONVILLE, MI

PREP: 25 MIN. • **BAKE:** 10 MIN.
MAKES: ABOUT 3 DOZEN MINI MUFFINS
OR 10 REGULAR MUFFINS

- 1   can (8 ounces) crushed pineapple
- 1½ cups all-purpose flour
- ¾   cup sugar
- 2   teaspoons baking powder
- ¼   teaspoon salt
- 2   eggs
- ½   cup vanilla yogurt
- ¼   cup canola oil
- 5   teaspoons brown sugar
- 18 to 20 maraschino cherries, halved

1. Preheat oven to 400°. Drain crushed pineapple, reserving 1 tablespoon juice. Set crushed pineapple aside.

2. In a large bowl, whisk flour, sugar, baking powder and salt. In another bowl, whisk the eggs, vanilla yogurt, canola oil and reserved pineapple juice. Add to flour mixture; stir just until moistened. Fold in the reserved crushed pineapple.

3. Fill greased mini-muffin cups two-thirds full. Sprinkle top of each with brown sugar; top with the halved maraschino cherries.

4. Bake 9-12 minutes or until toothpick inserted in the center comes out clean. Cool 5 minutes before removing from pans to wire racks. Serve warm.

NOTE *If using regular-size muffin cups, reduce the maraschino cherries to five and bake for 12-16 minutes.*

Roasted Butternut Squash Bread

Spread a thick slice of this squash bread with butter and savor a homey treat.

—SARAH MEUSER NEW MILFORD, CT

PREP: 40 MIN. • **BAKE:** 55 MIN. + COOLING
MAKES: 1 LOAF (16 SLICES)

- 3½ cups cubed peeled butternut squash (1-inch pieces)
- 2 tablespoons olive oil
- ½ cup butter, softened
- ½ cup sugar
- ½ cup packed brown sugar
- 2 eggs
- 1 teaspoon vanilla extract
- 1½ cups whole wheat pastry flour
- 1 teaspoon baking soda
- 1 teaspoon ground cinnamon
- ¾ teaspoon salt
- ½ cup fat-free plain Greek yogurt
- ¼ teaspoon fine sea salt

1. Preheat oven to 375°. Place the squash in a greased 15x10x1-in. baking pan. Drizzle with oil; toss to coat. Roast 25-30 minutes or until tender. Reduce oven setting to 325°.

2. Transfer roasted squash to a bowl; mash coarsely. In a large bowl, beat the butter and sugars until blended. Add the eggs, one at a time, beating well after each addition. Beat in mashed squash and vanilla.

3. In another bowl, whisk the flour, baking soda, cinnamon and salt; add to the butter mixture alternately with the plain Greek yogurt, beating well after each addition.

4. Transfer the batter to a greased 9x5-in. loaf pan; sprinkle with fine sea salt. Bake 55-65 minutes or until a toothpick inserted in center comes out clean. Cool in the pan 10 minutes before removing to a wire rack to cool.

Chocolate Chunk Pancakes with Raspberry Sauce

My sister and I love chocolate—and I love it even more with raspberries. So I decided to splurge and use both ingredients to dress up a stack of made-from-scratch pancakes. It's like having dessert for breakfast!

—KATHERINE NELSON CENTERVILLE, UT

PREP: 20 MIN. • **COOK:** 5 MIN./BATCH
MAKES: 12 PANCAKES (1½ CUPS SAUCE)

- 1 package (10 ounces) frozen sweetened raspberries, thawed
- ¼ cup orange juice
- 3 tablespoons lemon juice
- 2 tablespoons sugar

PANCAKES
- 1½ cups all-purpose flour
- 3 tablespoons sugar
- 1 teaspoon baking powder
- ½ teaspoon baking soda
- ¼ teaspoon salt
- 2 eggs
- 1 cup 2% milk
- ¾ cup (6 ounces) vanilla yogurt
- ¼ cup butter, melted
- ½ cup semisweet chocolate chunks or chips

1. Place the raspberries, orange juice, lemon juice and sugar in a blender; cover and process until pureed. Press through a fine-mesh strainer into a bowl; discard the seeds.

2. In a large bowl, whisk the flour, sugar, baking powder, baking soda and salt. In another bowl, whisk the eggs, milk, vanilla yogurt and melted butter until blended. Add to dry ingredients, stirring just until moistened. Fold in chocolate chunks.

3. Lightly grease a griddle; heat over medium heat. Pour batter by ¼ cupfuls onto the griddle. Cook until bubbles on top begin to pop and the bottoms are golden brown. Turn pancakes; cook until the second side is golden brown. Serve with sauce.

Sweet Potato & Andouille Hash

When my husband was training to compete in the Senior Olympics, I accumulated quite a collection of tasty yet nutritious recipes, including this sweet potato-sausage hash. Served with a fried egg or two on the side, it's an energizing way to start the day.

—MARLA CLARK ALBUQUERQUE, NM

PREP: 15 MIN. • **COOK:** 25 MIN.
MAKES: 6 SERVINGS

- 2 tablespoons olive oil
- ½ pound fully cooked andouille sausage or fully cooked Spanish chorizo, finely chopped
- 4 cups finely chopped sweet potatoes (about 2 medium)
- 4 celery ribs, finely chopped
- 1 medium onion, finely chopped
- 4 garlic cloves, minced
- ½ teaspoon salt
- ¼ teaspoon pepper

1. In a Dutch oven, heat the oil over medium-high heat. Add the sausage; cook and stir until browned.
2. Stir in the remaining ingredients. Reduce the heat to medium-low; cook, uncovered, 15-20 minutes or until the sweet potatoes are tender, stirring occasionally.

Carolina Shrimp & Cheddar Grits

Everyone in my family loves traditional shrimp and grits, but we couldn't agree on the perfect version. So I went into the kitchen and started experimenting. Luckily, the cheesy, Cajun-seasoned dish I came up with pleased the whole gang.

—CHARLOTTE PRICE RALEIGH, NC

PREP: 15 MIN. • **COOK:** 2¾ HOURS
MAKES: 6 SERVINGS

- 1 cup uncooked stone-ground grits
- 1 large garlic clove, minced
- ½ teaspoon salt
- ¼ teaspoon pepper
- 4 cups water
- 2 cups (8 ounces) shredded cheddar cheese
- ¼ cup butter, cubed
- 1 pound peeled and deveined cooked shrimp (31–40 per pound)
- 2 medium tomatoes, seeded and finely chopped
- 4 green onions, finely chopped
- 2 tablespoons chopped fresh parsley
- 4 teaspoons lemon juice
- 2 to 3 teaspoons Cajun seasoning

1. Place the first five ingredients in a 3-qt. slow cooker; stir to combine. Cook, covered, on high 2½ to 3 hours or until water is absorbed and grits are tender, stirring every 45 minutes.
2. Stir in the cheese and butter until melted. Stir in remaining ingredients; cook, covered, on high 15-30 minutes or until heated through.

Coconut Granola Parfaits

Easy to prepare in advance, the homemade granola makes these yogurt treats special.

—JULIE MERRIMAN SEATTLE, WA

PREP: 20 MIN. • **BAKE:** 25 MIN. + COOLING
MAKES: 8 PARFAITS PLUS 2½ CUPS GRANOLA

- ½ cup pomegranate juice
- 1 tablespoon sugar
- ¾ teaspoon lemon juice
- ¼ cup butter, cubed
- ¼ cup packed brown sugar
- ½ teaspoon salt
- ½ teaspoon each ground cardamom, cinnamon and allspice
- ½ teaspoon vanilla extract
- 2 cups old-fashioned oats
- 1 cup flaked coconut
- ½ cup coarsely chopped cashews
- ¼ cup dried cranberries
- ¼ cup dark chocolate chips

PARFAITS

- 4 cups fat-free plain Greek yogurt
- 6 tablespoons honey, divided
- 1 tablespoon grated lime peel
- 2 tablespoons lime juice
- 3 cups chopped Honeycrisp apples (about 2 large)
- 1 cup pomegranate seeds

1. Preheat oven to 325°. In a small saucepan, combine pomegranate juice, sugar and lemon juice. Bring to a boil; cook until liquid is reduced by half. Stir in butter and brown sugar until sugar is dissolved. Remove from heat; stir in salt, spices and vanilla.

2. In a large bowl, combine the oats, coconut and cashews. Drizzle with the juice mixture; toss to combine. Transfer to a greased 15x10x1-in. baking pan, spreading evenly.

3. Bake 20-25 minutes or until lightly browned, stirring halfway. Cool on a wire rack. When completely cooled, stir in cranberries and chocolate chips.

4. For parfaits, in a bowl, mix yogurt, 4 tablespoons honey, peel and juice until blended. Layer ¼ cup mixture, 2 tablespoons granola, 3 tablespoons apple and 1 tablespoon seeds in each of eight parfait glasses. Repeat layers. (Save remaining granola for another use; store in an airtight container.)

5. Drizzle parfaits with remaining honey. Serve immediately.

Cranberry Scones with Orange Butter

Dotted with dried cranberries, these flaky melt-in-your-mouth scones are even better with the accompanying orange-flavored butter. They're sure to brighten up any holiday brunch or afternoon tea.

—JOAN HALLFORD
NORTH RICHLAND HILLS, TX

PREP: 20 MIN. • **BAKE:** 25 MIN.
MAKES: 8 SCONES
(½ CUP ORANGE BUTTER)

- 2½ cups all-purpose flour
- ¼ cup sugar
- 3 teaspoons baking powder
- ½ cup cold butter, cubed
- 2 eggs
- ½ cup heavy whipping cream
- ¾ cup dried cranberries

EGG WASH

- 1 egg
- 1 tablespoon water

ORANGE BUTTER

- ½ cup butter, softened
- 1 tablespoon honey
- 1½ teaspoons grated orange peel
- 1 tablespoon orange juice

1. Preheat oven to 350°. In a large bowl, whisk flour, sugar and baking powder. Cut in butter until mixture resembles coarse crumbs. In another bowl, whisk the eggs and cream until blended; stir into crumb mixture just until moistened. Stir in cranberries.

2. Turn dough onto a floured surface; knead dough gently 10 times. Transfer to a greased baking sheet. Pat into an 8-in. circle. Cut into eight wedges, but do not separate. In a small bowl, whisk egg with water; brush over dough.

3. Bake 22-25 minutes or until golden brown. For orange butter, in a small bowl, mix remaining ingredients until blended. Serve with warm scones.

Tiny Bubbles

I often ordered a fizzy raspberry beverage at a restaurant and decided to try making a similar concoction at home. Garnish the glass with a simple fresh raspberry.
—**HILLARY TEDESCO** CROFTON, MD

START TO FINISH: 5 MIN.
MAKES: 1 SERVING

- 1 ounce raspberry liqueur
- ⅔ cup chilled champagne
- 1 fresh raspberry

Pour the raspberry liqueur into a champagne flute; top with the champagne. Garnish with berry.

Brunch Puff with Sausage Gravy

PREP: 25 MIN. • **BAKE:** 20 MIN.
MAKES: 9 SERVINGS

- 7 large eggs, divided use
- ¼ cup 2% milk
- ¼ teaspoon salt
- ¼ teaspoon plus ⅛ teaspoon pepper, divided
- 1 tablespoon butter
- 1 tablespoon water
- 1 package (17.3 ounces) frozen puff pastry, thawed
- 8 ounces sliced deli ham (¼ inch thick)
- 1 cup (4 ounces) shredded cheddar cheese

SAUSAGE GRAVY
- ¾ pound bulk pork sausage
- 1 envelope country gravy mix

1. Preheat oven to 400°. In a small bowl, whisk 6 eggs, milk, salt and ¼ teaspoon pepper until blended.
2. In a large nonstick skillet coated with cooking spray, heat butter over medium heat. Pour in egg mixture; cook and stir just until the eggs are thickened and no liquid egg remains. Remove from heat.
3. In a small bowl, whisk remaining egg with water. On a lightly floured surface, unfold one sheet of puff pastry and roll to a 10-in. square. Transfer to a parchment paper-lined baking sheet. Arrange ham over puff pastry to within 1 in. of edges; top with scrambled eggs. Sprinkle with cheese.

4. Brush the beaten egg mixture over the edges of puff pastry square. Roll the remaining puff pastry sheet to a 10-in. square; place over the filling. Press the edges with a fork to seal; cut slits in the top. Brush the top with additional beaten egg mixture; sprinkle with the remaining pepper. Bake 20-25 minutes or until golden brown.
5. Meanwhile, in a large skillet, cook sausage over medium heat 6-8 minutes or until no longer pink, breaking the sausage into crumbles. Remove with a slotted spoon; drain on paper towels. Discard the drippings, wiping skillet clean if necessary.
6. In the same pan, prepare the country gravy mix according to the package directions. Stir in the sausage. Serve with the pastry.

"My overnight guests wake up to a breakfast of Brunch Puff with Sausage Gravy. The home-style squares are hearty and delicious."

—**DANIELLE COCHRAN** GRAYLING, MI

Cranberry Orange Mimosas

Sparkling mimosas are perfect for special mornings. My recipe adds the tangy flavor and festive color of cranberries.
—**SHANNON STEPHENS** LAKE IN THE HILLS, IL

PREP: 10 MIN. • **MAKES:** 12 SERVINGS

- 2 **cups fresh or frozen cranberries**
- 3 **cups orange juice, divided**
- 2 **tablespoons lemon juice**
- 3 **bottles (750 milliliters each) champagne, chilled**
  Fresh mint leaves, optional

1. Place berries and 1 cup orange juice in a blender; cover and process until pureed, stopping to scrape down sides of jar with a rubber spatula as needed. Add lemon juice and remaining orange juice; cover and process until blended.
2. Pour ⅓ cup berry mixture into each champagne flute. Top with ¾ cup champagne; serve with mint if desired.

Cinnamon-Sugar Spread

In just five minutes, you can whip up this yummy topper for toast or bagels.
—**TERRI CHRISTENSEN** MONTAGUE, MI

START TO FINISH: 5 MIN.
MAKES: 18 SERVINGS (6 TABLESPOONS)

- ¼ **cup butter, softened**
- ¼ **cup packed brown sugar**
- 1 **teaspoon ground cinnamon**
- ¼ **teaspoon ground nutmeg**
  Assorted breads and bagels

In a small bowl, beat butter, brown sugar, cinnamon and nutmeg until smooth. Spread on breads and bagels.

Holiday Helper

Whenever we host family and friends, I record the date, which recipes I used and which were especially popular. That way, I can change things up the next time if I want—or pull together a meal in a pinch using the complete menus listed in my journal.

—**RUTH K.** TYRONE, PA

Bananas Foster French Toast

Classic Bananas Foster has always seemed to be one of those special treats reserved for dining at fine restaurants. With this dessert-like French toast, we enjoy the same indulgent flavors at home.

—ANGELA HACKER HENDERSONVILLE, TN

PREP: 25 MIN. • **BAKE:** 25 MIN. + STANDING
MAKES: 8 SERVINGS

- 4 **medium firm bananas, halved lengthwise**
- ½ **cup butter, cubed**
- 1 **cup packed brown sugar**
- 2 **teaspoons rum extract**
- 4 **eggs**
- 1 **cup 2% milk**
- 2 **teaspoons ground cinnamon**
- 1 **teaspoon vanilla extract**
- 15 **slices French bread (½ inch thick)**
  Sweetened whipped cream

1. Preheat oven to 350°. Arrange the bananas in a greased 13x9-in. baking dish. In a small saucepan, melt butter over medium heat; remove from heat. Stir in brown sugar and extract; spoon evenly over bananas.

2. In a shallow bowl, whisk eggs, milk, cinnamon and vanilla until blended. Dip both sides of French bread slices in the egg mixture. Arrange over the bananas. Pour the remaining egg mixture over the top.

3. Bake 25-30 minutes or until a knife inserted near the center comes out clean. Let stand 10 minutes before serving. Serve with whipped cream.

HOLIDAY
DINNERS

Lobster Dinner

Lobster alla Diavola
pg. 41

Roasted Broccoli & Cauliflower
pg. 41

Onion & Garlic Rolls
pg. 42

Jeweled Endive Salad
pg. 43

Sparkling Celebration Punch
pg. 44

Meringue Shells with Lemon Curd
pg. 44

Lobster alla Diavola

I've cooked lobster *alla diavola* (devil's style) since I was newly married. I often serve it over a bed of linguine or angel hair pasta at family celebrations.

—MARCIA WHITNEY GAINESVILLE, FL

PREP: 20 MIN. • **COOK:** 35 MIN.
MAKES: 6 SERVINGS

- 6 fresh or frozen lobster tails (4 to 5 ounces each), thawed
- 3 tablespoons olive oil
- 1 jalapeno pepper, seeded and minced
- 3 garlic cloves, minced
- 1 can (28 ounces) whole plum tomatoes, undrained
- ½ cup julienned soft sun-dried tomatoes (not packed in oil)
- ½ cup dry red wine
- 1 teaspoon sugar
- 2 teaspoons salt-free Italian herb seasoning
- ½ teaspoon smoked paprika, optional
- ¼ teaspoon salt
- ⅛ teaspoon pepper
- 1 tablespoon red wine vinegar
- 2 tablespoons butter
- 3 tablespoons finely chopped shallots
  Hot cooked linguine and minced fresh parsley

1. Using kitchen scissors, cut through bottom of lobster tail lengthwise down the center. Place the tail, cut side up, on a cutting board. Using a chef's knife, cut through the lobster meat and shell. Carefully remove the meat from shell; cut into 1-in. pieces. Set shells aside.

2. In a 6-qt. stockpot, heat the oil over medium-high heat. Add jalapeno; cook and stir 1-2 minutes or until tender. Add garlic; cook 1 minute longer.

3. Add plum tomatoes, dried tomatoes, wine, sugar and seasonings, breaking up the tomatoes with a spoon. Add the reserved lobster shells. Bring to a boil. Reduce the heat; simmer, covered, 25-30 minutes, stirring occasionally. Remove shells; set aside. Stir in vinegar.

4. In a large skillet, heat butter over medium-high heat. Add shallots; cook and stir until tender. Add lobster meat; cook and stir 2-4 minutes or until meat is opaque. Stir into the tomato mixture. Bring to a boil. Reduce heat; simmer, uncovered, 2-3 minutes or until meat is firm but tender.

5. To serve, fill the lobster shells with tomato mixture. Serve with linguine; sprinkle with parsley.

NOTE *Wear disposable gloves when cutting hot peppers; the oils can burn skin. Avoid touching your face.*

Roasted Broccoli & Cauliflower

When we're making an entree that requires a bit more time, we rely on this simple side. It's delicious and ready in just 25 minutes.

—DEBRA TOLBERT DEVILLE, LA

START TO FINISH: 25 MIN.
MAKES: 8 SERVINGS

- 4 cups fresh cauliflowerets
- 4 cups fresh broccoli florets
- 10 garlic cloves, peeled and halved
- 2 tablespoons olive oil
- ½ teaspoon salt
- ½ teaspoon pepper

Preheat oven to 425°. In a large bowl, combine all ingredients; toss to coat. Transfer to two greased 15x10x1-in. baking pans. Roast 15-20 minutes or until tender.

Preparing Tails for Lobster alla Diavola

1. Place the tail on a cutting board. Using kitchen shears, cut lengthwise through the shell on the underside of the lobster to expose the meat.

2. With a sharp chef's knife, cut the lobster tail in half lengthwise. Then carefully remove the meat from the shell and cut the meat into pieces.

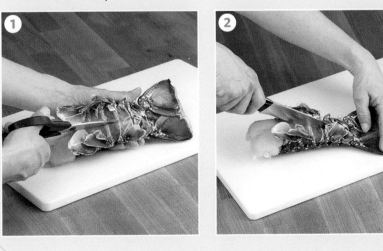

Onion & Garlic Rolls

For a change from the usual garlic toast, I mixed up a yeast dough with dried minced onion. Sprinkling on mozzarella cheese and parsley makes the rolls even yummier.

—BRENDA CAUGHELL DURHAM, NC

PREP: 45 MIN. + RISING • **BAKE:** 20 MIN.
MAKES: 20 ROLLS

- ⅓ **cup dried minced onion**
- ⅓ **cup water**
- 1 **package (¼ ounce) active dry yeast**
- 2 **tablespoons warm water (110° to 115°)**
- 1 **cup warm 2% milk (110° to 115°)**
- ¼ **cup toasted wheat germ**
- 1 **tablespoon canola oil**
- 1 **tablespoon honey**
- 1 **teaspoon garlic powder**
- ¾ **teaspoon salt**
- 3 **to 3¼ cups all-purpose flour**
- 2 **tablespoons butter, melted**
- 1 **cup (4 ounces) shredded part-skim mozzarella cheese**
  Minced fresh parsley, optional

1. In a small bowl, mix onion and water. Let stand 10 minutes or until onion is softened. In a small bowl, dissolve yeast in warm water.

2. In a large bowl, combine milk, wheat germ, oil, honey, garlic powder, salt, onion mixture, yeast mixture and 1½ cups flour; beat on medium speed until smooth. Stir in enough remaining flour to form a stiff dough (dough will be sticky).

3. Turn dough onto a floured surface; knead until smooth and elastic, about 6-8 minutes. Place in a greased bowl, turning once to grease the top. Cover with plastic wrap and let rise in a warm place until doubled, about 1 hour.

4. Punch down dough. Turn onto a lightly floured surface; divide and shape into 20 balls. Place in a greased 13x9-in. baking pan. Cover with a kitchen towel; let rise in a warm place until almost doubled, about 45 minutes.

5. Preheat oven to 375°. Bake for 15-18 minutes or until lightly browned. Brush rolls with butter; sprinkle with cheese. Bake 5-7 minutes longer or until cheese is melted and rolls are golden brown. Sprinkle with parsley if desired. Serve warm.

Jeweled Endive Salad

Every year during the Christmas season, friends of mine host a big holiday potluck. When I wanted to contribute something a little different, I tossed together a salad of watercress and endive, then drizzled on a made-from-scratch dressing. Ruby red pomegranate seeds add festive color.
—**ALYSHA BRAUN** ST. CATHARINES, ON

START TO FINISH: 15 MIN.
MAKES: 8 SERVINGS

- 1 **bunch watercress (4 ounces)**
- 2 **heads endive, halved lengthwise and thinly sliced**
- 1 **cup pomegranate seeds (about 1 pomegranate)**
- 1 **shallot, thinly sliced**

DRESSING
- ⅓ **cup olive oil**
- 3 **tablespoons lemon juice**
- 2 **teaspoons grated lemon peel**
- ¼ **teaspoon salt**
- ⅛ **teaspoon pepper**

1. In a large bowl, combine watercress, endive, pomegranate seeds and shallot.
2. In a small bowl, whisk the dressing ingredients. Drizzle over the salad and toss to coat.

Holiday Helper

Pomegranates are available from late September to November. Whole pomegranates keep well in a cool, dark place at room temperature for several days. They will last for 3 months in the refrigerator. You can refrigerate the seeds for up to 3 days. When buying, choose pomegranates that have fresh, leather-like skin free from cracks and splits.

Sparkling Celebration Punch

Every special spread of food deserves an equally special drink to go with it. This bubbly concoction of wine, champagne and brandy looks festive garnished with slices of citrus fruits.

—SHARON TIPTON CASSELBERRY, FL

START TO FINISH: 10 MIN. • **MAKES:** 8 SERVINGS (¾ CUP EACH)

- ½ to 1 cup brandy
- ½ cup light corn syrup
- 1 bottle (750 milliliters) riesling or other sweet white wine, chilled
- 1 bottle (750 milliliters) champagne, chilled
  Ice cubes
  Orange, lemon or lime slices

In a punch bowl, mix the brandy and light corn syrup until blended. Stir in the riesling; add the champagne. Serve over ice with citrus slices.

Meringue Shells with Lemon Curd

Pipe light-as-a-feather meringue into little cups, then fill them with homemade lemon curd and fresh berries. Your guests will love the contrasting flavors and textures. For a little extra sweetness and creaminess, dollop each serving with whipped topping.

—KRIS BRILL MILWAUKEE, WI

PREP: 25 MIN. + CHILLING • **BAKE:** 45 MIN. + STANDING
MAKES: 12 SERVINGS

- 6 egg whites
- 1 teaspoon white vinegar
- 1 teaspoon vanilla extract
- ¼ teaspoon salt
- ¼ teaspoon cream of tartar
- 1½ cups sugar

LEMON CURD
- ½ cup sugar
- 2 tablespoons potato starch
- 1 cup water
- ½ cup plus 1 tablespoon lemon juice, divided
- 3 eggs, beaten
- 2 teaspoons grated lemon peel
  Whipped topping and fresh berries, optional

1. Place the egg whites in a large bowl; let stand at room temperature 30 minutes.

2. Preheat oven to 225°. Add the vinegar, vanilla, salt and cream of tartar to the egg whites; beat on medium speed until foamy. Gradually add the sugar, 1 tablespoon at a time, beating on high after each addition until sugar is dissolved. Continue beating until stiff glossy peaks form.

3. Cut a small hole in the tip of a pastry bag or in a corner of a food-safe plastic bag; insert a large star tip. Transfer the meringue to bag. On a parchment paper-lined baking sheet, pipe the meringue into twelve 3-in. round disks, building up the sides with meringue to form shells. Bake 45-50 minutes or until set and dry. Turn off the oven (do not open the door); leave the meringues in oven 1 hour. Remove from oven; cool completely on baking sheet.

4. Meanwhile, in a small heavy saucepan, mix sugar and potato starch. Whisk in the water and ½ cup lemon juice until smooth. Cook and stir over medium-high heat until thickened and bubbly. Reduce the heat to low; cook and stir 2 minutes longer.

5. Remove from heat. Stir a small amount of the hot mixture into the eggs; return all to the pan, stirring constantly. Bring to a gentle boil; cook and stir 2 minutes. Remove from the heat. Gently stir in lemon peel and remaining lemon juice. Transfer to a small bowl; cool without stirring. Refrigerate, covered, until cold.

6. Spoon ¼ cup curd into each meringue shell. If desired, top with whipped topping and berries.

Pork Roast Dinner

Holiday Crown Pork Roast
pg. 47

Cream of Butternut Squash Soup
pg. 47

**Roasted Apple Salad with
Spicy Maple-Cider Vinaigrette**
pg. 48

**Sherried Mushroom Baked
Potatoes**
pg. 49

Parmesan-Herb Dinner Rolls
pg. 50

Tangy Apple-Ginger Chutney
pg. 50

Cranberry Eggnog Cake
pg. 51

Holiday Crown Pork Roast

Crown roast of pork always has such a "wow" factor. If you've never served this meat before, you might be surprised at how simple it can be to prepare.

—**LISA SPEER** PALM BEACH, FL

PREP: 15 MIN. • **BAKE:** 2 HOURS + STANDING
MAKES: 12 SERVINGS

- 1 tablespoon paprika
- 1½ teaspoons kosher salt
- 1 teaspoon dried thyme
- 1 teaspoon dried rosemary, crushed
- 1 teaspoon pepper
- ½ teaspoon rubbed sage
- 1 pork crown roast (12 ribs and about 8 pounds)
  Apples, fresh rosemary sprigs and dried sage leaves, optional

1. Preheat oven to 350°. Mix the first six ingredients; rub over roast. Place on a rack in a large shallow roasting pan. Cover the rib ends with foil. Roast 2 to 2½ hours or until a thermometer reads at least 145°.
2. Remove roast from oven; tent with foil. Let stand 15 minutes. Remove foil; carve between ribs to serve. If desired, serve with apples, rosemary and sage.

Cream of Butternut Squash Soup

Butternut squash and potatoes combine perfectly in this comforting cream soup.

—**TIFFANY SMITH** CINCINNATI, OH

PREP: 15 MIN. • **COOK:** 40 MIN.
MAKES: 6 SERVINGS (1½ QUARTS)

- 4 cups cubed peeled butternut squash (about 1 pound)
- 2 medium potatoes (about 1 pound), peeled and cubed
- 1 medium onion, chopped
- 4 cups water
- 1 carton (2½ ounces) chicken noodle soup mix
- 1 cup half-and-half cream
- ¼ teaspoon salt
- ¼ teaspoon pepper
  Chopped fresh parsley, optional

1. Place the first five ingredients in a large saucepan; bring to a boil. Reduce heat; simmer, covered, 40-45 minutes or until squash and potatoes are tender.
2. Puree the soup using an immersion blender. Or, cool the soup slightly and puree in batches in a blender; return to the pan. Stir in the cream, salt and pepper; heat through. If desired, sprinkle servings with parsley.

Nutshell Candles

Turn walnut shells into adorable floating candles for your table. It's easy—just follow these steps!

1. To make perfectly split shells, use long-handled pliers or a wide clamp to hold each nut, then cut along the seam using a rotary tool such as a Dremel with a cutting attachment. (You need to cut only partway.) Use a spatula or flat screwdriver to pry the shell apart. Clean out the halved shells.

2. Place a 4-inch pre-waxed wire wick in the center of each shell. Put a bit of candle mold or putty on the bottom of the wick and press it onto the shell to secure.

3. Following the manufacturer's instructions, melt microwavable soy wax in the microwave or melt beeswax in a double boiler on the stovetop.

4. Pour the melted wax into each shell up to the top edge. Let the wax solidify.

5. Trim each wick to about ½ inch above the solidified wax.

6. Fill decorative bowls or glasses with water and carefully place the candles in the water, making sure not to get the wicks wet. Light each candle. (Approximate burn time per candle is one hour.)

Roasted Apple Salad with Spicy Maple-Cider Vinaigrette

When we had an overabundance of apples, this salad became a fast favorite. I roasted the apples to enhance their flavor.
—**JANICE ELDER** CHARLOTTE, NC

PREP: 15 MIN. • **BAKE:** 20 MIN. + COOLING
MAKES: 8 SERVINGS

- 4 medium Fuji, Gala or other firm apples, quartered
- 2 tablespoons olive oil

DRESSING
- 2 tablespoons cider vinegar
- 2 tablespoons olive oil
- 1 tablespoon maple syrup
- 1 teaspoon Sriracha Asian hot chili sauce
- ½ teaspoon salt
- ¼ teaspoon pepper

SALAD
- 1 package (5 ounces) spring mix salad greens
- 4 pitted dates, quartered
- 1 log (4 ounces) fresh goat cheese, crumbled
- ½ cup chopped pecans, toasted

1. Preheat oven to 375°. Place the apples in a foil-lined 15x10x1-in. baking pan; drizzle with the olive oil and toss to coat. Roast 20-30 minutes or until tender, stirring occasionally. Cool completely.

2. In a small bowl, whisk dressing ingredients until blended. In a large bowl, combine the salad greens and dates. Drizzle the dressing over salad and toss to coat.

3. Divide the mixture among eight plates. Top with the goat cheese and roasted apples; sprinkle with pecans. Serve immediately.

NOTE *To toast nuts, bake in a shallow pan in a 350° oven for 5-10 minutes or cook in a skillet over low heat until lightly browned, stirring occasionally.*

Sherried Mushroom Baked Potatoes

PREP: 1¼ HOURS • **BAKE:** 25 MIN.
MAKES: 8 SERVINGS

- 4 **large baking potatoes (about 3¼ pounds)**
- ¼ **cup butter, cubed**
- 1 **cup sliced fresh mushrooms**
- 1 **small onion, chopped**
- 1 **garlic clove, minced**
- ½ **cup sherry**
- ⅓ **cup 2% milk**
- ½ **cup sour cream**
- 2 **tablespoons minced fresh chives**

1. Preheat oven to 375°. Scrub the potatoes; pierce several times with a fork. Place in a foil-lined 15x10x1-in. baking pan; bake 1 hour or until tender.

2. Meanwhile, in a large skillet, heat the butter over medium-high heat. Add the mushrooms, onion and garlic; cook and stir until tender. Stir in the sherry. Bring to a boil. Reduce heat; simmer, uncovered, 14-16 minutes or until the liquid is almost evaporated.

3. When the potatoes are cool enough to handle, cut each potato lengthwise in half. Scoop out the pulp, leaving ¼-in.-thick shells.

4. In a large bowl, mash the pulp with milk, sour cream and chives. Stir in the mushroom mixture. Spoon into potato shells. Return to the baking pan. Bake 25-30 minutes or until heated through.

"*My husband and I regularly choose Sherried Mushroom Baked Potatoes as a side dish for dinner, no matter what the occasion.*"

—**CHARLENE CHAMBERS** ORMOND BEACH, FL

Holiday Helper

Have a melon baller? When making twice-baked potatoes, try using that utensil to scoop the cooked potato pulp out of the shells. The pulp will come out quickly and neatly without the skins tearing. I once prepared 40 potatoes this way in no time!

—**FAY GRIMES** EVERETT, PA

Tangy Apple-Ginger Chutney

Here's a wonderful condiment for a pork entree. We even spread the spiced chutney over bagels with cream cheese as a snack. If you'd prefer a little more kick, add some black pepper, red pepper and cumin.

—AYSHA SCHURMAN AMMON, ID

PREP: 20 MIN. • **COOK:** 40 MIN.
MAKES: 3 CUPS

- 2 tablespoons olive oil
- 1 medium red onion, chopped
- ½ cup chopped sweet red pepper
- 2 green onions, finely chopped
- 2 medium McIntosh apples, peeled and chopped
- 1 small Granny Smith apple, peeled and finely chopped
- ⅓ cup finely chopped pickled banana peppers
- 1 cup golden raisins
- 1 cup apple cider or juice
- ⅔ cup cider vinegar
- ½ cup packed brown sugar
- 3 tablespoons minced fresh gingerroot
- ½ teaspoon salt
- ½ teaspoon ground cardamom
- ½ teaspoon ground cinnamon
- ¼ teaspoon ground allspice
- ¼ teaspoon white pepper

1. In a 6-qt. stockpot, heat the olive oil over medium-high heat. Add the red onion, red pepper and green onions; cook and stir 3 minutes. Add the apples and pickled banana peppers; cook and stir 3 minutes longer.

2. Stir in the remaining ingredients. Bring to a boil, stirring occasionally. Reduce heat to medium-low; simmer, uncovered, 30-35 minutes or until the liquid is almost evaporated, stirring occasionally. Serve warm or cold. Refrigerate leftovers.

Parmesan-Herb Dinner Rolls

Whether you're preparing an elaborate holiday meal or need a fuss-free way to round out dinner on a weeknight, these rolls are a busy cook's dream. They use convenient frozen bread dough and just five other ingredients.

—CHRISTINA HASELMAN MILLER CITY, OH

PREP: 10 MIN. + RISING • **BAKE:** 15 MIN.
MAKES: 1 DOZEN

- 12 frozen bread dough dinner rolls
- ½ cup grated Parmesan cheese
- 2 garlic cloves, minced
- 1½ teaspoons Italian seasoning
- ¼ teaspoon dill weed
- ¼ cup butter, melted

1. Place the frozen dinner rolls on a greased baking sheet; thaw, covered, in refrigerator overnight or at room temperature 2 hours.

2. In a small bowl, mix the Parmesan cheese, garlic, Italian seasoning and dill. Brush rolls with melted butter; sprinkle with the Parmesan cheese mixture. Cover loosely with plastic wrap; let rise in a warm place until doubled, about 1 hour.

3. Preheat the oven to 350°. Bake 15-20 minutes or until golden brown. Remove from the pan to a wire rack; serve warm.

Cranberry Eggnog Cake

Are cranberries and eggnog always in your kitchen during the Christmas season? I stir both into the batter for this yuletide cake. It's especially yummy with the topping of whipped cream and Mascarpone.

—ROXANNE PEELEN FRANKLIN, WI

PREP: 15 MIN. • **BAKE:** 40 MIN. + COOLING
MAKES: 12 SERVINGS

- 1 **package yellow cake mix (regular size)**
- 1½ **cups eggnog**
- 3 **eggs**
- ¼ **cup butter, softened**
- 2 **teaspoons ground nutmeg**
- 1 **teaspoon vanilla extract**
- 1 **cup dried cranberries**
MASCARPONE TOPPING
- ½ **cup heavy whipping cream**
- 1 **carton (8 ounces) Mascarpone cheese**
- 2 **tablespoons confectioners' sugar**
- ½ **teaspoon vanilla extract**
  Additional ground nutmeg

1. Preheat oven to 350°. Grease and flour a 10-in. fluted tube pan. In a large bowl, combine cake mix, eggnog, eggs, softened butter, nutmeg and vanilla; beat on low speed 30 seconds. Beat on medium 2 minutes. Fold in berries.

2. Transfer to prepared pan. Bake 40-45 minutes or until a toothpick inserted in center comes out clean. Cool in the pan 10 minutes before removing from pan to a wire rack to cool completely.

3. For the Mascarpone topping, in a small bowl, beat the heavy whipping cream until stiff peaks form. In another small bowl, mix Mascarpone cheese, confectioners' sugar and vanilla just until combined. Fold in the whipped cream. Serve with cake; sprinkle with additional nutmeg.

NOTE *This recipe was tested with commercially prepared eggnog.*

Chicken Dinner

Roast Chicken with Vegetables
pg. 53

Hungarian-Style Green Beans
pg. 53

Sweet & Moist Corn Bread
pg. 54

Tomato-Bacon Dip with Focaccia
pg. 55

Mango Gelatin Salad
pg. 56

Fudge-Filled Vanilla Cake
pg. 56

Roast Chicken with Vegetables

This home-style main course offers the convenience of roasting the chicken and vegetables together in one cooking bag. And you'll need only 15 minutes to get everything into the oven.

—TASTE OF HOME TEST KITCHEN

PREP: 15 MIN. • **BAKE:** 1¼ HOURS + STANDING
MAKES: 6 SERVINGS

- 1 tablespoon all-purpose flour
- 1 large oven roasting bag
- 8 small red potatoes, halved
- 6 medium carrots, cut into 2-inch pieces
- 6 half-ears frozen corn on the cob, thawed
- 1 teaspoon salt, divided
- ½ teaspoon pepper, divided
- ¼ teaspoon paprika, divided
- 1 medium onion, quartered
- 3 fresh rosemary sprigs or 1 tablespoon dried rosemary, crushed
- 1 roasting chicken (6 to 7 pounds)
- 2 tablespoons olive oil
- 2 teaspoons minced fresh rosemary or ½ teaspoon dried rosemary, crushed

1. Preheat oven to 350°. Sprinkle the flour into the oven bag; shake to coat. Add the potatoes, carrots, corn, ½ teaspoon salt, ¼ teaspoon pepper and ⅛ teaspoon paprika. Shake bag to coat vegetables; place in a 13x9-in. baking pan.
2. Place onion and rosemary sprigs in the cavity of the chicken. Rub the skin with oil; sprinkle with the minced rosemary and remaining salt, pepper and paprika. Skewer chicken openings; tie drumsticks together. Place chicken in the center of the bag, breast side up; place vegetables around chicken.
3. Cut six ½-in. slits in top of bag; close with tie provided. Bake 1¼ to 1½ hours or until a thermometer inserted in the thickest part of thigh reads 170°-175°. Let stand in oven bag 15 minutes before carving chicken. Discard the onion and rosemary sprigs.

Hungarian-Style Green Beans

After a vacation to Hungary, I was inspired to make a flavorful stovetop dish of green beans, garlic, paprika and mushrooms. It's a nice side for a variety of menus.

—SHERRY JOHNSTON
GREEN COVE SPRINGS, FL

START TO FINISH: 25 MIN.
MAKES: 6 SERVINGS

- 1 pound fresh green beans, trimmed
- ¼ cup butter, cubed
- ½ pound sliced fresh mushrooms
- 1½ teaspoons paprika
- 2 garlic cloves, minced
- ¾ teaspoon salt

1. In a large saucepan, place a steamer basket over 1 in. of water. Place green beans in basket. Bring water to a boil. Reduce the heat to maintain a low boil; steam, covered, 8-10 minutes or until crisp-tender.
2. Meanwhile, in a large skillet, heat the butter over medium-high heat. Add the mushrooms and paprika; cook and stir 4-6 minutes or until mushrooms are tender. Add garlic; cook 1 minute longer. Add beans and salt; toss to coat.

Sweet & Moist Corn Bread

We like traditional versions of corn bread, but sometimes we want it a touch sweeter. This simple recipe has just the right amount of sugar. Cut pieces fresh from the oven for dinner and let your guests slather on butter...or serve the warm squares for breakfast with honey, syrup or jam.

—STACEY FEATHER JAY, OK

PREP: 10 MIN. • **BAKE:** 25 MIN.
MAKES: 15 SERVINGS

- 2½ cups all-purpose flour
- 1½ cups cornmeal
- 1 cup sugar
- 4 teaspoons baking powder
- 1½ teaspoons salt
- ¾ cup shortening
- 2 eggs
- 2½ cups whole milk

1. Preheat oven to 400°. In a large bowl, combine first five ingredients. Cut in shortening until the mixture resembles coarse crumbs. In another bowl, whisk eggs and milk; stir into crumb mixture just until moistened.

2. Pour into a greased 13x9-in. baking pan. Bake 25-30 minutes or until a toothpick inserted in the center comes out clean. Serve warm.

Tomato-Bacon Dip with Focaccia

My friends rave about the fresh flavor of this creamy appetizer. With a combination of crispy bacon, tomato and mayonnaise, it reminds everyone of a BLT. We enjoy the zesty dip with toasted focaccia bread and even as a spread on sandwiches.

—MARSHA POSTAR LUBBOCK, TX

PREP: 20 MIN. + CHILLING
MAKES: 12 SERVINGS (¼ CUP EACH)

- 1 cup mayonnaise
- 1 cup (8 ounces) sour cream
- ½ pound bacon strips, cooked and crumbled
- 1 large tomato, seeded and finely chopped
- ½ small onion, finely chopped
  Crumbled cooked bacon and minced fresh parsley, optional
  Focaccia bread, sliced and lightly toasted

1. In a small bowl, mix mayonnaise and sour cream. Stir in bacon, tomato and onion. Refrigerate until cold, about 1 hour.
2. If desired, sprinkle with bacon and parsley; serve with focaccia bread.

Holiday Helper

Instead of frying strips of bacon, cook them in the oven. Lay the bacon strips on a jelly roll pan and bake them at 350° for about 30 minutes. Prepared this way, bacon comes out crisp and flat. Plus, the pan cleans easily, and there's no stovetop spattering.

—LOU H. MOBRIDGE, SD

1. Preheat oven to 350°. Grease a 13x9-in. baking pan. In a large bowl, combine the white cake mix, water, canola oil, eggs and vanilla; beat on low speed 30 seconds. Beat on medium 2 minutes. Stir in the melted white chips until combined.

2. Transfer the cake batter to the prepared pan. Bake 25-30 minutes or until a toothpick inserted in center comes out clean. Meanwhile, in a small saucepan, melt semisweet chocolate chips and butter with milk over low heat. Stir in the confectioners' sugar, corn syrup and vanilla until smooth. Spread over warm cake. Cool cake completely in pan on a wire rack.

3. For the mousse topping, in a large bowl, whisk the cold milk and white chocolate pudding mix for 2 minutes. Let stand 5 minutes or until soft-set. Fold in whipped topping and vanilla until combined. Spread over the cake. If desired, top with chocolate curls. Refrigerate leftovers.

Mango Gelatin Salad

My Aunt Nannette shared her recipe for a gelatin mold full of refreshing mango.

—**DEBRA SULT** CHANDLER, AZ

PREP: 30 MIN. + CHILLING
MAKES: 8 SERVINGS

- 1 jar (24 ounces) refrigerated mango slices, drained
- 1 package (8 ounces) cream cheese, softened and cubed
- 2 cups boiling water
- 2 packages (3 ounces each) lemon gelatin
- 1 package (3 ounces) apricot gelatin
- 2 cups cold water
  Fresh mint leaves and cranberries, optional

1. Place mango and cream cheese in a food processor; process until blended.
2. In a large bowl, add the boiling water to gelatins; stir 2 minutes to completely dissolve. Stir in the cold water, then the mango mixture. Pour into an 8-cup ring mold coated with cooking spray or a 2-qt. serving bowl. Refrigerate until firm, about 4 hours. If using a ring mold, unmold onto a serving plate. If desired, serve with mint and cranberries.

Fudge-Filled Vanilla Cake

This luscious cake has both a fudge layer and a white chocolate mousse topping.

—**LINNEA LEDGISTER** WAUSAU, WI

PREP: 15 MIN. • **BAKE:** 25 MIN. + COOLING
MAKES: 12 SERVINGS

- 1 package white cake mix (regular size)
- 1¼ cups water
- ⅓ cup canola oil
- 2 eggs
- 1 teaspoon vanilla extract
- ½ cup white baking chips, melted

FUDGE FILLING
- 1 cup (6 ounces) semisweet chocolate chips
- 3 tablespoons butter
- 2 tablespoons 2% milk
- ¼ cup confectioners' sugar
- 2 tablespoons light corn syrup
- 1 teaspoon vanilla extract

MOUSSE TOPPING
- 1½ cups cold 2% milk
- 1 package (3.3 ounces) instant white chocolate pudding mix
- 1 carton (8 ounces) frozen whipped topping, thawed
- 1 teaspoon vanilla extract
  Chocolate curls, optional

Curling Chocolate

Garnishing Fudge-Filled Vanilla Cake (at left) with chocolate curls is a cinch. Use a vegetable peeler to "peel" curls from a solid block of chocolate. To keep the strips intact, allow them to fall gently onto a plate or single layer of waxed paper. If you get only shavings, your chocolate may be too hard, so warm it slightly.

More Choices for Christmas Menus

If you like the three yuletide menus showcased in this chapter but want even more options for entrees, sides and desserts, page through this extra-special section. You'll find bonus recipes that can make wonderful substitutions in any of the featured dinners.

Prime Rib with Fresh Herb Sauce

Few entrees say "special occasion" like perfectly seasoned prime rib. I start by roasting mine with onions, garlic, sage, thyme and bay leaves. Then I take things up a notch by preparing a complementary herb sauce made with beef stock, vinegar and red wine. We love it!

—TONYA BURKHARD PALM COAST, FL

PREP: 40 MIN.
BAKE: 3¼ HOURS + STANDING
MAKES: 10 SERVINGS (1½ CUPS SAUCE)

- 1 bone-in beef rib roast (6 to 8 pounds)
- 1 teaspoon kosher salt
- 1 teaspoon freshly ground pepper
- 3 cups water
- 2 small onions, halved
- 7 garlic cloves, crushed
- 5 fresh sage sprigs
- 5 fresh thyme sprigs
- 2 bay leaves

SAUCE
- 2 tablespoons butter
- 2 shallots, thinly sliced
- 4 garlic cloves, thinly sliced
- 5 fresh sage sprigs
- 5 fresh thyme sprigs
- 2 bay leaves
- 1 tablespoon all-purpose flour
- 2 tablespoons cracked black pepper
- ¼ teaspoon kosher salt
- 1½ to 2½ cups beef stock, divided
- ½ cup dry red wine or beef stock
- ½ teaspoon red wine vinegar
  Fresh thyme sprigs, optional

1. Preheat oven to 450°. Place roast in a shallow roasting pan, fat side up; rub with kosher salt and pepper. Add 1 cup water, onions, garlic and herbs to the roasting pan. Roast 15 minutes.
2. Reduce the oven setting to 325°. Roast 3 to 3½ hours longer or until the meat reaches the desired doneness (for medium-rare, a thermometer should read 145°; medium, 160°; well-done, 170°), adding 1 cup water every hour.
3. For the sauce, in a large saucepan, heat the butter over medium-high heat. Add the shallots; cook and stir 5-6 minutes or until tender. Add the garlic and herbs; cook 1 minute longer. Stir in flour, cracked black pepper and kosher salt until blended. Gradually stir in 1½ cups beef stock. Remove from the heat.
4. Remove roast to a serving platter; tent with foil. Let stand 15 minutes before carving. Meanwhile, strain any pan juices through a sieve into a measuring cup; discard onions and herbs. Skim the fat from the pan juices. If necessary, add additional beef stock to the pan juices to measure 1 cup. Add to the shallot mixture.
5. Place the roasting pan over two burners; add the dry red wine. Bring to a boil; cook 2-3 minutes, stirring to loosen the browned bits from the pan. Add to sauce. Bring to a boil, stirring occasionally; cook until the mixture is reduced to about 1½ cups, about 10-15 minutes.
6. Stir in the red wine vinegar; strain, discarding shallots and herbs. Serve with roast and, if desired, thyme.

Brown Sugar Pineapple Ham

PREP: 10 MIN. • **BAKE:** 2 HOURS
MAKES: 12 SERVINGS

- 1 fully cooked bone-in ham (7 to 9 pounds)
- 1 can (20 ounces) crushed pineapple, undrained
- 1 cup packed brown sugar
- 1 tablespoon Dijon mustard
- ¼ teaspoon ground cloves

1. Preheat oven to 325°. Place ham on a rack in a shallow roasting pan. Using a sharp knife, score surface of ham with ½-in.-deep cuts in a diamond pattern. Cover and bake 1½ hours.
2. In a small bowl, mix the remaining ingredients. Spread over ham, pressing the mixture into the cuts. Bake ham, uncovered, 30-60 minutes longer or until a thermometer reads 140°.

"Enjoy the best of both worlds with Brown Sugar Pineapple Ham. It's easy enough for beginners to prepare, yet it looks and tastes like a holiday-worthy main course."

—TASTE OF HOME TEST KITCHEN

Fettuccine Shrimp Casserole

To our Louisiana family, this creamy seafood fettuccine is the perfect pasta entree. It can be made with either shrimp or crawfish. If you like, garnish servings with sour cream or salsa.
—**JUDY ARMSTRONG** PRAIRIEVILLE, LA

PREP: 25 MIN. • **BAKE:** 40 MIN. • **MAKES:** 8 SERVINGS

- 6 **ounces uncooked fettuccine**
- 1 **egg**
- ¾ **cup half-and-half cream**
- ½ **cup sour cream**
- ½ **teaspoon salt**
- 2 **cups (8 ounces) shredded cheddar cheese**
- ¼ **cup canned chopped green chilies**
- 3 **green onions, thinly sliced**
- 1 **tablespoon each minced fresh cilantro, basil and marjoram**
- 1 **pound uncooked shrimp (31-40 per pound), peeled and deveined or frozen cooked crawfish tail meat, thawed**
- 1 **cup salsa**
- ½ **cup shredded pepper jack cheese**
- 2 **cups tortilla chips, crushed**
- 2 **plum tomatoes, chopped**
- 1 **medium ripe avocado, peeled and sliced**

1. Preheat oven to 350°. Cook fettuccine according to the package directions. In a large bowl, whisk egg, cream, sour cream and salt. Stir in cheddar cheese, chilies, green onions and herbs. Drain fettuccine.
2. In a greased 13x9-in. baking dish, layer half of fettuccine, shrimp, cream mixture and salsa. Repeat the layers.

3. Bake, covered, 35 minutes. Sprinkle with pepper jack cheese, tortilla chips and plum tomatoes. Bake, uncovered, 5-10 minutes longer or until bubbly and cheese is melted. Serve with avocado slices.

Peachy Cranberry Sauce

When I was a newlywed, my mother-in-law gave me her cranberry sauce recipe so I could bring it to our holiday feast. The peaches are a pleasantly mellow complement to the tart berries.
—**HEIDI AZAR** SAN DIEGO, CA

PREP: 10 MIN. • **COOK:** 10 MIN. + CHILLING
MAKES: 16 SERVINGS (¼ CUP EACH)

- 1 **can (15¼ ounces) peach halves**
- 1 **package (12 ounces) fresh or frozen cranberries, thawed**
- 1 **large onion, chopped**
- ¾ **cup sugar**
- ½ **teaspoon ground cinnamon**
- ¼ **teaspoon ground ginger**
- 1 **cup chopped pecans**

1. Drain the peaches, reserving the syrup; coarsely chop the peaches. In a large saucepan, combine the cranberries, onion, sugar, cinnamon, ginger and reserved syrup. Bring to a boil, stirring to dissolve sugar. Reduce heat to medium; cook, uncovered, 8-10 minutes or until the cranberries pop, stirring occasionally.
2. Stir in the chopped peaches; remove from heat. Transfer to a small bowl; refrigerate, covered, until cold. Just before serving, stir in pecans.

Creamy Mashed Potatoes with Cabbage

These buttery mashed potatoes with chunks of cabbage and onion may remind you of traditional Irish colcannon.
—**PEGGY GOODRICH** ENID, OK

PREP: 15 MIN. • **COOK:** 20 MIN. • **MAKES:** 9 SERVINGS

- 6 **medium potatoes (about 2¾ pounds), peeled and quartered**
- 3 **cups chopped cabbage**
- 1 **medium onion, chopped**
- ¼ **cup water**
- ¼ **cup 2% milk**
- ¼ **cup butter, cubed**
- 1¼ **teaspoons salt**
- ½ **teaspoon pepper**

1. Place the potatoes in a 6-qt. stockpot; add water to cover. Bring to a boil. Reduce heat; cook, uncovered, 20-25 minutes or until tender.
2. Meanwhile, in a large saucepan, combine cabbage, onion and ¼ cup water; bring to a boil. Reduce the heat; simmer, covered, 10-12 minutes or until tender. Drain the potatoes; return to pan. Mash potatoes, gradually adding milk, butter, salt and pepper. Drain cabbage; stir into potato mixture.

Orange Roasted Turkey

When we want to roast a turkey, we always choose this one. Orange peel, juice and marmalade combine for a citrusy glaze.
—**LEE BREMSON** KANSAS CITY, MO

PREP: 20 MIN. • **BAKE:** 3 HOURS + STANDING
MAKES: 16 SERVINGS

- 1 turkey (14 to 16 pounds)
- 1 tablespoon canola oil
- ½ teaspoon salt
- ¼ teaspoon pepper
  Orange and onion wedges, optional

GLAZE

- ½ cup orange juice
- ½ cup orange marmalade
- ¼ cup butter, cubed
- 2 teaspoons grated orange peel
- 2 teaspoons minced fresh thyme or
  ½ teaspoon dried thyme
  Fresh parsley sprigs, optional

1. Preheat oven to 325°. Place the turkey on a rack in a shallow roasting pan, breast side up. Tuck wings under the turkey; tie the drumsticks together. Rub oil over turkey; sprinkle with salt and pepper. If desired, add orange and onion wedges to roasting pan.

2. Roast turkey, uncovered, 2¾ hours. Meanwhile, for the glaze, in a small saucepan, bring juice, marmalade and butter to a boil. Reduce heat; simmer, uncovered, 15-20 minutes or until slightly thickened, stirring occasionally. Stir in orange peel and thyme.
Brush turkey with some of the glaze. Roast 15-30 minutes longer or until a thermometer inserted in the thickest part of thigh reads 170°-175°, brushing occasionally with the remaining glaze. (Cover loosely with foil if the turkey browns too quickly.) Remove turkey from oven; tent with foil. Let stand 20 minutes before carving. If desired, skim fat and thicken pan drippings for gravy. Serve with turkey and, if desired, orange and onion wedges and parsley.

Orange and Beet Salad

This vibrant green salad is sure to attract attention on your holiday table. I started with a slightly different version of the recipe and kept altering the ingredients until I got it just the way I wanted it.

—**JESSIE APFE** BERKELEY, CA

PREP: 20 MIN. • **BAKE:** 55 MIN. + COOLING
MAKES: 6 SERVINGS

- 4 **medium fresh beets (about 1 pound)**
- 1 **tablespoon olive oil**
- 8 **cups spring mix salad greens**
- 2 **medium oranges, peeled and sectioned**
- ½ **cup crumbled feta cheese**

DRESSING
- ⅓ **cup orange juice**
- 2 **tablespoons mayonnaise**
- 1 **tablespoon grated orange peel**
- 1 **tablespoon brown sugar**
- 1 **tablespoon cider vinegar**
- ½ **teaspoon ground cinnamon**
- ¼ **teaspoon ground coriander**
- ¼ **teaspoon ground cardamom**
- ⅛ **teaspoon ground allspice**

1. Preheat oven to 400°. Scrub beets and trim the tops to 1 in. Place beets on a double thickness of heavy-duty foil (about 24x12 in.); drizzle with oil. Fold foil around beets, sealing tightly. Place on a baking sheet. Roast 55-65 minutes or until tender. Open foil carefully to allow steam to escape.

2. When cool enough to handle, peel and slice the beets. Divide the salad greens, beets and oranges among six salad plates. Sprinkle with crumbled feta cheese. In a small bowl, whisk the dressing ingredients; serve with salads.

Sweet Potato, Pear and Fig Crisp

My unusual but yummy dessert crisp celebrates the flavors of Christmastime. With vanilla ice cream or whipped cream, a just-baked scoop is a real treat.

—**DEANNA MCDONALD** MUSKEGON, MI

PREP: 25 MIN. • **BAKE:** 35 MIN.
MAKES: 8 SERVINGS

- 2 cans (15¾ ounces each) cut sweet potatoes in syrup, undrained
- 2 medium pears, peeled and chopped
- 8 ounces dried figs, quartered
- ¼ cup maple syrup
- 1 teaspoon lemon juice
- ½ teaspoon ground allspice

TOPPING
- 1 cup old-fashioned oats
- 1 cup chopped pecans
- ⅓ cup all-purpose flour
- ¼ cup packed brown sugar
- 1 teaspoon ground cinnamon
- ¼ teaspoon ground allspice
- ⅛ teaspoon salt
- ⅓ cup canola oil
- 1 tablespoon maple syrup
  Vanilla ice cream or sweetened whipped cream, optional

1. Preheat oven to 350°. Drain sweet potatoes, reserving 3 tablespoons syrup. Place sweet potatoes in a large bowl. Stir in pears, figs, maple syrup, lemon juice, allspice and reserved sweet potato syrup. Transfer to a greased 8-in.-square baking dish.
2. In a small bowl, mix the first seven topping ingredients. Stir in the oil and maple syrup; sprinkle over filling.
3. Bake, uncovered, 35-40 minutes or until the fruit is tender. If desired, serve warm with vanilla ice cream or whipped cream.

Butternut Apple Casserole

Fall and winter favorites come together perfectly in this warm, comforting side dish. The spiced chunks of butternut squash and apples are sprinkled with a buttery streusel and chopped pecans before going into the oven.

—**LORRAINE DAROCHA** MOUNTAIN CITY, TN

PREP: 25 MIN. • **BAKE:** 50 MIN.
MAKES: 12 SERVINGS (⅔ CUP EACH)

- 1 medium butternut squash (3 pounds), peeled and cut into ½-inch cubes
- ¼ cup packed brown sugar
- ½ teaspoon ground cinnamon
- ¼ teaspoon ground ginger
- ¼ teaspoon ground nutmeg
- 2 large apples, peeled and cut into ½-inch cubes

TOPPING
- ¾ cup all-purpose flour
- ¼ cup sugar
- ½ teaspoon ground cinnamon
- 2 tablespoons maple syrup
- ½ cup cold butter, cubed
- ⅔ cup chopped pecans

1. Preheat oven to 350°. In a 6-qt. stockpot, bring 1 in. of water to a boil. Add squash; cook, covered, 5 minutes or just until crisp-tender. Drain.
2. Meanwhile, in a large bowl, mix the brown sugar, cinnamon, ginger and nutmeg. Add the apples and cooked squash; toss to coat. Transfer to a greased 13x9-in. baking dish.
3. In a small bowl, mix the flour, sugar and cinnamon; stir in the maple syrup. Cut in butter until crumbly; sprinkle over the casserole. Bake, uncovered, 50-60 minutes or until the squash is tender, sprinkling with pecans during the last 10 minutes.

Cranberry & Walnut Pie

When it comes to dessert for a Christmas get-together, you just can't go wrong with a homemade pie. This one combines tart cranberries, rich semisweet chocolate and crunchy walnuts—plus a splash of dark rum for extra holiday spirit!

—LORRIE MELERINE HOUSTON, TX

PREP: 30 MIN. + CHILLING
BAKE: 30 MIN. + COOLING
MAKES: 8 SERVINGS

> Pastry for single-crust pie (9 inches)
> 3 eggs
> ¾ cup sugar
> ½ cup butter, melted
> 3 tablespoons all-purpose flour
> 1 cup chopped walnuts
> 1 cup fresh or frozen cranberries
> 1 cup (6 ounces) semisweet chocolate chips
> 2 tablespoons dark rum

1. On a lightly floured surface, roll pastry dough to a ⅛-in.-thick circle; transfer to a 9-in. pie plate. Trim pastry to ½ in. beyond the rim of the pie plate; flute the edge. Refrigerate 30 minutes. Preheat oven to 450°.

2. Line unpricked pastry with a double thickness of foil. Fill with pie weights, dried beans or uncooked rice. Bake on a lower oven rack 15-20 minutes or until edges are light golden brown. Remove the foil and weights; bake 3-6 minutes longer or until bottom is golden brown. Cool on a wire rack. Reduce the oven setting to 350°.

3. In a large bowl, beat the eggs, sugar and melted butter until well blended. Gradually add the flour until blended. Stir in the remaining ingredients; pour into the crust.

4. Bake 30-35 minutes or until top is bubbly and crust is golden brown. Cool on a wire rack. Refrigerate leftovers.

PASTRY FOR SINGLE-CRUST PIE (9 INCHES) *Combine 1¼ cups all-purpose flour and ¼ teaspoon salt; cut in ½ cup cold butter until crumbly. Gradually add 3-5 tablespoons ice water, tossing with a fork until dough holds together when pressed. Wrap in plastic wrap and refrigerate 1 hour.*

NOTE *Let the pie weights cool before storing. Beans and rice may be reused for pie weights, but not for cooking.*

JOLLY GINGERBREAD

Gingerbread Coffee Cake

The ginger, cinnamon and allspice really come through in this tongue-tingling cake. For a sweet drizzle, follow the directions for icing at the end of the recipe.

—**BARBARA HUMISTON** TAMPA, FL

PREP: 20 MIN. • **BAKE:** 20 MIN. + COOLING
MAKES: 8 SERVINGS

- 1 **cup all-purpose flour**
- ½ **cup plus 1 tablespoon sugar, divided**
- 1¾ **teaspoons ground cinnamon, divided**
- 1 **teaspoon ground ginger**
- ¼ **teaspoon salt**
- ¼ **teaspoon ground allspice**
- ¼ **cup cold butter**
- ¾ **teaspoon baking powder**
- ½ **teaspoon baking soda**
- 1 **egg**
- ½ **cup buttermilk**
- 2 **tablespoons molasses**

1. Preheat oven to 350°. In a large bowl, mix the flour, ½ cup sugar, ¾ teaspoon cinnamon, ginger, salt and allspice; cut in cold butter until crumbly. Reserve ⅓ cup for topping.
2. Stir the baking powder and baking soda into the remaining flour mixture. In a small bowl, whisk egg, buttermilk and molasses. Add to the flour mixture; stir just until moistened. Transfer batter to a greased 8-in. round baking pan.
3. Add remaining sugar and cinnamon to reserved topping; sprinkle over the batter. Bake 20-25 minutes or until a toothpick inserted in center comes out clean. Cool completely in pan on a wire rack.
CONFECTIONERS' SUGAR ICING (OPTIONAL) *Mix ¾ cup confectioners' sugar, 1 tablespoon 2% milk and ½ teaspoon vanilla extract. Drizzle icing over cooled coffee cake. Sprinkle with 2 tablespoons finely chopped crystallized ginger.*

Apple-Pecan Gingerbread Cobbler

My favorite cobbler is a scrumptious mix of gingerbread, crunchy pecans and tender apples. Dish up big bowlfuls warm from the oven and add a scoop of ice cream on top.
—**LOIS HENDRIX** REDONDO BEACH, CA

PREP: 15 MIN. • **BAKE:** 20 MIN. • **MAKES:** 12 SERVINGS

- 2 cans (21 ounces each) apple pie filling
- ½ cup cold butter, divided
- 1 package (14½ ounces) gingerbread cake/cookie mix, divided
- ¾ cup water
- ¼ cup packed brown sugar
- ½ cup chopped pecans
  Cinnamon ice cream or ice cream of your choice

1. Preheat oven to 375°. In a large saucepan, combine the apple pie filling and ¼ cup cold butter. Cook and stir over medium heat until heated through. Pour into a greased 13x9-in. baking dish.

2. In a large bowl, mix 2 cups gingerbread mix and water; spoon over pie filling. In a small bowl, mix the brown sugar and remaining gingerbread mix; cut in the remaining butter until crumbly. Stir in the pecans; sprinkle over the top.

3. Bake, uncovered, 20-25 minutes or until filling is bubbly and topping is golden brown. Serve warm with ice cream.

Pumpkin Toffee Trifle

With smooth pumpkin layers and crunchy cookies, this yummy trifle will have guests coming back for a second scoop.
—**JODIE JENSEN** DRAPER, UT

START TO FINISH: 25 MIN. • **MAKES:** 14 SERVINGS

- 2 packages (8 ounces each) cream cheese, softened
- ¾ cup sugar
- 1 can (15 ounces) solid-pack pumpkin
- 2 tablespoons ground cinnamon
- 2 teaspoons ground nutmeg
- ½ teaspoon ground cloves
- 1 carton (16 ounces) frozen whipped topping, thawed
- 2 teaspoons vanilla extract
- 1 package (11.3 ounces) toffee shortbread cookies, crushed
- 1 package (5¼ ounces) thin ginger cookies, crushed
- ½ cup plus 2 tablespoons hot caramel ice cream topping, divided
- 1 cup milk chocolate English toffee bits, divided

1. In a large bowl, beat the cream cheese and sugar until blended. Beat in pumpkin, cinnamon, nutmeg and cloves. In another bowl, mix whipped topping and vanilla.

2. In a 4-qt. glass bowl, layer half of the shortbread cookies, pumpkin mixture and ginger cookies. Drizzle with ¼ cup caramel topping. Top with half of the whipped topping and ¾ cup toffee bits. Repeat layers, adding remaining toffee bits. Drizzle with remaining caramel topping.

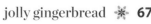

Chocolate-Ginger Pumpkin Muffins

A special breakfast calls for special muffins! Stir chocolate chips, orange peel, pumpkin and spices into the batter, and you'll have goodies worthy of Christmas morning.

—EVA AMUSO CHESHIRE, MA

PREP: 15 MIN. • **BAKE:** 20 MIN.
MAKES: 20 MUFFINS.

- 1¾ cups all-purpose flour
- 1 cup packed brown sugar
- 1½ teaspoons ground ginger
- 1½ teaspoons ground cinnamon
- 1 teaspoon baking soda
- ½ teaspoon salt
- ½ teaspoon ground nutmeg
- ⅛ teaspoon ground cloves
- 2 eggs
- ¾ cup canned pumpkin
- ½ cup canola oil
- ½ cup plain yogurt
- 4 teaspoons grated orange peel
- 1 cup (6 ounces) miniature semisweet chocolate chips
- ⅓ cup finely chopped crystallized ginger

1. Preheat oven to 375°. In a large bowl, whisk the first eight ingredients. In another bowl, whisk eggs, pumpkin, oil, plain yogurt and orange peel until blended. Add to flour mixture; stir just until moistened. Fold in the chocolate chips and crystallized ginger.
2. Fill greased muffin cups three-fourths full. Bake 18-20 minutes or until a toothpick inserted in center comes out clean. Cool 5 minutes before removing from the pans to wire racks. Serve warm.

Holiday Helper

Want fresh-baked muffins for breakfast? Make things easier in the morning by doing some prep work the night before. Combine dry ingredients in a plastic bag and measure other ingredients that will hold. In the morning, just stir together the batter and pop the muffins into the oven.

Apple Crumb Tart with Cinnamon Cream

Anyone who likes apple pie is sure to love this elegant tart dolloped with flavored whipped cream. The crumb topping and crust are easy to make with a cookie mix.

—KIM VAN DUNK CALDWELL, NJ

PREP: 30 MIN. • **BAKE:** 20 MIN. + COOLING
MAKES: 12 SERVINGS
(1 CUP WHIPPED CREAM)

- 1 package (17½ ounces) sugar cookie mix
- 1½ teaspoons ground cinnamon, divided
- ¾ teaspoon ground ginger
- ½ teaspoon ground nutmeg
- ¼ teaspoon ground cloves
- ½ cup cold butter, cubed
- 4 large apples, peeled and finely chopped (about 6 cups)
- ¼ cup packed brown sugar
- ½ cup all-purpose flour, divided
- ¼ cup raisins
- ½ cup heavy whipping cream
- 1 tablespoon maple syrup

1. Preheat oven to 350°. In a large bowl, whisk the cookie mix, 1 teaspoon cinnamon, ginger, nutmeg and cloves; cut in the butter until crumbly. Reserve 1 cup for topping; press remaining onto bottom and up sides of an ungreased 9-in. tart pan. Bake 8-10 minutes or until lightly browned. Remove to a wire rack.
2. Meanwhile, in a large saucepan, combine apples and sugar. Cook and stir over medium heat 7-9 minutes or until apples are tender and sugar is dissolved. Remove from heat; stir in ¼ cup flour, raisins and ¼ teaspoon cinnamon.
3. Increase the oven setting to 400°. Pour the apple mixture into the crust. Add the remaining flour to reserved topping and sprinkle over apples. Bake 20-22 minutes longer or until filling is bubbly and topping is golden brown. Cool on a wire rack at least 20 minutes.
4. In a small bowl, beat the cream until it begins to thicken. Add the syrup and remaining cinnamon; beat until soft peaks form. Serve tart warm or at room temperature with whipped cream.

Chocolate Gingerbread Cupcakes

It's no secret that these fun chocolate cupcakes have a fluffy filling—it overflows from the top! I sprinkle on confectioners' sugar for the finishing touch, then watch my family snatch them up.

—PATRICIA HARMON BADEN, PA

PREP: 40 MIN. • **BAKE:** 15 MIN. + COOLING
MAKES: 1 DOZEN

- 1 package (8 ounces) cream cheese, softened
- ½ cup white baking chips, melted and cooled
- ½ teaspoon vanilla extract
- ¼ teaspoon salt
- 1½ cups confectioners' sugar
- ½ cup marshmallow creme
- 1 package (14½ ounces) gingerbread cake/cookie mix
- 2 teaspoons pumpkin pie spice
- ½ teaspoon ground ginger
- 2 ounces semisweet chocolate, melted
  Grated semisweet chocolate and additional confectioners' sugar

1. Preheat oven to 375°. In a small bowl, beat cream cheese, melted white chips, vanilla and salt until blended. Gradually beat in confectioners' sugar until smooth. Fold in the marshmallow creme. Refrigerate until ready to use.

2. Line 12 muffin cups with paper liners. Prepare the gingerbread cake mix batter according to the package directions, adding the pumpkin pie spice and ginger before mixing the batter. Stir in the melted semisweet chocolate.

3. Fill prepared cups three-fourths full. Bake for 15-18 minutes or until a toothpick inserted in the center comes out clean. Cool in the pan for 10 minutes before removing to a wire rack to cool completely.

4. Using a sharp knife, cut a 1½-in. circle, 1 in. deep, in top of each cupcake. Carefully remove cut portion of cake and set aside. Fill the cavity with about 2 tablespoons filling; sprinkle with the grated semisweet chocolate. Replace the tops of cupcakes, pressing down lightly; dust with confectioners' sugar. Refrigerate leftovers.

Holiday Ginger Cookies

These classic boy and girl cutout cookies will look adorable not only on your Christmas treat platter, but also strung together on ribbon as a decorative holiday garland.
—**CHERYL WILT** EGLON, WV

PREP: 45 MIN. + CHILLING • **BAKE:** 10 MIN./BATCH + COOLING
MAKES: ABOUT 4 DOZEN

- 1 cup sugar
- 1 cup molasses
- ½ cup water
- ⅓ cup canola oil
- 1 egg
- 5½ cups all-purpose flour
- 3 teaspoons baking soda
- 3 teaspoons cream of tartar
- 3 teaspoons ground ginger
- 1 teaspoon ground cinnamon
  Frosting of your choice, optional

1. In a large bowl, beat the first five ingredients until blended. In another bowl, whisk the flour, baking soda, cream of tartar, ginger and cinnamon; gradually beat into the molasses mixture. Divide the dough into four portions. Shape each into a disk; wrap in plastic wrap. Refrigerate 1 hour or until firm enough to roll.

2. Preheat oven to 375°. On a well-floured surface, roll each portion of dough to ¼-in. thickness. Cut with a floured 4-in. gingerbread man cookie cutter. Place 1 in. apart on greased baking sheets. Using a plastic straw, make two holes at the neckline, about ½ in. apart.

3. Bake 10-12 minutes or until edges are lightly browned. Use straw to reopen holes in cookies. Remove to wire racks to cool completely.

4. If desired, decorate with frosting. Let dry completely. Tie a ribbon bow through the holes of each cookie or thread a long strand of ribbon through the holes of several cookies to create a decorative garland.

Creating a Cookie Garland

Holiday Ginger Cookies (above) are too good not to eat. But they're so cute, you'll want to turn some into a decorative garland, too! Follow the directions in the recipe and use the tips here:

When punching the holes, be sure to position them about ½ inch apart so the center is sturdy enough for hanging. (You may also wish to bake the cookies longer—for up to 15 minutes—to produce crispier, sturdier cookies.) Handle the baked cookies carefully and do not pull the garland too tight. For best results, do not freeze them before creating the garland.

Cranberry-Gingerbread Scones

Cranberry-studded scones are perfect for a December brunch. I bake them as guests arrive because the aroma is so welcoming.
—**LISA VARNER** EL PASO, TX

PREP: 20 MIN. • **BAKE:** 15 MIN. • **MAKES:** 8 SERVINGS

- 2 cups all-purpose flour
- 2 teaspoons baking powder
- 1 teaspoon ground ginger
- 1 teaspoon ground cinnamon
- ¼ teaspoon salt
- ¼ teaspoon baking soda
- ¼ teaspoon ground nutmeg
- ½ cup cold butter
- ⅓ cup heavy whipping cream
- ⅓ cup molasses
- ½ cup dried cranberries

TOPPING

- 1 tablespoon sugar
- ¼ teaspoon ground cinnamon
- 1 tablespoon finely chopped pecans

1. Preheat oven to 400°. In a large bowl, whisk the first seven ingredients. Cut in butter until mixture resembles coarse crumbs. In another bowl, whisk the whipping cream and molasses; stir into crumb mixture just until moistened. Stir in cranberries.

2. Turn onto a lightly floured surface; knead gently five times. Pat dough into an 8-in. circle. Cut into eight wedges. Place wedges on an ungreased baking sheet. Combine sugar and cinnamon; sprinkle over scones. Top with pecans. Bake 12-14 minutes or until light brown. Serve warm.

Gingerbread Cookie Bites

These creative goodies always stand out on a holiday platter. I press the dough into miniature muffin cups to form treats that resemble little tarts. With a cream cheese filling piped into the center, they're fun to serve and scrumptious, too.

—SHENAE PULLIAM SWANSEA, SC

PREP: 30 MIN. • **BAKE:** 10 MIN. + COOLING
MAKES: ABOUT 3 DOZEN

- 1 package (14½ ounces) gingerbread cake/cookie mix
- ½ cup butter, softened
- ¼ cup sugar
- 1 egg
- 2 tablespoons all-purpose flour
- 1 tablespoon water
- ¼ teaspoon ground ginger, optional

FILLING

- 4 ounces cream cheese, softened
- ¼ cup butter, softened
- ½ teaspoon vanilla extract
- 1¾ cups confectioners' sugar
  Ground cinnamon and nutmeg
  Crystallized ginger, chopped, optional

1. In a large bowl, beat the gingerbread cake/cookie mix, butter, sugar, egg, flour, water and, if desired, ginger until blended. Refrigerate 30 minutes or until firm.

2. Preheat oven to 350°. Shape the cookie dough into 1-in. balls; place in ungreased mini muffin cups. Press the balls evenly onto the bottoms and up the sides of cups. Bake 10-12 minutes or until the edges are lightly golden. Cool in the pans 2 minutes. Remove to wire racks to cool completely.

3. For the filling, in a large bowl, beat the cream cheese, butter and vanilla until blended. Gradually beat in the confectioners' sugar until smooth. Pipe into cookie cups; sprinkle with the cinnamon, nutmeg and, if desired, crystallized ginger. Refrigerate in an airtight container.

Gingerbread Peppermint Pinwheels

I roll two seasonal flavors—peppermint and gingerbread—into my little pinwheels. Friends and family love the combination.

—**JOANNA QUELCH** BURLINGTON, VT

PREP: 1 HOUR + CHILLING
BAKE: 10 MIN./BATCH
MAKES: ABOUT 6 DOZEN

GINGERBREAD DOUGH

- ½ cup butter, softened
- ½ cup packed brown sugar
- 1 egg
- ¼ cup molasses
- 2¼ cups all-purpose flour
- 1 teaspoon ground ginger
- ½ teaspoon ground cinnamon
- ¼ teaspoon baking soda
- ¼ teaspoon ground cloves

PEPPERMINT DOUGH

- ⅓ cup butter, softened
- 3 ounces cream cheese, softened
- 1 cup sugar
- 1 egg
- ½ teaspoon vanilla extract
- ⅛ teaspoon peppermint extract
- 2¼ cups all-purpose flour
- ½ teaspoon baking powder
- 2 tablespoons crushed peppermint candies

1. In a large bowl, cream butter and brown sugar until light and fluffy. Beat in egg and molasses. In another bowl, whisk flour, ginger, cinnamon, baking soda and cloves; gradually beat into creamed mixture. Divide dough in half. Shape each into a disk; wrap in plastic wrap. Refrigerate 1 hour or until firm enough to roll.

2. For peppermint dough, in a large bowl, cream butter, cream cheese and sugar until light and fluffy. Beat in egg and extracts. In another bowl, whisk flour and baking powder; gradually beat into creamed mixture. Stir in candies. Divide dough in half. Shape each into a disk; wrap in plastic wrap. Refrigerate 1 hour or until firm enough to roll.

3. On a baking sheet, roll one portion of gingerbread dough between two sheets of waxed paper into a 10x8-in. rectangle. Roll one portion of peppermint dough between two sheets of waxed paper into a 10x8-in. rectangle. Remove the top sheets of waxed paper; invert peppermint dough over gingerbread dough. Refrigerate 30 minutes.

4. Remove waxed paper from dough. Roll up tightly jelly-roll style, starting with a long side. Wrap in plastic wrap. Repeat with the remaining dough. Refrigerate 2 hours or until firm.

5. Preheat oven to 375°. Unwrap and cut dough crosswise into ¼-in. slices. Place 2 in. apart on greased baking sheets. Bake 10-12 minutes or until set. Remove from pans to wire racks to cool.

Gingerbread with Lime Cream Cheese Icing

Moist, tender gingerbread gets a tangy twist when you add a burst of refreshing lime to the icing. I sprinkle on toasted pecans for crunch, too.

—**CHARLENE CHAMBERS** ORMOND BEACH, FL

PREP: 25 MIN. • **BAKE:** 35 MIN. + COOLING
MAKES: 8 SERVINGS

- ¾ cup butter, softened
- 1¼ cups sugar, divided
- ⅓ cup molasses
- 1 egg
- 2 tablespoons water
- 2 teaspoons grated fresh gingerroot
- 1¼ cups all-purpose flour
- 1 teaspoon ground cinnamon
- ¼ teaspoon ground nutmeg
- ¼ teaspoon ground allspice
- ½ teaspoon salt
- ¼ teaspoon baking soda
- 1 package (8 ounces) cream cheese, softened
- 2 tablespoons lime juice
- 1 teaspoon grated lime peel
- 2 tablespoons chopped pecans, toasted

1. Preheat oven to 350°. Grease an 11x7-in. baking dish.

2. In a large bowl, cream butter and ¾ cup sugar until light and fluffy. Beat in the molasses, egg, water and ginger. In another bowl, whisk flour, spices, salt and baking soda; gradually beat into the creamed mixture. Transfer batter to prepared dish.

3. In a small bowl, beat cream cheese, lime juice, lime peel and remaining sugar until blended. Set aside ¾ cup for icing. Drop the remaining mixture by tablespoonfuls over the batter; cut through batter with a knife to blend slightly (mixture will not swirl).

4. Bake 35-40 minutes or until a toothpick inserted in the center comes out clean. Cool completely in the pan on a wire rack. Spread reserved icing over the cake; sprinkle with pecans. Refrigerate leftovers.

Gingerbread-Pumpkin Cheesecake Bars

Cheesecake lovers will go crazy for these rich, smooth cream-cheese squares.

—**KATHLEEN RHODEBECK** PENACOOK, NH

PREP: 30 MIN. • **BAKE:** 25 MIN. + CHILLING
MAKES: 16 SERVINGS

- ½ cup butter, softened
- ½ cup packed dark brown sugar
- 1 egg
- ¼ cup molasses
- 1½ cups all-purpose flour
- 1¼ teaspoons ground ginger
- 1 teaspoon ground cinnamon
- ½ teaspoon baking soda
- ¼ teaspoon ground cloves

CHEESECAKE BATTER
- 1 package (8 ounces) cream cheese, softened
- ¼ cup plus 1 tablespoon sugar, divided
- ½ cup canned pumpkin
- ½ teaspoon ground cinnamon
- ¼ teaspoon ground ginger
- ⅛ teaspoon ground cloves
- 1 egg

1. Preheat oven to 350°. In a large bowl, cream butter and brown sugar until light and fluffy. Beat in egg and molasses. In a small bowl, whisk flour, ginger, cinnamon, baking soda and cloves; gradually beat into creamed mixture. Reserve 1 cup dough for the topping; press remaining mixture onto bottom of a greased 9-in.-square baking pan.

2. For cheesecake batter, in a small bowl, beat cream cheese and ¼ cup sugar until light and fluffy. Beat in the pumpkin and spices. Add the egg; beat on low speed just until blended. Pour over the crust.

3. Drop the reserved dough by tablespoonfuls over the cheesecake batter. Sprinkle with remaining sugar.

4. Bake 25-30 minutes or until the center is almost set. Cool 1 hour on a wire rack. Refrigerate at least 2 hours. Cut into bars.

Winter Spice Bundt Cake

Dotted with fruits and nuts, this seasonal cake is perfect for a holiday tea.

—**RENEE ROBERTS** SLEEPY HOLLOW, NY

PREP: 30 MIN. + COOLING
BAKE: 50 MIN. + COOLING
MAKES: 12 SERVINGS

- 1 **cup golden raisins**
- 1 **cup dried cranberries**
- ½ **cup dark rum or ¼ cup orange juice and ¼ cup apple cider**
- 2 **teaspoons grated orange peel**
- 1 **teaspoon ground cinnamon**
- 1 **teaspoon ground ginger**
- ½ **teaspoon ground allspice**
- ½ **teaspoon ground cloves**
- ½ **teaspoon ground nutmeg**
- 1½ **cups apple cider or juice**
- 1 **cup packed dark brown sugar**
- ⅔ **cup butter, cubed**
- 2 **eggs, lightly beaten**
- 2 **cups all-purpose flour**
- 1 **teaspoon salt**
- 1 **teaspoon baking powder**
- 1 **teaspoon baking soda**
- ½ **cup chopped walnuts**
- ½ **cup chopped pecans**
   Sweetened whipped cream

1. In a large saucepan, combine first nine ingredients. Bring to a boil. Cook and stir 2-3 minutes or until the fruit is softened. Stir in the cider, brown sugar and butter. Bring to a boil. Reduce the heat; simmer, uncovered, 8-10 minutes or until slightly thickened, stirring frequently. Transfer to a large bowl; cool to room temperature, about 1 hour, stirring occasionally.

2. Preheat oven to 325°. Grease and flour a 10-in. fluted tube pan. Add eggs to fruit mixture; mix well. In another bowl, whisk flour, salt, baking powder and baking soda. Add to fruit mixture; stir just until moistened. Stir in nuts.

3. Transfer batter to prepared pan. Bake 50-60 minutes or until a toothpick inserted in center comes out clean. Cool in the pan 10 minutes before removing to a wire rack to cool. Serve warm or at room temperature with whipped cream.

NOTE *To remove cakes easily, use solid shortening to grease plain and fluted tube pans.*

Gingerbread Belgian Waffles

Mmm, homemade waffles! A sweet drizzle takes the place of the usual maple syrup.

—**JANNINE FISK** MALDEN, MA

PREP: 25 MIN. • **COOK:** 5 MIN./BATCH
MAKES: 6 ROUND WAFFLES (1½ CUPS ICING)

- 2 **cups all-purpose flour**
- ¼ **cup packed brown sugar**
- 3 **teaspoons baking powder**
- 1½ **teaspoons ground ginger**
- 1 **teaspoon baking soda**
- 1 **teaspoon ground cinnamon**
- ½ **teaspoon salt**
- ¼ **teaspoon ground nutmeg**
- 4 **eggs, separated**
- 2 **cups buttermilk**
- ½ **cup butter, melted**
- ½ **cup molasses**
- 2 **teaspoons vanilla extract**

ICING

- 1½ **cups confectioners' sugar**
- ½ **cup butter, softened**
- ¼ **cup cream cheese, softened**
- 2 **tablespoons 2% milk**
- ½ **teaspoon vanilla extract**
- ⅛ **teaspoon salt**

1. In a large bowl, combine the first eight ingredients. In another bowl, whisk egg yolks, buttermilk, butter, molasses and vanilla. Add to the dry ingredients; stir just until combined.

2. In a small bowl, beat egg whites until stiff. Gently fold into batter.

3. Bake batter in a preheated round Belgian waffle iron according to the manufacturer's directions until golden brown. Meanwhile, in a small bowl, combine all icing ingredients; beat until smooth. Serve icing with waffles.

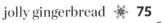

Pumpkin Bread with Gingerbread Topping

This delectable loaf with a ginger-spiced topping won first prize in a bread contest.

—RENEE' NANEZ FREDERIC, WI

PREP: 35 MIN. • **BAKE:** 30 MIN. + COOLING
MAKES: 5 LOAVES (6 SLICES EACH)

- ¾ cup butter, cubed
- 2¼ cups sugar
- 1½ cups canned pumpkin
- 3 eggs
- 2¼ cups all-purpose flour
- 1 teaspoon ground cinnamon
- 1 teaspoon ground nutmeg
- ¾ teaspoon baking soda
- ½ teaspoon baking powder
- ½ teaspoon salt
- ½ cup chopped walnuts
- ½ cup finely chopped crystallized ginger

TOPPING

- 10 gingersnap cookies
- ⅓ cup packed brown sugar
- 2 tablespoons all-purpose flour
- ¼ teaspoon ground cinnamon
- ¼ teaspoon ground nutmeg
- 6 tablespoons cold butter
- ¼ cup finely chopped walnuts, optional

1. Preheat oven to 350°. In a large heavy saucepan, melt the butter over medium heat. Heat 5-7 minutes or until golden brown, stirring constantly. Remove from heat. Transfer to a large bowl; cool slightly. Add sugar, pumpkin and eggs; beat until well blended.

2. In another bowl, whisk the flour, cinnamon, nutmeg, baking soda, baking powder and salt; gradually beat into the pumpkin mixture. Fold in the walnuts and crystallized ginger.

3. Transfer to five greased 5¾x3x2-in. loaf pans. Place cookies, brown sugar, flour, cinnamon and nutmeg in a food processor; pulse until cookies are finely ground. Add butter; pulse until crumbly. Sprinkle cookie mixture and, if desired, walnuts over batter.

4. Bake 30-35 minutes or until a toothpick inserted in the center comes out clean. Cool in the pans 10 minutes before removing to wire racks to cool.

SEASONAL
GET-TOGETHERS

Christmas Coffee & Dessert

Home sweet coffeehouse! Become a barista for a day and gather together
the espresso lovers in your life for good conversation, specialty beverages
and scrumptious treats. You're sure to perk up the holiday season.

Fudgy Turtle Pie

Indulge! A slice of this incredibly decadent, ooey-gooey dessert is impossible to resist. With rich chocolate, caramel and pecans, it captures all the delights of turtle candy.

—DOLORES VACCARO PUEBLO, CO

PREP: 55 MIN. + CHILLING
MAKES: 16 SERVINGS

1½ cups chocolate wafer crumbs
   (32 wafers)
⅓ cup butter, melted

FILLING

20 caramels
¼ cup heavy whipping cream
2 cups chopped pecans
4 Snickers candy bars (1.86 ounces
   each), chopped

TOPPING

2 cups (12 ounces) semisweet
   chocolate chips
1 cup heavy whipping cream
   Caramel ice cream topping,
   optional
   Additional chopped Snickers
   candy bars, optional

1. Preheat oven to 375°. In a small bowl, mix the chocolate wafer crumbs and butter. Press onto the bottom and up the sides of a greased 9-in. fluted tart pan with a removable bottom. Bake 8-10 minutes or until set. Cool on a wire rack.

2. For the filling, in a small heavy saucepan, combine the caramels and heavy whipping cream. Cook and stir over low heat until the caramels are melted. Stir in pecans. Remove from the heat; pour into the crust. Top with chopped Snickers candy.

3. For the topping, place semisweet chocolate chips in a small bowl. In a small saucepan, bring the heavy cream just to a boil. Pour over the chocolate; stir with a whisk until smooth. Pour and spread, if necessary, over the top. Refrigerate 1 hour or until set.

4. If desired, drizzle ice cream topping over individual pieces and top with additional chopped candy.

Comforting Coffee Milk

This drink is one of my favorites because the simple, wholesome ingredients speak for themselves. Each sip has a little maple, molasses and cocoa flavor—just the right comforting combo on a chilly afternoon.

—BRENDA SCHRAG FARMINGTON, NM

START TO FINISH: 20 MIN.
MAKES: 6 SERVINGS

4 cups whole milk
1⅓ cups strong brewed coffee
½ cup maple syrup
2 tablespoons molasses
2 teaspoons baking cocoa

WHIPPED CREAM

1 cup heavy whipping cream
1 tablespoon maple syrup
1 teaspoon vanilla extract
   Additional baking cocoa

1. In a large saucepan, combine the first five ingredients over medium heat to just simmering (do not boil), stirring occasionally.

2. Meanwhile, in a small bowl, beat the heavy cream until it begins to thicken. Add maple syrup and vanilla; beat until soft peaks form. Serve with coffee milk. Dust with additional cocoa.

Making Foam for Frothy Cafe Bombon

1. Vigorously whisk the heated milk to create foam for each mug. Milk that is too hot won't froth up as much, so be sure the milk is just shy of boiling. Feel free to use skim, 1% or 2% milk in place of whole milk if you prefer.

2. Stop whisking when the foam reaches almost the top of the 2-cup measuring cup. Remove as much foam as possible so you have room in the same cup to make more foam as needed.

Frothy Cafe Bombon

While visiting Spain on my honeymoon, I discovered this delightful coffee beverage. The sweetened condensed milk, java and foam create a fun layered look.

—KERI HESEMANN ST. CHARLES, MO

START TO FINISH: 10 MIN.
MAKES: 4 SERVINGS

> 1 **cup whole milk**
> ¾ **cup sweetened condensed milk**
> 4 **cups hot strong brewed coffee**
> **Ground cinnamon**

1. Place milk in a 2-cup microwave-safe measuring cup. Microwave, uncovered, on high for 1-2 minutes or until the milk is hot and small bubbles form around the edge of the cup.

2. Divide the sweetened condensed milk among four glass mugs; carefully pour the coffee over the milk.

3. Place a metal whisk in the warm milk; whisk vigorously by holding the whisk handle loosely between your palms and quickly rubbing your hands back and forth to create foam. Remove the foam to another 2-cup measuring cup as it forms. Continue whisking the milk until the foam measures 2 cups. Spoon the foam over coffee. Discard any remaining milk.

4. Sprinkle the foam with cinnamon; serve with a spoon.

Sweet Almond Twists

These delicate almond pastries make lovely light-as-air accompaniments for just about any warm drink. Guests will never guess the recipe calls for packaged frozen dough.

—**GLORIA DEVENDITTIS** WATERFORD, CT

PREP: 25 MIN. • **BAKE:** 15 MIN.
MAKES: 32 TWISTS

- 1 **package (17.3 ounces) frozen puff pastry, thawed**
- 1 **egg**
- 1 **tablespoon water**
- ¼ **cup almond cake and pastry filling**
- 1 **cup sliced almonds**

1. Preheat oven to 400°. Unfold pastry sheets on a lightly floured surface; roll each sheet into a 15x10-in. rectangle.
2. In a small bowl, whisk egg and water; brush over rectangles. Spread the pastry filling over one rectangle to within ¼ in. of the edges; sprinkle with the almonds. Top with remaining pastry, egg wash side down, pressing lightly.
3. Brush the top with egg wash. Cut in half lengthwise; cut each rectangle crosswise into sixteen strips. Twist each strip 2-3 times. Place 1 in. apart on baking sheets. Bake 12-14 minutes or until golden brown. Serve warm.

Mint Creme Cookies

A minty filling sandwiched between rich chocolate cookies—what's not to love?

—**GAYLENE ANDERSON** SANDY, UT

PREP: 20 MIN. • **BAKE:** 10 MIN. + COOLING
MAKES: 4 DOZEN

- 1½ **cups packed brown sugar**
- ¾ **cup butter, cubed**
- 2 **tablespoons water**
- 2 **cups (12 ounces) semisweet chocolate chips**
- 2 **eggs**
- 3 **cups all-purpose flour**
- 1¼ **teaspoons baking soda**
- 1 **teaspoon salt**

FILLING
- ⅓ **cup butter, softened**
- 3 **cups confectioners' sugar**
- 3 **to 4 tablespoons milk**
- ⅛ **teaspoon peppermint extract**
  Dash salt

1. In a small saucepan, combine the brown sugar, butter and water. Cook and stir over medium heat until sugar is dissolved. Remove from heat; stir in the chips until melted and smooth. Transfer to a large bowl; cool slightly.
2. Add eggs, one at a time, beating well after each addition. Combine the flour, baking soda and salt; gradually add to the chocolate mixture and mix well.
3. Drop cookie dough by rounded teaspoonfuls onto greased baking sheets. Bake at 350° for 8-10 minutes or until set. Remove to wire racks; flatten slightly. Cool completely.
4. Combine the filling ingredients; spread on the bottoms of half of the cookies; top with remaining cookies. Store in the refrigerator.

> ### "The word 'noisette' means
> *hazelnut, and mini French Noisette Cups*
> *have a yummy toasted nut flavor."*
>
> —**MARIE RIZZIO** INTERLOCHEN, MI

French Noisette Cups

PREP: 20 MIN. + CHILLING • **BAKE:** 20 MIN.
MAKES: 2 DOZEN

- ½ cup butter, softened
- 3 ounces cream cheese, softened
- 1 cup all-purpose flour
- 1⅓ cups hazelnuts
- ⅔ cup packed brown sugar
- 1 egg
- 1 tablespoon butter, melted
- 1 teaspoon vanilla extract

1. In a large bowl, cream the butter and cream cheese. Beat in the flour. Refrigerate, covered, 30 minutes or until easy to handle.

2. Preheat oven to 350°. Spread the hazelnuts in a 15x10x1-in. baking pan. Bake 7-10 minutes or until fragrant and lightly browned, stirring occasionally. To remove skins, wrap the hazelnuts in a tea towel; rub with towel to loosen skins. Reserve 24 nuts for topping.

3. Shape dough into 24 balls. With floured fingers, press evenly onto the bottom and up the sides of ungreased mini-muffin cups.

4. Place brown sugar and remaining hazelnuts in a food processor; pulse until hazelnuts are finely ground. In a small bowl, whisk egg, melted butter and vanilla; stir in hazelnut mixture. Fill cups with 2 teaspoons; top each with a reserved hazelnut.

5. Bake 18-22 minutes or until set. Remove to wire racks to cool.

Caramel-Chai Tea Latte

Inspired by the spicy chai drinks served at coffee shops, I whipped up a caramel-drizzled latte I can enjoy at home anytime.
—**KATELYN KELLY** PERRYVILLE, MD

START TO FINISH: 25 MIN. • **MAKES:** 4 SERVINGS

- 3½ cups water
- 1½ cups whole milk
- 10 chai-flavored black tea bags
- ⅓ cup caramel flavoring syrup
  Sweetened whipped cream and hot caramel ice cream topping, optional

1. In a large saucepan, bring water and milk to a boil over medium heat, stirring occasionally. Add the tea bags. Reduce the heat; simmer, covered, 5 minutes. Remove from the heat; continue steeping, covered, 5 minutes.

2. Squeeze excess liquid from all tea bags into tea; discard tea bags. Stir in caramel syrup. If desired, top servings with whipped cream and caramel topping.

NOTE *This recipe was tested with Torani brand flavoring syrup. Look for it in the coffee section.*

Raspberry-Almond Coffee Cake

Applesauce makes this moist, berry-filled cake a little bit lighter. The brown sugar topping adds the perfect touch of sweetness.
—**LISA VARNER** EL PASO, TX

PREP: 20 MIN. • **BAKE:** 30 MIN. + COOLING • **MAKES:** 15 SERVINGS

- 2 cups all-purpose flour
- ¾ cup sugar
- ¼ cup packed brown sugar
- 1 teaspoon baking powder
- ½ teaspoon baking soda
- ½ teaspoon salt
- 2 eggs
- 1 cup buttermilk
- ⅓ cup unsweetened applesauce
- ⅓ cup butter, melted
- ½ teaspoon almond extract
- 2 cups fresh or frozen unsweetened raspberries

TOPPING
- ⅔ cup sliced almonds
- ½ cup packed brown sugar
- 1 teaspoon ground cinnamon

1. Preheat oven to 350°. In a large bowl, whisk the first six ingredients. In another bowl, whisk the eggs, buttermilk, applesauce, butter and extract; stir into the dry ingredients just until moistened. Gently fold in raspberries.

2. Transfer the batter to a 13x9-in. baking pan coated with cooking spray. In a small bowl, mix the topping ingredients; sprinkle over batter. Bake 30-35 minutes or until a toothpick inserted in center comes out clean. Cool 10 minutes in pan on a wire rack. Serve warm.

Tree Trimming Party

A stately evergreen tree stands tall and proud in your home for Christmas. Now for the decorating! Enlist friends and family, then reward your helpers with a delicious, satisfying meal that shines as bright as the ornaments.

Potluck Sausage Casserole

Whenever my husband digs in to this pasta casserole full of Italian sausage and veggies, he gets a big smile on his face. I love that!
—**JANE DAVIS** MARION, IN

PREP: 25 MIN. • **BAKE:** 25 MIN. + STANDING
MAKES: 10 SERVINGS

- 1 package (16 ounces) penne pasta
- 1 pound bulk Italian sausage
- 1 tablespoon butter
- 1 tablespoon olive oil
- 1 medium onion, finely chopped
- 1 medium carrot, finely chopped
- 1½ teaspoons dried oregano
- 1 teaspoon salt
- ½ teaspoon pepper
- 1 small zucchini, halved lengthwise and sliced
- 1 cup chopped fresh mushrooms
- 6 garlic cloves, minced
- 1 can (15 ounces) tomato sauce
- 1 jar (14 ounces) pasta sauce with meat
- 2 cups (8 ounces) shredded part-skim mozzarella cheese

1. Preheat oven to 350°. Cook pasta according to package directions for al dente; drain and transfer to a greased 13x9-in. baking dish. Meanwhile, in a large skillet, cook Italian sausage over medium heat 6-8 minutes or until no longer pink, breaking into crumbles; drain and remove from pan.
2. In same skillet, heat butter and oil over medium-high heat. Add onion, carrot, oregano, salt and pepper; cook and stir 5 minutes. Add the zucchini, mushrooms and garlic; cook and stir 6-8 minutes longer or until vegetables are tender.
3. Stir in tomato sauce, pasta sauce and sausage; pour over penne pasta. Sprinkle with the mozzarella cheese (dish will be full). Cover the casserole with a piece of foil coated with cooking spray. Bake 10 minutes. Uncover; bake 15-20 minutes longer or until golden brown and cheese is melted. Let stand 10 minutes before serving.

Meatball & Pasta Soup

Warm up cold winter days with bowlfuls of hearty soup. We like crusty French bread or dinner rolls on the side.
—**LAURA GREENBERG** LAKE BALBOA, CA

START TO FINISH: 30 MIN.
MAKES: 8 SERVINGS (3 QUARTS)

- 8 cups vegetable stock
- 1 garlic clove, minced
- 1 teaspoon salt, divided
- 1 egg
- ½ cup dry bread crumbs
- ¼ cup 2% milk
- 2 tablespoons ketchup
- 2 teaspoons Worcestershire sauce
- 1 teaspoon onion powder
- ½ teaspoon pepper
- 1 pound lean ground beef (90% lean)
- 4 medium carrots, chopped
- 1 cup uncooked orzo pasta
- 1 package (6 ounces) fresh baby spinach

1. In a 6-qt. stockpot, bring vegetable stock, garlic and ¾ teaspoon salt to a boil. Meanwhile, in a large bowl, mix the egg, bread crumbs, milk, ketchup, Worcestershire sauce, onion powder, pepper and remaining salt. Add beef; mix lightly but thoroughly. Shape into 1-in. balls.
2. Add the carrots, pasta and meatballs to boiling stock. Reduce heat; simmer, uncovered, 10-12 minutes or until the meatballs are cooked through and the pasta is tender, stirring occasionally. Stir in spinach until wilted.

Cherry Cheese Logs

Our Christmas guests flock to this gem of an appetizer. The recipe makes two logs of sweetened cream cheese studded with cherries and coated with pecans. Great on graham crackers, the yummy spread would also be good on sliced apples and pears.

—**LIBBY WALP** CHICAGO, IL

PREP: 15 MIN. + CHILLING
MAKES: 2 LOGS (1¾ CUPS EACH)

- 3 **packages (8 ounces each) cream cheese, softened**
- 2 **tablespoons sugar**
- 1 **tablespoon orange juice**
- ¼ **teaspoon ground ginger**
- 1 **jar (10 ounces) maraschino cherries, well drained and chopped**
- 1 **cup chopped pecans, toasted Graham crackers**

1. In a large bowl, beat the cream cheese, sugar, orange juice and ginger until smooth. Fold in the maraschino cherries. Refrigerate, covered, at least 1 hour.

2. Place the pecans in a shallow bowl. Shape the cream cheese mixture into two 7-in.-long logs; roll in the pecans to coat evenly. Wrap in plastic wrap; refrigerate at least 1 hour. Serve with graham crackers.

NOTE *To toast nuts, bake in a shallow pan in a 350° oven for 5-10 minutes or cook in a skillet over low heat until lightly browned, stirring occasionally.*

Romaine & Cherry Tomato Salad

My mother fixed this colorful dish for me when I was a child, and it was my favorite. The layers of vegetables, Parmesan, bacon and mayonnaise all add up to a refreshing but hearty side salad. We've even served it as the main course!

—**BLYTHE TWIGGS** BUFORD, GA

START TO FINISH: 20 MIN.
MAKES: 8 SERVINGS

- 1 **small bunch romaine, torn**
- 2 **cups grape tomatoes, halved**
- 1 **package (12 ounces) frozen peas, thawed**
- 1 **small red onion, thinly sliced**
- 1½ **cups reduced-fat mayonnaise**
- 1 **cup shredded Parmesan cheese**
- 8 **bacon strips, cooked and crumbled**

In a 3-qt. trifle bowl or glass bowl, layer the romaine, grape tomatoes, peas and red onion. Spread the mayonnaise over the onion. Sprinkle with the cheese and bacon. Refrigerate until serving.

Monkey Bread Biscuits

Traditional monkey bread is a sweet, cinnamony breakfast treat. I came up with a simple dinner version featuring Italian seasoning and garlic to complement a variety of entrees.
—**DANA JOHNSON** SCOTTSDALE, AZ

START TO FINISH: 20 MIN. • **MAKES:** 1 DOZEN

- **1 tube (16.3 ounces) large refrigerated flaky biscuits**
- **3 tablespoons butter, melted**
- **1 garlic clove, minced**
- **½ teaspoon Italian seasoning**
- **¼ cup grated Parmesan cheese**
  Additional Italian seasoning

1. Preheat oven to 425°. Separate the biscuits; cut each into six pieces. In a large bowl, combine butter, garlic and Italian seasoning; add biscuit pieces and toss to coat.

2. Place four pieces in each of twelve greased muffin cups. Sprinkle with the cheese and additional Italian seasoning. Bake 8-10 minutes or until golden brown. Serve warm.

Retro Paper Ornaments

This child-friendly craft is simple to create, but the result makes a surprisingly sophisticated addition to a Christmas tree. Start by gathering as many 12-inch squares of double-sided card stock as you'd like (one sheet makes four ornaments).

1. For each ornament, use a paper cutter or scissors to cut one 4x1-inch strip, two 5x1-inch strips and two 6x1-inch strips.

2. Layer the strips with the shortest in the center, two medium-length strips on either side and the two longest on the outer layer.

3. Position the layered strips so that they line up at one short end.

4. Cut a 6-inch length of narrow ribbon. Fold the ribbon in half and place the two ends between the layered paper strips at the flush end. Staple all the layers at the flush end in place.

5. Hold the stapled end with one hand and use your other hand to pinch the opposite ends of the longest strips. Push the pinched ends up toward the stapled end, capturing the medium-length strips as you go. Continue pushing up until all ends meet at the end of the shortest strip, then staple the ends in place.

Chocolate, Peanut & Pretzel Toffee Crisps

Just try to stop munching these chocolaty crackers piled with peanuts, pretzels and candy. The sweet-salty treats disappear so quickly, you may want to make extra!

—**JENNIFER BUTKA** LIVONIA, MI

PREP: 25 MIN. • **BAKE:** 10 MIN. + CHILLING
MAKES: 2½ POUNDS

- 40 **saltines**
- ¾ **cup butter, cubed**
- ¾ **cup packed brown sugar**
- 1 **teaspoon vanilla extract**
- 2 **cups (12 ounces) semisweet chocolate chips**
- 1 **cup cocktail peanuts**
- 1 **cup broken pretzel sticks**
- ¾ **cup M&M's minis**

1. Preheat oven to 350°. Line a 15x10x1-in. baking pan with foil; grease foil. Arrange saltine crackers in a single layer on foil.

2. In a large heavy saucepan, melt the butter over medium heat. Stir in the brown sugar. Bring to a boil; cook and stir 2-3 minutes or until brown sugar is dissolved. Remove from heat; stir in the vanilla. Spread evenly over the saltine crackers.

3. Bake 8-10 minutes or until bubbly. Immediately sprinkle with semisweet chocolate chips. Allow chocolate chips to soften 2 minutes, then spread over the top. Sprinkle with peanuts, pretzels and M&M's minis; shake pan to settle toppings into chocolate. Cool.

4. Refrigerate, uncovered, 1 hour or until set. Break into pieces. Store in an airtight container.

Festive Holiday Punch

Wondering what beverage to present on a Christmas buffet? Here's a wonderful choice. The tangy fruit flavor and gorgeous red color always go over well. For extra flair, garnish glasses with lime wedges.

—**TAHNIA FOX** TRENTON, MI

START TO FINISH: 5 MIN.
MAKES: 14 SERVINGS (¾ CUP EACH)

- 1 **bottle (64 ounces) cranberry-raspberry juice, chilled**
- 1 **can (12 ounces) frozen raspberry lemonade concentrate, thawed**
- 1 **bottle (2 liters) lemon-lime soda, chilled**
  Fresh raspberries
  Ice cubes
  Lime wedges, optional

In a punch bowl, mix the juice and raspberry lemonade concentrate. Stir in the lemon-lime soda; top with raspberries. Serve over ice. If desired, garnish glasses with lime wedges.

Holiday Helper

Instead of serving holiday punch in a traditional punch bowl, I use a two-piece cake stand. I simply invert the base, set the domed lid inside, then add my punch. The cake stand "bowl" makes an interesting centerpiece on a Christmas buffet table.

—**SHERRY RENNICK** ZEELAND, MI

New Year's Eve Buffet

Cheers! Ring in the New Year with an elegant buffet for the occasion. Your guests will raise their glasses to a memorable dinner featuring beef tenderloin and stuffed salmon. Don't forget the champagne!

Beef Tenderloin with Sauteed Vegetables

A rich, creamy Hollandaise sauce makes beef tenderloin and veggies extra special.

—CLEO GONSKE REDDING, CA

PREP: 20 MIN. • **BAKE:** 50 MIN. + STANDING
MAKES: 12 SERVINGS

- 1 beef tenderloin (5 pounds), trimmed
- 2 teaspoons salt
- ½ teaspoon pepper

VEGETABLES

- ¼ cup butter, cubed
- 8 medium carrots, julienned
- 6 celery ribs, julienned
- ¼ teaspoon salt
- ¼ teaspoon pepper
- 3 cans (14 ounces each) water-packed artichoke hearts, drained and quartered

HOLLANDAISE SAUCE

- 3 egg yolks
- 3 tablespoons heavy whipping cream
- 2 teaspoons Dijon mustard
- ¼ teaspoon cayenne pepper
- 1 cup butter, melted
- 1 tablespoon lemon juice

1. Preheat oven to 425°. Tuck thin tail end of tenderloin under; tie beef at 2-in. intervals with kitchen string. Sprinkle with salt and pepper.

2. Place the beef on a rack in a shallow roasting pan. Roast 50-60 minutes or until meat reaches desired doneness (for medium-rare, a thermometer should read 145°; medium, 160°; well-done, 170°). Remove the beef from oven; tent with foil. Let stand 15 minutes before slicing.

3. In a large skillet, heat butter over medium-high heat. Add carrots; cook and stir 5 minutes. Add the celery, salt and pepper; cook and stir 5-7 minutes longer or until the vegetables are crisp-tender. Stir in artichokes.

4. In top of a double boiler or a metal bowl over simmering water, whisk egg yolks, cream, mustard and cayenne until blended; cook until mixture is just thick enough to coat a metal spoon and temperature reaches 160°, whisking constantly. Remove from heat. Very slowly drizzle in warm melted butter, whisking constantly. Whisk in juice.

5. Transfer the sauce to a small bowl if necessary. Place bowl in a larger bowl of warm water. Keep warm, stirring occasionally, until ready to serve, up to 30 minutes. Serve sauce with the beef and vegetables.

Tequila Vinaigrette with Greens

Sometimes I drizzle this zingy dressing over greens tossed with mandarin oranges, feta cheese, apples and candied walnuts.

—JANELLE LEE APPLETON, WI

START TO FINISH: 20 MIN.
MAKES: 12 SERVINGS

DRESSING

- ¼ cup olive oil
- 2 tablespoons orange juice
- 2 tablespoons honey
- 1 tablespoon tequila
- 1 tablespoon lemon juice
- 1 tablespoon lime juice
- 1 tablespoon red wine vinegar
- ⅛ teaspoon salt
- ⅛ teaspoon pepper

SALAD

- 12 cups spring mix salad greens
- 4 cups seedless red grapes, halved
- ½ cup sliced almonds, toasted
- ½ cup shredded Swiss cheese

In a small bowl, whisk the dressing ingredients. In a large bowl, combine the salad ingredients. Drizzle with dressing; toss to coat.

NOTE *To toast nuts, bake in a shallow pan in a 350° oven for 5-10 minutes or cook in a skillet over low heat until lightly browned, stirring occasionally.*

Seafood-Stuffed Salmon Fillets

These baked salmon fillets are loaded with cream cheese, crab, rice and savory herbs. It's definitely a decadent way to eat fish!

—MARY COKENOUR MONTICELLO, UT

PREP: 25 MIN. • **BAKE:** 20 MIN.
MAKES: 12 SERVINGS

- 1½ cups cooked long grain rice
- 1 package (8 ounces) imitation crabmeat
- 2 tablespoons cream cheese, softened
- 2 tablespoons butter, melted
- 2 garlic cloves, minced
- ½ teaspoon each dried basil, marjoram, oregano, thyme and rosemary, crushed
- ½ teaspoon celery seed, crushed
- 12 salmon fillets (8 ounces each and 1½ inches thick)
- 3 tablespoons olive oil
- 2 teaspoons dill weed
- 1½ teaspoons salt

1. Preheat oven to 400°. In a large bowl, combine rice, crab, cream cheese, butter, garlic, basil, marjoram, oregano, thyme, rosemary and celery seed.
2. Cut a pocket horizontally in each salmon fillet to within ½ in. of the opposite side. Fill with the stuffing mixture; secure with toothpicks. Place the salmon on two greased 15x10x1-in. baking pans. Brush with oil; sprinkle with dill and salt.
3. Bake 18-22 minutes or until the fish just begins to flake easily with a fork. Discard toothpicks before serving.

Candied Bacon-Wrapped Figs

Everyone will love the sweet-salty flavor combination of these stuffed figs wrapped with bacon. Cinnamon and cocoa chile blend add a bit of spice, too.

—SHELLY BEVINGTON HERMISTON, OR

START TO FINISH: 30 MIN.
MAKES: 2 DOZEN

- 12 bacon strips
- 24 dried figs
- ¼ cup cream cheese, softened
- ¼ cup packed brown sugar
- 2 tablespoons cocoa chile blend powder
- 1 teaspoon ground cinnamon

1. Preheat oven to 375°. Cut bacon strips in half crosswise. In a large skillet, cook bacon over medium heat until partially cooked but not crisp. Remove to paper towels to drain.
2. Cut a lengthwise slit down the center of each fig; fill with ½ teaspoon cream cheese. In a small bowl, mix the brown sugar, chile blend powder and cinnamon. Dip one side of each bacon piece in the brown sugar mixture; wrap each fig with a bacon piece, sugar side out. Secure with a toothpick.
3. Transfer to a greased 15x10x1-in. baking pan. Bake 12-15 minutes or until bacon is crisp.
NOTE *The following ingredients may be substituted for 2 tablespoons cocoa chile blend powder: 2 teaspoons sugar, 2 teaspoons baking cocoa, 2 teaspoons chili powder and ½ teaspoon paprika.*

Nutella-Stuffed Strawberries

Gourmet strawberries are expensive to buy but simple to make yourself for a fraction of the price. Featuring a hazelnut spread, this version is always a hit as an appetizer or dessert.

—**DARLENE BRENDEN** SALEM, OR

PREP: 15 MIN. + CHILLING • **MAKES:** 1 DOZEN

- 12 **large fresh strawberries**
- ¼ **cup Nutella**
- 1 **cup milk chocolate chips, melted**
- ¼ **cup chopped hazelnuts**
  Confectioners' sugar

1. Remove stems from strawberries. Using a paring knife, cut out centers; pipe Nutella into strawberries.

2. Insert a toothpick into the side of each strawberry. Holding the toothpick, quickly dip the stem end of strawberry into melted chocolate; allow the excess to drip off. Sprinkle with the hazelnuts; place strawberries on a waxed paper-lined baking sheet, point side up. Remove toothpicks; refrigerate strawberries until set. Just before serving, dust berries with confectioners' sugar.

Lemon-Basil Roasted Potatoes

Two of my favorite ingredients, onion and garlic, make lemony herbed potatoes even more delicious. The versatile side dish will complement just about any main course.

—**LYNELLE MARTINSON** PLOVER, WI

PREP: 15 MIN. • **BAKE:** 25 MIN. • **MAKES:** 8 SERVINGS

- 2½ **pounds small Yukon Gold potatoes, cut into eighths**
- 8 **tablespoons olive oil, divided**
- 3 **tablespoons lemon juice**
- 1 **tablespoon Dijon mustard**
- 3 **garlic cloves, minced**
- ¾ **teaspoon salt**
- ½ **teaspoon pepper**
- ½ **medium red onion, thinly sliced**
- ⅓ **cup chopped fresh basil**

1. Preheat oven to 450°. In a large bowl, toss the potatoes with 2 tablespoons oil. Transfer to a greased 15x10x1-in. baking pan. Bake 22-28 minutes or until tender, stirring occasionally.

2. In a large bowl, whisk the lemon juice, mustard, garlic, salt, pepper and remaining oil. Stir in the onion and basil. Add roasted potatoes; toss to coat.

Lovely Lemon Cheesecake

Get ready for raves when guests taste this luxurious dessert. The combination of tangy lemon and cheesecake is divine!

—MARGARET ALLEN ABINGDON, VA

PREP: 25 MIN. • **BAKE:** 70 MIN. + CHILLING
MAKES: 14 SERVINGS

- ¾ cup graham cracker crumbs
- 2 tablespoons sugar
- 3 teaspoons ground cinnamon
- 2 tablespoons butter, melted

FILLING

- 5 packages (8 ounces each) cream cheese, softened
- 1⅔ cups sugar
- ⅛ teaspoon salt
- ¼ cup lemon juice
- 1½ teaspoons vanilla extract
- 5 eggs, lightly beaten
  Thin lemon slices, optional

1. Preheat oven to 325°. Place a greased 10-in. springform pan on a double thickness of heavy-duty foil (about 18 in. square). Wrap the foil securely around pan.

2. In a small bowl, mix cracker crumbs, sugar and cinnamon; stir in the butter. Press onto the bottom of prepared pan; refrigerate while preparing filling.

3. In a large bowl, beat cream cheese, sugar and salt until smooth. Beat in lemon juice and vanilla. Add the eggs; beat on low speed just until blended. Pour over crust. Place springform pan in a larger baking pan; add 1 in. of hot water to larger pan.

4. Bake 70-80 minutes or until the center is just set and the top appears dull. Remove springform pan from water bath. Cool cheesecake on a wire rack 10 minutes. Loosen sides of pan with a knife; remove foil. Cool 1 hour longer. Refrigerate overnight, covering when completely cooled.

5. Remove rim from pan. Garnish with lemon slices if desired.

Shimmering Paper Party Garland

Can you do simple machine-sewing? Then you can make this easy party decoration that will bring a festive flourish to New Year's Eve.

1. Using a star or circle craft punch, punch shapes from double-sided metallic card stock in coordinating shades.

2. Pull a tail about 8 inches long of coordinating thread before sewing the first shape. Begin sewing at the top center of a circle or point of a star. Push each shape through the machine, one at a time.

3. At the end of the garland, leave an 8-inch tail of thread.

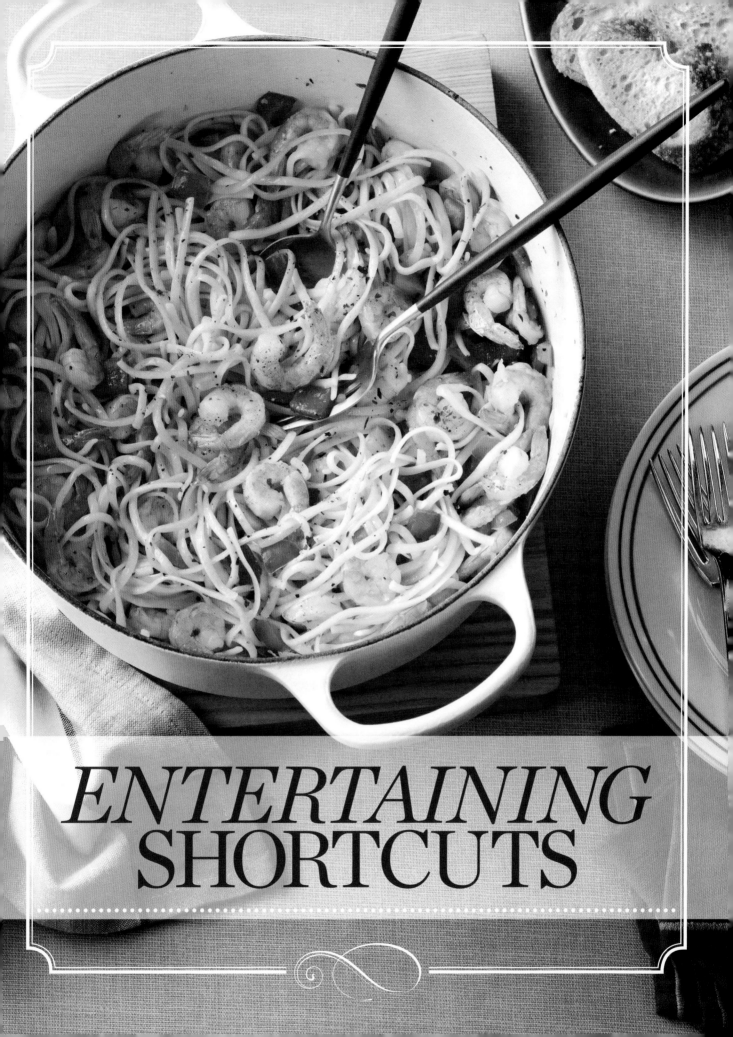

ENTERTAINING
SHORTCUTS

Creamy Microwave Scalloped Potatoes

This goes-with-everything dish is a tradition at our get-togethers. When I double the recipe, I use two kinds of soup—cream of chicken and cream of mushroom.

—BETTY MENEREY AUBURN, MI

START TO FINISH: 30 MIN.
MAKES: 8 SERVINGS

- 1 can (10¾ ounces) condensed cream of chicken soup, undiluted
- ¾ cup evaporated milk
- 4 medium potatoes, peeled and cut into ⅛-inch slices
- 1 cup (4 ounces) shredded cheddar cheese
- ¼ cup chopped onion
- ½ teaspoon salt
- ⅛ teaspoon pepper
- 1 tablespoon grated Parmesan cheese, optional

1. In a 3-qt. microwave-safe dish, combine the cream of chicken soup and evaporated milk until blended. Stir in the potatoes, cheddar cheese, onion, salt and pepper.
2. Cover and microwave on high for 7-8 minutes; stir. Cook 7-9 minutes longer or until the potatoes are tender; stir. Sprinkle with Parmesan cheese if desired.
NOTE *This recipe was tested in a 1,100-watt microwave.*

Microwave Corn 'n' Bean Bake

One of the simplest sides I make is loaded with pure veggie goodness. To finish it off, I sprinkle on a cheesy crumb topping.

—NELLIE PERDUE SUMMER SHADE, KY

START TO FINISH: 20 MIN.
MAKES: 6 SERVINGS

- 1 package (16 ounces) frozen cut green beans
- 1 can (15¼ ounces) whole kernel corn, drained
- 1 can (10¾ ounces) condensed cream of mushroom soup, undiluted
- 1 cup (4 ounces) shredded cheddar cheese, divided
- ½ cup crushed butter-flavored crackers (about 12 crackers)

1. In a large bowl, combine the green beans, corn, cream of mushroom soup and ½ cup cheddar cheese. Spoon into a greased 2-qt. microwave-safe dish.
2. Cover and microwave on high for 10 minutes, stirring once. Combine the butter-flavored cracker crumbs and remaining cheddar cheese; sprinkle over green bean mixture. Microwave, uncovered, on high for 3-5 minutes or until beans are tender.
NOTE *This recipe was tested in a 1,100-watt microwave.*

Veggie Ranch Tortilla Pinwheels

START TO FINISH: 25 MIN.
MAKES: ABOUT 5 DOZEN

- 2 packages (8 ounces each) cream cheese, softened
- 1 envelope ranch salad dressing mix
- 5 green onions, chopped
- 1 can (4 ounces) chopped green chilies, drained
- 1 can (3.8 ounces) sliced ripe olives, drained
- 1 celery rib, chopped
- ¼ cup chopped sweet red pepper
- 2 to 3 tablespoons real bacon bits
- 8 flour tortillas (10 inches)

In a small bowl, beat the cream cheese and dressing mix until blended. Beat in the onions, green chilies, ripe olives, celery, red pepper and bacon. Spread over tortillas. Roll up. Cut each into 1-in. slices. Refrigerate leftovers.

"My guests love snacking on Veggie Ranch Tortilla Pinwheels. The zesty roll-ups always disappear at parties."

—LORI KOSTECKI WAUSAU, WI

Beef Tenderloin with Mushroom Sauce

Treat family and friends to a spectacular entree of grilled steaks with mushrooms. The garlicky red wine sauce goes together on the stovetop while the meat cooks.

—**TERESA SEAMAN** PICKERINGTON, OH

START TO FINISH: 20 MIN.
MAKES: 4 SERVINGS

- 1 tablespoon coarsely ground pepper
- 4 beef tenderloin steaks (1½ inches thick and 6 ounces each)
- ½ pound sliced fresh mushrooms
- ⅓ cup butter, cubed
- ½ teaspoon minced garlic
- 2 tablespoons all-purpose flour
- 1 cup beef broth
- ¾ cup dry red wine or additional beef broth
- ⅛ teaspoon salt

1. Rub pepper onto both sides of the steaks. Grill, covered, over medium heat or broil 4 in. from the heat for 6-8 minutes on each side or until the meat reaches the desired doneness (for medium-rare, a thermometer should read 145°; medium, 160°; well-done, 170°).

2. Meanwhile, in a large skillet, saute mushrooms in butter for 3-4 minutes or until tender. Add the garlic; cook 1 minute longer.

3. Stir in flour until blended. Gradually stir in the beef broth, dry red wine and salt. Bring to a boil; cook and stir for 2-3 minutes or until thickened. Serve sauce with steaks.

Cherry Cream Cheese Dessert

Bright red cherries, smooth cream cheese and graham crackers make festive parfaits for the yuletide season. At other times of year, we sometimes substitute blueberry pie filling or another variety.

—**MELODY MELLINGER** MYERSTOWN, PA

START TO FINISH: 15 MIN.
MAKES: 8 SERVINGS

- ¾ cup graham cracker crumbs (about 12 squares)
- 2 tablespoons sugar
- 2 tablespoons butter, melted

FILLING
- 1 package (8 ounces) cream cheese, softened
- 1 can (14 ounces) sweetened condensed milk
- ⅓ cup lemon juice
- 1 teaspoon vanilla extract
- 1 can (21 ounces) cherry pie filling

1. In a small bowl, combine the graham cracker crumbs, sugar and butter. Divide among eight dessert dishes, about 4 rounded teaspoonfuls in each.

2. In a small bowl, beat the cream cheese until smooth. Gradually add the sweetened condensed milk until blended. Beat in the lemon juice and vanilla. Spoon ¼ cup into each dish. Top with the cherry pie filling, about ¼ cup in each.

Crisp Waldorf Salad

Our Christmas dinner menu includes this refreshing salad of apples, vanilla yogurt, crunchy walnuts and more. It's the perfect way to balance a rich holiday entree.

—**SUE FALK** WARREN, MI

START TO FINISH: 15 MIN.
MAKES: 9 SERVINGS

- 2 large green apples, chopped
- 2 large red apples, chopped
- ½ cup chopped walnuts
- ¼ cup flaked coconut
- ¼ cup raisins
- 1 cup vanilla yogurt
- 1 tablespoon honey
- ½ teaspoon ground cinnamon

In a large bowl, combine the first five ingredients. In a small bowl, whisk the vanilla yogurt, honey and cinnamon until blended. Pour over apple mixture; toss to coat. Refrigerate until serving.

Coconut-Layered Pound Cake

A 10-minute dessert that's special enough for company? Yes! The flavor reminds us of coconut-and-almond chocolate bars.
—**LINDA NICHOLS** STEUBENVILLE, OH

START TO FINISH: 10 MIN.
MAKES: 8 SERVINGS

- 1 loaf (16 ounces) frozen pound cake, thawed
- 2⅔ cups flaked coconut
- 1 can (14 ounces) sweetened condensed milk
- ½ cup chopped almonds, toasted
- 1 cup chocolate fudge frosting

Cut the pound cake horizontally into four layers. In a small bowl, combine the coconut, sweetened condensed milk and almonds. Place the bottom cake layer on a serving plate; top with half of the coconut mixture, one cake layer and ½ cup chocolate fudge frosting. Repeat layers.

Chili with Barley

Simmer up a pot of beefy chili whenever your family craves it. This recipe is ready to enjoy in just half an hour.
—**SHIRLEY MCCLANAHAN** FALMOUTH, KY

START TO FINISH: 30 MIN.
MAKES: 8 SERVINGS (2¼ QUARTS)

- 1 pound ground beef
- 1 medium onion, chopped
- 2 garlic cloves, minced
- 4 cups water
- 1 cup quick-cooking barley
- 1 can (16 ounces) chili beans, undrained
- 1 can (14½ ounces) diced tomatoes, undrained
- 1 can (6 ounces) tomato paste
- 1 envelope chili seasoning

1. In a large saucepan, cook beef and onion over medium heat until the meat is no longer pink, breaking meat into crumbles. Add the garlic; cook 1 minute longer. Drain. Add water; bring to a boil.
2. Stir in the barley. Reduce heat; cover and simmer for 10 minutes or until the barley is tender. Stir in the chili beans, diced tomatoes, tomato paste and chili seasoning; heat through.

Apple-Topped Ham Steak

Don't have time to prepare your usual oven-baked ham? Here's an absolutely delicious alternative. I cook the steaks in a skillet, then prepare a tangy sauce using sliced apples, onion, mustard and sage. It's an entree we enjoy any time of year.
—**ELEANOR CHORE** ATHENA, OR

START TO FINISH: 30 MIN.
MAKES: 8 SERVINGS

- 4 **fully cooked boneless ham steaks (8 ounces each)**
- 1 **cup chopped onion**
- 3 **cups apple juice**
- 2 **teaspoons Dijon mustard**
- 2 **medium green apples, thinly sliced**
- 2 **medium red apples, thinly sliced**
- 2 **tablespoons cornstarch**
- ¼ **cup cold water**
- 1 **tablespoon minced fresh sage or 1 teaspoon rubbed sage**
- ¼ **teaspoon pepper**

1. In a large skillet coated with cooking spray, brown the ham steaks in batches over medium heat; remove and keep warm.

2. In the same skillet, saute the onion until tender. Stir in the apple juice and Dijon mustard; bring to a boil. Add the apples. Reduce the heat; cover and simmer for 4 minutes or until the apples are tender.

3. Combine the cornstarch and cold water until smooth; stir into the apple juice mixture. Bring to a boil; cook and stir for 2 minutes. Stir in the sage and pepper. Return the ham steaks to the skillet; heat through.

Holiday Helper

To make savory turnovers for lunch or dinner, I dice leftover chicken and mixed vegetables, then toss it all with a seasoned white sauce. I enclose mounds of the mixture in refrigerated crescent roll dough and bake the turnovers until golden.

—**BARBARA T.** PEBBLE BEACH, CA

Quick Cherry Turnovers

Refrigerated crescent roll dough is the key to these quick-as-can-be pastries. Just add cherry pie filling and drizzle on a basic icing of confectioners' sugar and milk. It's that simple! My family can't get enough.
—**ELLEEN OBERRUETER** DANBURY, IA

START TO FINISH: 20 MIN.
MAKES: 4 SERVINGS

- 1 **tube (8 ounces) refrigerated crescent rolls**
- 1 **cup cherry pie filling**
- ½ **cup confectioners' sugar**
- 1 **to 2 tablespoons milk**

1. Preheat oven to 375°. Unroll the crescent roll dough and separate into four rectangles; place on an ungreased baking sheet. Press the perforations to seal.

2. Place ¼ cup cherry pie filling on one half of each dough rectangle. Fold the dough over cherry pie filling; pinch the edges to seal. Bake 10-12 minutes or until golden.

3. Place the confectioners' sugar in a small bowl; stir in enough milk to achieve a drizzling consistency. Drizzle icing over cherry turnovers. Serve warm.

Sweet Potato Tartlets

Here's a before-dinner spin on traditional holiday sweet potatoes. Your appetizer buffet may never be the same once you try these marshmallow-topped tarts.
—**MARLA CLARK** MORIARTY, NM

START TO FINISH: 30 MIN.
MAKES: 15 TARTLETS

- 1 medium sweet potato, peeled and chopped
- 1 tablespoon butter
- 1 tablespoon maple syrup
- ⅛ teaspoon ground cinnamon
- ⅛ teaspoon ground nutmeg
- 1 package (1.9 ounces) frozen miniature phyllo tart shells
- 15 miniature marshmallows

1. Place the sweet potato in a small saucepan; cover with water. Bring to a boil. Reduce heat; cover and simmer for 10-15 minutes or until tender. Drain.
2. In a small bowl, mash sweet potato with butter, syrup, cinnamon and nutmeg. Place 1 tablespoon potato mixture in each tart shell. Place on an ungreased baking sheet. Top with mini marshmallows. Bake at 350° for 8-12 minutes or until marshmallows are lightly browned.

Holiday Rum Balls

With a splash of rum, these goodies rolled in sugar are a cheery choice for the season.
—**DIANE DUSCHANEK** COUNCIL BLUFFS, IA

START TO FINISH: 30 MIN.
MAKES: ABOUT 2½ DOZEN

- 2 cups confectioners' sugar
- ¼ cup baking cocoa
- 1 package (12 ounces) vanilla wafers, finely crushed
- 1 cup finely chopped walnuts
- ½ cup light corn syrup
- ¼ cup rum
  Additional confectioners' sugar

1. In a large bowl, mix confectioners' sugar and cocoa until blended. Add the wafers and walnuts; toss to combine. In another bowl, mix corn syrup and rum; stir into wafer mixture.
2. Shape the mixture into 1-in. balls. Roll in additional confectioners' sugar. Store in an airtight container.

Puffed Apple Pastries

It's a cinch to make these wonderful little treats for dessert, breakfast or brunch. The secret? Store-bought puff pastry! It forms a cute and crunchy "nest" that holds the spiced apple pie filling inside. For extra appeal, add a scoop of vanilla ice cream as the finishing touch.
—*TASTE OF HOME* TEST KITCHEN

START TO FINISH: 25 MIN.
MAKES: 6 SERVINGS

- 1 package (10 ounces) frozen puff pastry shells
- 1 can (21 ounces) apple pie filling
- ½ teaspoon ground cinnamon
- ¼ teaspoon ground nutmeg
  Vanilla ice cream, optional

1. Bake puff pastry shells according to the package directions. Meanwhile, in a small saucepan, combine apple pie filling, cinnamon and nutmeg; mix well. Cook and stir over medium-low heat 3-4 minutes or until heated through.
2. Remove the tops from the puff pastry shells; fill with the apple pie filling mixture. Replace the tops of the pastry shells. Serve warm, with vanilla ice cream if desired.

Skillet Sausage Stuffing

I transformed stuffing mix using pork sausage, mushrooms, celery and onion. The dressed-up dish impressed my in-laws.
—**JENNIFER LYNN CULLEN** TAYLOR, MI

START TO FINISH: 25 MIN.
MAKES: 8 SERVINGS

- 1 pound bulk pork sausage
- 1¼ cups chopped celery
- ½ cup chopped onion
- ½ cup sliced fresh mushrooms
- 1 large garlic clove, minced
- 1½ cups reduced-sodium chicken broth
- 1 teaspoon rubbed sage
- 1 package (6 ounces) stuffing mix

1. In a large skillet, cook the sausage, celery, onion and mushrooms over medium heat until meat is no longer pink, breaking meat into crumbles. Add garlic; cook 1 minute longer; drain. Stir in broth and sage.
2. Bring to a boil. Stir in stuffing mix. Cover and remove from the heat; let stand for 5 minutes. Fluff with a fork.

Fluffy Pumpkin Pie

Children love this pie—marshmallows and whipped topping make the filling light and fluffy. It's an easy recipe that I've shared many times over the years.

—PHYLLIS RENFRO WHITE BEAR LAKE, MN

PREP: 1 HOUR + CHILLING
COOK: 10 MIN. + CHILLING
MAKES: 8 SERVINGS

- **Pastry for single-crust pie (9 inches)**
- 24 **large marshmallows**
- 1 **can (15 ounces) solid-pack pumpkin**
- ½ **teaspoon ground cinnamon**
- ½ **teaspoon ground allspice**
- ¼ **teaspoon salt**
- 1 **carton (8 ounces) frozen whipped topping, thawed**
  Additional whipped topping and ground cinnamon, optional

1. On a lightly floured surface, roll pastry to a ⅛-in.-thick circle; transfer to a 9-in. pie plate. Trim to ½ in. beyond rim of plate; flute edge. Refrigerate 30 minutes. Preheat oven to 425°.

2. Line pastry with a double thickness of foil. Fill with pie weights, dried beans or uncooked rice. Bake on a lower oven rack 20-25 minutes or until edges are golden brown. Remove the foil and weights; bake 3-6 minutes longer or until bottom is golden brown. Cool completely on a wire rack.

3. In a small heavy saucepan, melt marshmallows over low heat. Remove from the heat. Stir in the pumpkin, cinnamon, allspice and salt; cool to room temperature.

4. Fold in whipped topping. Spoon into pastry shell. Refrigerate for at least 4 hours before serving. Garnish with additional whipped topping and cinnamon if desired.

PASTRY FOR SINGLE-CRUST PIE (9 INCHES) *Combine 1-¼ cups all-purpose flour and ¼ teaspoon salt; cut in ½ cup cold butter until crumbly. Gradually add 3-5 tablespoons ice water, tossing with a fork until dough holds together when pressed. Wrap in plastic wrap and refrigerate 1 hour.*

Potato Bacon Chowder

On winter days, the sight of bowls filled with this chowder instantly cheers my family. The flavor reminds us of loaded baked potatoes.

—JACQUE MANNING BURBANK, CA

START TO FINISH: 30 MIN. • **MAKES:** 6 SERVINGS

- 1 **pound potatoes, peeled and cubed (about 2 medium)**
- 1 **cup water**
- 8 **bacon strips**
- 1 **medium onion, chopped**
- 1 **celery rib, chopped**
- 1 **can (10¾ ounces) condensed cream of chicken soup, undiluted**
- 1¾ **cups whole milk**
- 1 **cup (8 ounces) sour cream**
- ½ **teaspoon salt**
  Dash pepper
- 1 **tablespoon minced fresh parsley**

1. Place potatoes in a small saucepan and cover with the water. Bring to a boil. Reduce the heat; cover and cook for 10-15 minutes or until tender.

2. Meanwhile, in a large skillet, cook the bacon until crisp; remove to paper towels to drain and set aside.

3. In the same skillet, saute onion and celery in drippings until tender; drain. Add to undrained potatoes. Stir in the soup, milk, sour cream, salt and pepper. Cook over low heat for 10 minutes or until heated through (do not boil).

4. Crumble bacon; set aside ¼ cup. Add remaining bacon to soup along with parsley. Sprinkle with reserved bacon.

Hot Apple Pie Sipper

When my daughters wanted to throw a party, we concocted a warm-you-up drink that tastes like apple pie with ice cream. Garnish each mug with a cinnamon stick for extra fun.

—CONNIE YOUNG PONY, MT

PREP: 10 MIN. + FREEZING • **MAKES:** 6 SERVINGS

- ¼ **cup butter, softened**
- ⅓ **cup packed brown sugar**
- 2 **teaspoons ground cinnamon**
- 1 **teaspoon ground nutmeg**
- ¼ **teaspoon ground cloves**
- 1 **pint vanilla ice cream, softened**
- 4 **cups hot apple cider or unsweetened apple juice**
  Brandy, optional

1. In a large bowl, cream the butter, brown sugar and spices until light and fluffy. Beat in the ice cream. Cover and freeze until firm.

2. For each serving, place ⅓ cup ice cream mixture in a mug; add ⅔ cup cider. Stir in brandy if desired.

Baked Onion Cheese Dip

Three kinds of cheese, sweet onions and thyme make this dip so rich and indulgent. The wonderful aroma as it bakes hints of the yummy appetizer to come.
—**BONNIE HAWKINS** ELKHORN, WI

START TO FINISH: 30 MIN. • **MAKES:** 3 CUPS

- 2 cups (8 ounces) shredded cheddar cheese
- 1 cup (4 ounces) shredded pepper Jack cheese
- 4 ounces cream cheese, cubed
- ¼ teaspoon dried thyme
- 2 cups chopped sweet onions, divided
  Assorted crackers

1. In a food processor, combine the cheeses, thyme and 1 cup onions; cover and process until blended. Stir in the remaining onions.

2. Transfer mixture to a greased 3-cup baking dish. Bake, uncovered, at 375° for 20-25 minutes or until bubbly. Serve with crackers.

Cranberry-Orange Sangria

I refrigerate my colorful sangria overnight to build the fruitiness. If you're feeling bold, stir in a splash of brandy.
—**MARIA REGAKIS** SAUGUS, MA

PREP: 15 MIN. + CHILLING
MAKES: 10 SERVINGS

- 1 medium orange, halved and thinly sliced
- 1 medium apple, quartered and thinly sliced
- ½ cup fresh or frozen cranberries
- 1 bottle (32 ounces) cranberry juice
- 1 bottle (750 ml) Zinfandel or other fruity red wine
- 1 cup simple syrup
- ½ cup orange liqueur
  Ice cubes

GARNISHES
  Additional thinly sliced oranges and fresh cranberries, optional

In a large pitcher, combine the first seven ingredients; refrigerate sangria overnight. Serve over ice; garnish with orange slices and fresh cranberries if desired.

Creamy Hazelnut Dip

This irresistibly decadent treat boasts the chocolate-hazelnut flavor of Nutella. With strawberries, cookies and biscotti as dippers, your guests will dive right in.
—*TASTE OF HOME* TEST KITCHEN

START TO FINISH: 15 MIN.
MAKES: ABOUT 3 CUPS

- 2 packages (3 ounces each) cream cheese, softened
- ½ cup Nutella
- 1 teaspoon vanilla extract
- ½ cup confectioners' sugar
- 1 cup heavy whipping cream, whipped
- ½ cup chopped hazelnuts
  Fresh strawberries, biscotti and Milano cookies

In a small bowl, combine the cream cheese, Nutella and vanilla. Beat in the confectioners' sugar until smooth. Fold in the whipped cream and hazelnuts. Serve with fresh strawberries, biscotti and cookies.

Bacon Swiss Squares

Want to serve a hearty egg bake for the holiday but don't have time for anything complicated? Using Swiss cheese, bacon, biscuit mix and onion powder, we make a satisfying dish that's similar to breakfast pizza. When I'm cooking for a really big group, I double the recipe.
—AGARITA VAUGHAN FAIRBURY, IL

START TO FINISH: 30 MIN.
MAKES: 12 SERVINGS

- 2 cups biscuit/baking mix
- ½ cup cold water
- 8 ounces sliced Swiss cheese
- 1 pound sliced bacon, cooked and crumbled
- 4 eggs, lightly beaten
- ¼ cup milk
- ½ teaspoon onion powder

1. In a large bowl, combine the biscuit mix and water. Turn onto a floured surface; knead 10 times. Roll into a 14x10-in. rectangle.

2. Place the biscuit dough on the bottom and ½ in. up the sides of a greased 13x9-in. baking dish. Arrange the Swiss cheese over biscuit dough. Sprinkle with bacon. In a large bowl, whisk the eggs, milk and onion powder; pour over the bacon.

3. Bake at 425° for 15-18 minutes or until a knife inserted near the center comes out clean. Cut into squares; serve immediately.

Holiday Helper

Setting up a buffet table? Here are a few ideas to make your presentation even more festive:

- **Add visual interest** by placing serving dishes at varying heights. Use cake pedestals as trays for some of your foods.

- **Fill in empty spaces** around serving dishes on the table by tucking in tree ornaments, small wrapped boxes or pieces from your Christmas village. Or add natural items such as pinecones, evergreen boughs or fruit.

Confetti Pasta

One of our Christmas Eve traditions is to have linguine with red and green peppers and shrimp. We pair that delicious entree with a tossed salad and garlic bread.
—ELLEN FIORE MONTVALE, NJ

START TO FINISH: 25 MIN.
MAKES: 8 SERVINGS

- 1 package (16 ounces) linguine
- 1 cup chopped sweet red pepper
- 1 cup chopped green pepper
- ⅓ cup chopped onion
- 3 garlic cloves, peeled and thinly sliced
- ¼ teaspoon salt
- ¼ teaspoon dried oregano
- ⅛ teaspoon crushed red pepper flakes
- ⅛ teaspoon pepper
- ¼ cup olive oil
- 2 pounds cooked small shrimp, peeled and deveined
- ½ cup shredded Parmesan cheese

1. Cook pasta according to package directions. Meanwhile, in a Dutch oven, saute the peppers, onion, garlic and seasonings in oil until vegetables are tender.

2. Add the shrimp; cook and stir 2-3 minutes longer or until heated through. Drain the pasta; toss with shrimp mixture. Sprinkle with cheese.

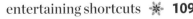

Orange Ricotta Pancakes

Give your Christmas morning pancakes a citrusy twist with orange juice and grated peel. Ricotta cheese adds richness, too.

—BREHAN KOHL ANCHORAGE, AK

START TO FINISH: 30 MIN.
MAKES: 12 PANCAKES

- 1½ cups all-purpose flour
- 3 tablespoons sugar
- 1½ teaspoons baking powder
- ½ teaspoon baking soda
- ¼ teaspoon salt
- 1 egg
- 1 cup part-skim ricotta cheese
- ¾ cup 2% milk
- ½ teaspoon grated orange peel
- ½ cup orange juice
- ¼ cup butter, melted
- ½ teaspoon vanilla extract
  Maple syrup and confectioners' sugar

1. In a bowl, whisk the first five ingredients. In another bowl, whisk egg, cheese, milk, orange peel, orange juice, melted butter and vanilla until blended. Add to dry ingredients; stir just until moistened.

2. Lightly grease a griddle; heat over medium heat. Pour batter by ¼ cupfuls onto griddle. Cook until bubbles on top begin to pop and bottoms are golden brown. Turn; cook until second side is golden brown. Serve with syrup and confectioners' sugar.

Caramelized Pork Tenderloin

This delectable tenderloin has a little bit of sweetness. Best of all, it tastes grilled even though it cooks on the stovetop.

—DEBI ARONE FORT COLLINS, CO

START TO FINISH: 20 MIN.
MAKES: 4 SERVINGS

- 1 pork tenderloin (1 pound)
- ¼ cup packed brown sugar
- 4 garlic cloves, minced
- 1 tablespoon Montreal steak seasoning
- 2 tablespoons butter

1. Cut the pork tenderloin into four pieces and pound with a meat mallet to ¼-in. thickness. In a shallow bowl, mix brown sugar, garlic and steak seasoning. Dip pork tenderloin in sugar mixture, patting to help coating adhere.

2. In a large skillet, heat the butter over medium-high heat. Add the pork tenderloin; cook 2-3 minutes on each side or until tender.

Feather-Light Biscuits

I always bake an extra batch of these fluffy goodies to send home with my children. They like to split the biscuits and fill them with cheese or peanut butter and jam.

—ELEANORE HILL FRESNO, CA

START TO FINISH: 30 MIN.
MAKES: ABOUT 2 DOZEN

- 6 **cups buttermilk baking mix**
- ¼ **cup sugar**
- 1 **package (¼ ounce) active dry yeast**
- ⅓ **cup shortening**
- 1 **to 1¼ cups warm water (120° to 130°)**
- ¼ **cup butter, melted**

1. In a large bowl, combine the baking mix, sugar and yeast. Cut in shortening until the mixture resembles coarse crumbs. Stir in enough warm water to form a soft and slightly sticky dough. Turn onto a floured surface; knead gently 3-4 times.

2. Roll the dough to ¾-in. thickness; cut with a 2½-in. round biscuit cutter. Place on ungreased baking sheets. Brush tops with melted butter. Bake at 400° for 10-12 minutes or until lightly browned.

Kneading Dough

Shape the dough into a ball on a lightly floured surface. Fold the top of the dough toward you. With your palms, push the dough with a rolling motion away from you. Turn the dough a quarter turn; continue folding, kneading and turning as many times as the recipe directs or until the dough is smooth and elastic.

Holiday Hot Browns

These traditional open-faced favorites originated at the Brown Hotel in Louisville, Kentucky. Hot from the oven, they're a nice change of pace from sloppy joes or other sandwiches. The homemade cheese sauce tastes special but is easy to whip up in just minutes on the stovetop.

—*TASTE OF HOME* TEST KITCHEN

START TO FINISH: 30 MIN.
MAKES: 12 SERVINGS

- ¼ cup butter, cubed
- ¼ cup all-purpose flour
- ¼ teaspoon salt
- ⅛ teaspoon white pepper
- 1 cup 2% milk
- ½ cup chicken broth
- ½ cup sherry or additional chicken broth
- 1 cup shredded Parmesan cheese, divided
- ⅓ cup shredded sharp cheddar cheese
- 12 slices pumpernickel bread, toasted
- 1½ pounds sliced cooked turkey
- 4 medium tomatoes, halved and sliced
- 12 cooked bacon strips, crumbled

1. In a large saucepan, melt the butter over low heat. Stir in the flour, salt and white pepper until smooth; gradually add the milk, chicken broth and sherry. Bring the mixture to a boil; cook and stir for 2 minutes or until thickened. Stir in ⅓ cup Parmesan cheese and cheddar cheese until melted. Remove sauce from the heat.

2. Place the pumpernickel toast slices on a baking sheet. Top each with sliced turkey, sauce, tomatoes and crumbled bacon. Sprinkle with the remaining Parmesan cheese. Broil 3-4 in. from the heat for 3-4 minutes or until the cheese is melted.

CUTE CONFECTIONS

Cherry Mice

'Twas the night before Christmas, and all through the house, not a creature was stirring—except maybe these sweet mice.
—*TASTE OF HOME* **TEST KITCHEN**

PREP: 45 MIN. + CHILLING
MAKES: 2 DOZEN

- 2 **cups (12 ounces) semisweet chocolate chips**
- 2 **teaspoons shortening**
- 24 **maraschino cherries with stems, well drained**
- 24 **milk chocolate kisses, unwrapped**
- 48 **almond slices**

1. In a microwave, melt the chips and shortening; stir until smooth. Holding each cherry by the stem, dip into the chocolate mixture. Place on a sheet of waxed paper; let stand until set.
2. Reheat remaining chocolate; dip cherries again, then press onto the bottom of a chocolate kiss. For ears, place almond slices between cherry and kiss. Refrigerate until set.

Crisp Button Cookies

Button button, who's got the button? You do when you bake these adorable cookies. What a way to dress up a treat tray!

—**BONNIE BUCKLEY** KANSAS CITY, MO

PREP: 20 MIN. + CHILLING • **BAKE:** 10 MIN./BATCH
MAKES: ABOUT 3 DOZEN

- ¾ **cup butter, softened**
- 1 **cup confectioners' sugar**
- 1 **egg**
- 1 **teaspoon vanilla extract**
- 2½ **cups all-purpose flour**
- ¼ **teaspoon salt**
- ¼ **teaspoon ground cardamom**
  Assorted food coloring, optional
  Multicolored pull-and-peel licorice

1. In a large bowl, cream the butter and confectioners' sugar until light and fluffy. Beat in the egg and vanilla. In another bowl, whisk the flour, salt and cardamom; gradually beat into the creamed mixture. If desired, divide dough into portions; tint with food coloring. Refrigerate, covered, 2 hours or until easy to handle.

2. Preheat oven to 350°. On a lightly floured surface, roll the dough to ¼-in. thickness. Cut with a floured 2½-in. round cookie cutter. Place 1 in. apart on ungreased baking sheets. With the top of a ¼-cup measuring cup dipped in flour, press an indented edge into each cookie. Using a plastic straw, cut out four holes near the center of each cookie.

3. Bake 10-15 minutes or until the edges are lightly browned. Remove to wire racks to cool. Lace licorice through the holes in each button; trim licorice.

Chocolate Reindeer

Whenever I round up a team of reindeer cutouts, they fly off the plate. A bright red candy nose is the perfect finishing touch.

—**LISA RUPPLE** KEENESBURG, CO

PREP: 30 MIN. + CHILLING • **BAKE:** 10 MIN./BATCH
MAKES: ABOUT 3 DOZEN

- 1 **cup butter, softened**
- 1 **cup sugar**
- ½ **cup packed brown sugar**
- 1 **egg**
- 1 **teaspoon vanilla extract**
- 2¼ **cups all-purpose flour**
- ½ **cup baking cocoa**
- 1 **teaspoon baking soda**
- 44 **Red Hots**

OPTIONAL ICING/DECORATION

- 1½ **cups confectioners' sugar**
- 2 **to 3 tablespoons milk**
  Blue pearl dragees

1. In a large bowl, cream butter and sugars until light and fluffy. Beat in egg and vanilla. In another bowl, whisk flour, cocoa and baking soda; gradually beat into creamed mixture. Refrigerate, covered, at least 2 hours or until easy to handle.

2. Preheat oven to 375°. On a lightly floured surface, roll dough to ⅛-in. thickness. Cut with a 3½-in. reindeer-shaped cookie cutter. Place on greased baking sheets.

3. Bake 8-9 minutes. Immediately press a Red Hot onto each nose. Cool on pans 2 minutes. Remove to wire racks to cool completely.

4. If desired, combine confectioners' sugar and enough milk to reach a piping consistency. Place mixture in a resealable plastic bag; cut a small hole in a corner of bag. Pipe around edges of cookies; add dragees for the eyes.

Peppermint Candy Cookies

Christmas guests can't resist peppermint cookies wrapped in cellophane to resemble candy. What could be sweeter?

—GLORIA MCKENZIE PANAMA CITY, FL

PREP: 25 MIN. • **BAKE:** 10 MIN./BATCH
MAKES: ABOUT 4 DOZEN

- 1¼ cups butter, softened
- ¾ cup confectioners' sugar
- 2½ cups all-purpose flour
- ½ teaspoon salt
- ½ teaspoon peppermint extract
  Green and red paste or gel food coloring

1. In a large bowl, cream butter and confectioners' sugar until light and fluffy. Add the flour, salt and extract and mix well. Divide the dough into four portions. Tint one portion green and one red; leave the remaining portions plain.

2. Divide each portion into thirds; shape each into a 6-in. log. Flatten into triangular logs, bending the top of one point slightly (to give finished cookies a pinwheel effect). Assemble one large roll by alternating three green and three plain logs. Wrap in plastic wrap. Repeat with red and remaining plain dough. Refrigerate 4 hours or until firm.

3. Preheat oven to 375°. Unwrap the dough and cut into ¼-in. slices. Place 2 in. apart on ungreased baking sheets. Bake 8-10 minutes or until edges are golden brown. Cool on pans 1 minute. Remove to wire racks to cool.

4. Cut 6-in.-square pieces of clear cellophane or plastic wrap to wrap each cookie; twist the ends securely or tie with a ribbon.

Neapolitan Fudge

I experimented with different flavors of fudge, and this variety reminded me of the vanilla, strawberry and chocolate combination in Neapolitan ice cream.

—FAITH LEONARD DELBARTON, WV

PREP: 35 MIN. + CHILLING
MAKES: ABOUT 6½ POUNDS

- 1½ teaspoons butter
- 1 package (8 ounces) cream cheese, softened
- 3 cups confectioners' sugar
- 16 ounces milk chocolate, melted and cooled

VANILLA LAYER
- 1 package (8 ounces) cream cheese, softened
- 3 cups confectioners' sugar
- 16 ounces white baking chocolate, melted and cooled
- 1 tablespoon vanilla extract

RASPBERRY LAYER
- 1 package (8 ounces) cream cheese, softened
- 3 cups confectioners' sugar
- 16 ounces white baking chocolate, melted and cooled
- 1 tablespoon raspberry extract
- 8 to 10 drops red food coloring, optional

1. Line a 13x9-in. pan with foil and grease foil with butter. In a large bowl, beat cream cheese until fluffy. Gradually beat in confectioners' sugar. Beat in melted milk chocolate. Spread into prepared pan. Refrigerate 10 minutes.

2. For vanilla layer, in a large bowl, beat the cream cheese until fluffy. Gradually beat in confectioners' sugar. Beat in melted white chocolate and vanilla. Spread over chocolate layer. Refrigerate 10 minutes.

3. For the raspberry layer, in a large bowl, beat cream cheese until fluffy. Gradually beat in the confectioners' sugar. Beat in melted white chocolate and extract. If desired, tint with food coloring. Spread over top. Refrigerate, covered, at least 8 hours or overnight.

4. Using the foil, lift the fudge out of the pan. Remove the foil; cut fudge into 1-in. squares. Store between layers of waxed paper in an airtight container in the refrigerator.

Meringue Santa Hats

My grandchildren love it when I make these meringues and call them Santa hats. The kids help by sprinkling on the red sugar. For extra fun, use similar shapes and more colors to create elf hats, too.

—BONNIE HAWKINS ELKHORN, WI

PREP: 30 MIN. • **BAKE:** 40 MIN. + STANDING
MAKES: 3 DOZEN

- 2 **egg whites**
- ½ **teaspoon cream of tartar**
- ¼ **teaspoon vanilla extract**
- ½ **cup sugar**
  Red colored sugar

1. Place egg whites in a small bowl; let stand at room temperature 30 minutes.
2. Preheat oven to 250°. Add cream of tartar and vanilla to the egg whites; beat on medium speed until foamy. Gradually add the sugar, 1 tablespoon at a time, beating on high after each addition until the sugar is dissolved. Continue beating until stiff glossy peaks form.
3. Cut a small hole in the tip of a pastry bag or in a corner of a food-safe plastic bag; insert a #8 round tip. Fill the bag with one-fourth of the meringue; set aside. Prepare a second piping bag, using a #12 round tip; fill the bag with the remaining meringue.
4. Using the bag with the #12 tip, pipe 36 Santa hat triangles (2 in. tall) onto parchment paper-lined baking sheets. Sprinkle with red sugar. Use the first bag to pipe white trim and pompoms on Santa hats.
5. Bake 40-45 minutes or until firm to the touch. Turn off oven (do not open the oven door); leave meringues in oven 1 hour.
6. Remove the Santa hats from the paper. Store in an airtight container at room temperature.

Sweet & Salty Snowmen

My young son and I built fun frosty treats by dressing up pretzel rods with white chocolate, candy and other decorations. For a whimsical centerpiece, arrange the snowmen in drinking glasses or vases filled with vanilla chips or coconut.

—**CAROL BERNDT** AVON, SD

START TO FINISH: 25 MIN.
MAKES: 8 SNOWMEN

- 8 pretzel rods
- 6 ounces white baking chocolate, melted

  Assorted candies and decorations:
  Miniature chocolate chips, sprinkles, black decorating gel, candy cane chocolate kisses, white nonpareils, Fruit by the Foot fruit rolls

1. Dip a pretzel rod two-thirds of the way into the melted white chocolate, or drizzle chocolate over pretzel with a spoon. Attach miniature chocolate chips for the eyes and buttons; attach a sprinkle for a nose. Using decorating gel, add a mouth.

2. For a hat, attach a chocolate kiss to the top of the pretzel. Sprinkle the snowman with nonpareils. Carefully stand the snowman upright in a tall glass or press the bottom of the pretzel into a 2-in.-thick piece of Styrofoam. For scarves, cut the fruit rolls into thin strips; tie around snowmen.

Pinwheels and Checkerboards

Every Christmas season, my mother baked playful pinwheel and checkerboard cookies using the same dough. I loved them!

—**JILL HEATWOLE** PITTSVILLE, MD

PREP: 30 MIN. + CHILLING
BAKE: 10 MIN./BATCH
MAKES: 6 DOZEN PINWHEEL AND
4 DOZEN CHECKERBOARD COOKIES

- 1¼ cups butter, softened
- 1 cup packed brown sugar
- ½ cup sugar
- 2 eggs
- ¼ teaspoon vanilla extract
- 4 cups all-purpose flour
- 1 teaspoon baking powder
- 1 teaspoon salt

- ¼ teaspoon baking soda
  Red and green gel food coloring
- 1 ounce unsweetened chocolate, melted and cooled

1. In a large bowl, cream the butter and sugars until light and fluffy. Beat in eggs and vanilla. In another bowl, whisk flour, baking powder, salt and baking soda; gradually beat into the creamed mixture.

2. Divide dough into four portions. Tint one portion red and one portion green. Stir chocolate into another portion. Wrap chocolate and plain portions in plastic wrap; refrigerate 1 hour or until easy to handle.

3. For pinwheel cookies, divide the red and green portions of dough in half. Roll out each portion of dough between waxed paper into a 9x6-in. rectangle. Refrigerate 30 minutes.

4. Remove the waxed paper. Place one green rectangle over a red rectangle.

Roll up tightly jelly-roll style, starting with a long side of the rectangle; wrap in plastic wrap. Repeat. Refrigerate 2 hours or until firm.

5. For checkerboard cookies, divide the plain and chocolate portions of dough in half. Roll out each portion between waxed paper into a 6x4-in. rectangle. Cut each rectangle lengthwise into eight ½-in. strips.

6. Stack the strips in groups of four, alternating plain and chocolate strips and forming eight separate stacks. Form a four-stack block by alternating chocolate-topped and plain-topped stacks. Repeat. Press each together gently. Wrap in plastic. Refrigerate at least 2 hours.

7. Preheat oven to 375°. Unwrap and cut pinwheel dough and checkerboard dough into ¼-in. slices. Place slices 1 in. apart on ungreased baking sheets. Bake 9-11 minutes or until set. Remove to wire racks to cool.

Cinnamon Candy Cane Cookies

Set aside ordinary candy canes for a new holiday favorite. These two-tone twists get their spiced flavor from crushed Red Hots and a dash of cinnamon.

—TASTE OF HOME TEST KITCHEN

PREP: 25 MIN. • **BAKE:** 10 MIN./BATCH
MAKES: 4 DOZEN

- 1 **cup butter, softened**
- 1 **cup confectioners' sugar**
- 1 **egg**
- 1 **teaspoon vanilla extract**
- 2½ **cups all-purpose flour**
- ¾ **teaspoon salt**
- ½ **cup Red Hots, crushed**
- ½ **teaspoon ground cinnamon**
  Red food coloring, optional
- 2 **tablespoons coarse sugar**

1. Preheat oven to 375°. In a large bowl, cream butter and confectioners' sugar until light and fluffy. Beat in the egg and vanilla. In another bowl, whisk the flour and salt; gradually beat into creamed mixture.

2. Divide the dough in half. Mix the Red Hots and cinnamon into one half; tint with red food coloring if desired. Shape 1½ teaspoons plain dough into a 4½-in. rope. Shape 1½ teaspoons red dough into a 4½-in. rope.

3. On an ungreased baking sheet, place the ropes side by side; press together lightly and twist. Curve the top of each cookie down to form handle of candy cane. Repeat with remaining plain and red dough, placing 2 in. apart on baking sheets. Sprinkle with coarse sugar.

4. Bake 7-10 minutes or until lightly browned. Cool on pans 1 minute. Remove to wire racks to cool.

Santa Claus Sugar Cookies

My mom taught me how to bake tender, buttery Santa cookies and hang them on the tree. Her tradition has lasted 40 years. (Use this dough to make any other cutout shapes you like, such as the snowflake and scalloped circle shown on the front cover.)

—ANN BUSH COLORADO CITY, CO

PREP: 45 MIN. + CHILLING
BAKE: 10 MIN./BATCH + COOLING
MAKES: 4 DOZEN

- 1 **cup unsalted butter**
- 1½ **cups sugar**
- 2 **eggs**
- 1 **teaspoon vanilla extract**
- 3½ **cups all-purpose flour**
- 1 **teaspoon baking soda**
- 1 **teaspoon cream of tartar**
- ½ **teaspoon ground nutmeg**
- ¼ **teaspoon salt**

FROSTING
- ¾ **cup unsalted butter, softened**
- 6 **tablespoons 2% milk**
- 2¼ **teaspoons vanilla extract**
- ¼ **teaspoon salt**
- 6¾ **cups confectioners' sugar**

Optional decorations: red colored sugar, miniature semisweet chocolate chips and Red Hots

1. In a large bowl, cream the butter and sugar until light and fluffy. Beat in the eggs and vanilla. In another bowl, whisk the flour, baking soda, cream of tartar, nutmeg and salt; gradually beat into creamed mixture.

2. Divide cookie dough in half. Shape each portion into a disk; wrap in plastic wrap. Refrigerate 1 hour or until firm enough to roll.

3. Preheat oven to 375°. On a lightly floured surface, roll each portion of dough to ¼-in. thickness. Cut with a floured 3-in. Santa-shaped cookie cutter. Place 2 in. apart on greased baking sheets.

4. Bake 8-10 minutes or until light brown. Remove from pans to wire racks to cool completely.

5. For the frosting, in a large bowl, beat the butter until creamy. Beat in milk, vanilla and salt. Gradually beat in the confectioners' sugar until smooth. Pipe onto cookies and decorate as desired.

> ### *"Charm your seasonal guests*
> *with a flock of Sugar Doves. They're beautifully*
> *decorated and absolutely scrumptious."*
>
> **—PEGGY PRESTON** FENTON, IA

Sugar Doves

PREP: 30 MIN. + CHILLING
BAKE: 10 MIN./BATCH + COOLING
MAKES: 7½ DOZEN

- 1 **cup butter, softened**
- 2 **cups sugar**
- 2 **eggs**
- 2 **tablespoons milk**
- 2 **teaspoons vanilla extract**
- 4¼ **cups all-purpose flour**
- 2 **teaspoons baking powder**
- ¼ **teaspoon salt**

FROSTING
- ½ **cup shortening**
- 3¾ **cups confectioners' sugar**
- 2 **tablespoons milk**
- 1 **teaspoon almond extract**
- ½ **teaspoon vanilla extract**
- 1 **to 2 tablespoons water**
- 4½ **cups sliced almonds**
- 3½ **cups finely chopped walnuts**
  Miniature semisweet chocolate chips

1. In a large bowl, cream the butter and sugar until light and fluffy. Add the eggs, one at a time, beating well after each addition. Beat in milk and vanilla.

2. In another bowl, whisk the flour, baking powder and salt; gradually beat into the creamed mixture. Refrigerate cookie dough, covered, 2 hours or until easy to handle.

3. Preheat oven to 350°. On a lightly floured surface, roll out cookie dough to ⅛-in. thickness. Cut with a 3-in. bird-shaped cookie cutter. Place 1 in. apart on greased baking sheets. Bake 7-9 minutes or until set. Remove from pans to wire racks to cool completely.

4. For the frosting, in a small bowl, combine shortening, confectioners' sugar, milk, extracts and enough water to achieve spreading consistency.

5. Frost cookies. Arrange almonds and walnuts over the bodies; add miniature chocolate chips for eyes.

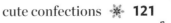

Elf Cookies

Santa's helpers make everything merry! With colorful hats and cute expressions, these spirited little elves are guaranteed to spread Christmas cheer.
—**TASTE OF HOME** TEST KITCHEN

PREP: 45 MIN. • **BAKE:** 10 MIN.
MAKES: 28 COOKIES

- ½ **tube refrigerated sugar cookie dough, softened**
- ⅓ **cup all-purpose flour**
- 2½ **cups confectioners' sugar**
- 10 **teaspoons water**
- 4 **teaspoons meringue powder**
  Assorted food coloring
  Assorted sprinkles, candies and almond slices

1. Preheat oven to 350°. In a small bowl, beat cookie dough and flour until combined. Roll out on a lightly floured surface to ⅛-in. thickness. Cut with a floured 1¾x3¼-in. diamond cookie cutter. Place 2 in. apart on ungreased baking sheets. Bake 7-9 minutes or until edges are golden brown. Remove to wire racks to cool.

2. For the icing, in a large bowl, combine confectioners' sugar, water and meringue powder; beat on low speed just until blended. Beat on high 4-5 minutes or until stiff peaks form. Divide into portions; tint as desired. Keep unused icing covered at all times with a damp cloth. If necessary, beat again on high speed to restore texture.

3. Frost and decorate the cookies as desired with assorted sprinkles and candies; add almonds for ears.

Sweetheart Coconut Cookies

Celebrate a season of peace and love with ruby red hearts. (If you want to give your cookie tray extra variety, cut some squares like those shown on the front cover.)
—JO ELLEN HELMLINGER COLUMBUS, OH

PREP: 30 MIN. • **BAKE:** 10 MIN./BATCH
MAKES: ABOUT 3½ DOZEN

- 1 **cup flaked coconut**
- 1 **cup sugar**
- ¾ **cup cold butter, cubed**
- 2¼ **cups all-purpose flour**
- 2 **eggs, lightly beaten**
- ½ **teaspoon vanilla extract**

GLAZE

- ¾ **cup confectioners' sugar**
- 1 **tablespoon water**
- ½ **teaspoon vanilla extract**
  Coarse white sugar, optional
- ½ **cup seedless raspberry jam**

1. Place the coconut and sugar in a food processor; cover and process until the coconut is coarsely chopped. In a large bowl, cut the butter into flour until crumbly. Stir in coconut mixture. Stir in eggs and vanilla.

2. On a lightly floured surface, roll out cookie dough to ⅛-in. thickness. Cut the dough with a 2½-in. heart-shaped cookie cutter dipped in flour. Using a 1-in. heart-shaped cookie cutter, cut out the center of half of cookies. Reroll small cutouts if desired.

3. Place the solid and cutout cookies 1 in. apart on greased baking sheets. Bake at 375° for 7-9 minutes or until the edges are lightly browned. Remove to wire racks.

4. In a small bowl, combine the confectioners' sugar, water and vanilla; brush over warm cookies with cutout centers. Immediately sprinkle with coarse white sugar if desired. Spread ½ teaspoon of jam over the bottom of each solid cookie; place the cookies with cutout centers over jam.

Holly Butter Mints

These yuletide leaves and berries not only are festive all by themselves, but also can make holiday garnishes for plain desserts. I create different shapes for weddings, recitals and other special events.

—CARMA BLOSSER LIVERMORE, CO

PREP: 1½ HOURS
MAKES: ABOUT 12 DOZEN (1¾ POUNDS)

- ¼ **cup butter, softened**
- ¼ **cup water**
- 1 **teaspoon peppermint extract**
- 1 **teaspoon butter flavoring**
  Dash salt
- 5½ **to 6 cups confectioners' sugar**
- 2 **to 4 drops green paste food coloring**
- 3 **to 5 drops red paste food coloring**
  Granulated sugar

1. In a large bowl, cream the butter. Gradually add water, peppermint extract, butter flavoring and salt; beat in enough confectioners' sugar on medium speed until the dough achieves a stiff putty consistency, about 3 minutes.

2. Divide dough into three portions. Knead green food coloring into two portions. Knead red food coloring into remaining portion. For holly leaves, shape teaspoonfuls of the green dough into balls; roll in granulated sugar. Flatten the balls to ⅛-in. thickness; cut with a holly leaf cookie cutter.

3. For berries, shape ¼ teaspoonfuls of the red dough into balls; roll in granulated sugar. Arrange the leaves and berries on a serving platter. Store at room temperature.

Holiday Helper

Flavoring extracts can be difficult to pour from the bottle into a measuring spoon. Now I use an inexpensive medicine dropper I bought at the pharmacy. It fits nicely into the bottles, prevents overpouring and is easy to clean.

—VIVIAN COOK MURFREESBORO, TN

Beary Cute Cookies

Whatever the season, teddy bears make everyone smile. I make my cub-shaped cookies for holiday gatherings and other special occasions. Mini chocolate kisses, M&M's and colored icing form the faces.

—SUSAN SCHULLER BRAINERD, MN

PREP: 25 MIN. • **BAKE:** 10 MIN./BATCH
MAKES: 2½ DOZEN

- ¾ **cup shortening**
- ½ **cup sugar**
- ½ **cup packed brown sugar**
- 1 **egg**
- 1 **teaspoon vanilla extract**
- 2 **cups all-purpose flour**
- 1 **teaspoon salt**
- ½ **teaspoon baking soda**
  Additional sugar
- 30 **miniature milk chocolate kisses**
- 60 **M&M's miniature baking bits**
  Colored decorating icing, optional

1. Preheat oven to 375°. In a large bowl, cream shortening and sugars until light and fluffy. Beat in egg and vanilla. In another bowl, whisk flour, salt and baking soda; gradually beat into the creamed mixture (the dough will be crumbly).

2. Set aside about ½ cup dough for the ears. Shape the remaining dough into 1-in. balls; roll in additional sugar. Place 3 in. apart on ungreased baking sheets. Flatten to about ½-in. thickness. Roll the reserved dough into ½-in. balls; roll in sugar. Place two smaller balls of dough about 1 in. apart, touching each flattened ball of dough (do not flatten the smaller balls).

3. Bake 10-12 minutes or until set and the edges are lightly browned. Remove from the oven; immediately press one milk chocolate kiss and two baking bits into each cookie for the nose and eyes. Cool on the pans 5 minutes. Remove to wire racks to cool completely.

4. If desired, pipe ear details, fur and remaining facial features with colored decorating icing.

Coconut Yule Trees

Guests say they love these mini coconut candies because of the bright decorations. With chocolaty trunks and bright sprinkles, the Christmas trees are almost too cute to eat. But they're too yummy not to!

—**MICHELLE RETTERER** MARYSVILLE, OH

PREP: 15 MIN. + CHILLING
MAKES: 2 DOZEN

- **3 cups flaked coconut**
- **2 cups confectioners' sugar**
- **¼ cup butter, softened**
- **¼ cup half-and-half cream**
- **1 teaspoon almond extract**

- **2 to 4 ounces dark chocolate candy coating**
- **Vanilla frosting, green sugar and assorted sprinkles**

1. In a large bowl, combine the first five ingredients. Drop the mixture by tablespoonfuls onto a waxed paper-lined baking sheet; refrigerate, covered, 1 hour. Shape into trees; return to the baking sheet.

2. In a microwave, melt the chocolate candy coating; stir until smooth. Spoon over or dip the trunks of trees; allow excess to drip off. Place on waxed paper;

let stand until set. Decorate the trees as desired with vanilla frosting, green sugar and sprinkles.

NOTE *Dark, white or milk chocolate confectionery coating is found in the baking section of most grocery stores. It is sometimes labeled "almond bark" or "candy coating" and is often sold in bulk packages (1 to 1½ pounds). It is the product used for dipping chocolate. A substitute for 6 ounces chocolate coating would be 1 cup (6 ounces) semisweet, dark or white chocolate chips and 1 tablespoon shortening melted together.*

Melting Snowmen

These treats are guaranteed to melt hearts! Feel free to try different decorations.
—*TASTE OF HOME* TEST KITCHEN

PREP: 1½ HOURS + STANDING
MAKES: 2 DOZEN

- ¾ cup sweetened condensed milk
- 1½ teaspoons peppermint extract
- 2¼ to 2½ cups confectioners' sugar
- ½ cup baking cocoa
- 1 pound white candy coating, chopped, divided

- 7 to 8 Starburst candies (orange for noses and colors of your choice for earmuffs)
- ⅓ cup dark chocolate chips

1. In a small bowl, combine sweetened condensed milk and extract. Stir in 2 cups confectioners' sugar and cocoa to form a dough. Turn onto a surface lightly sprinkled with confectioners' sugar. Knead in enough remaining confectioners' sugar to form a soft dough (dough should not be sticky).

2. Divide into thirds. Shape one portion into twenty-four ½-in. balls. Shape remaining portions of dough into twenty-four 1-in. balls. On waxed paper-lined baking sheets, flatten each 1-in. ball into an irregular 1½-in. circle.

3. In a microwave-safe bowl, melt 2 oz. white candy coating. Using the melted coating, attach a ½-in. ball near an edge of each circle. Let dry 1 hour.

4. Using Starburst candies, cut out noses and earmuffs as desired. Melt the remaining white candy coating; cool slightly. Working in batches of six, spoon candy coating over snowmen, allowing the coating to drape over each until completely covered. Immediately attach noses and earmuffs. Let stand at room temperature until dry to the touch, about 1 hour.

5. In a microwave, melt the dark chocolate chips; stir until smooth. Using a toothpick and melted chips, form the eyes, mouths, buttons and tops of earmuffs.

Rudolph Treats

Here's a great way to get children involved in your Christmas preparations. Kids will see the simple reindeer candy as a fun project with a sweet reward.
—**ABIGAIL VANDERSAUL** ST. PAUL, MO

START TO FINISH: 15 MIN.
MAKES: 1 DOZEN

- 12 miniature pretzels, halved
- 12 fun-size Almond Joy candy bars
- 12 miniature marshmallows, halved
  Black decorating gel
- 12 red M&M's miniature baking bits

1. Insert an end from two miniature pretzel halves into each candy bar to form the antlers. Gently press the cut side of two miniature marshmallow halves onto each candy bar for the eyes; dot with decorating gel.

2. For nose, attach a baking bit to top of each candy bar with decorating gel. Use gel to form mouths. Store in an airtight container.

Bugle Cones

Who says the prime season for ice cream is summer? Your guests are sure to crave a cone at Christmastime when they see these tiny goodies. A simple frosting-like mixture forms the little scoops, which go into crunchy Bugles. You can decorate the tops with red and green sprinkles—or any kind you like for other occasions.

—DIANNE CONWAY LONDON, ON

START TO FINISH: 20 MIN.
MAKES: 2½ DOZEN

- 2 **tablespoons butter, softened**
- 1⅓ **cups confectioners' sugar**
- ¼ **teaspoon salt**
- ¼ **teaspoon vanilla extract**
- 2 **tablespoons sweetened condensed milk**
- 1 **package (6 ounces) Bugles**
- ½ **cup semisweet chocolate chips, melted, optional**
  Assorted sprinkles and/or ground nuts

1. In a small bowl, beat butter and confectioners' sugar until crumbly. Beat in the salt and vanilla. Add the sweetened condensed milk and mix well (mixture will be stiff).

2. Shape mixture into ½-in. balls. Place one ball on top of each Bugle. Dip the tops of some or all in melted chocolate if desired. Decorate with sprinkles and/or nuts.

Holiday Helper

When I melt chocolate or almond bark to coat candies, fruit or pretzels, I like to use my slow cooker instead of melting the chocolate in a bowl in the microwave. The slow cooker keeps the chocolate warm when I have a lot that needs dipping.

—C. M. HARRIS WALKER, MN

ELEGANT DESSERTS

Favorite Hazelnut-Mocha Torte

When my daughter was newly married, one of the recipes she received was this wonderful mocha torte. It looks gorgeous decorated with a mound of shaved dark chocolate or chopped hazelnuts.

—ELIZABETH CZISZLER CALGARY, AB

PREP: 30 MIN. • **BAKE:** 20 MIN. + COOLING
MAKES: 12 SERVINGS

- 4 **eggs**
- ¾ **cup sugar**
- 1 **cup finely chopped hazelnuts**
- 2 **tablespoons all-purpose flour**
- 2½ **teaspoons baking powder**

FILLING
- 1 **cup confectioners' sugar**
- 2 **tablespoons butter, softened**
- 2 **tablespoons strong hot brewed coffee**
- 1 **teaspoon baking cocoa**
- ½ **teaspoon vanilla extract**

WHIPPED CREAM
- 1½ **cups heavy whipping cream**
- 4 **teaspoons confectioners' sugar**
- ¾ **teaspoon vanilla extract**
  Shaved dark chocolate and chopped hazelnuts, optional

1. Preheat oven to 350°. Line bottom of a greased 9-in. springform pan with parchment paper; grease paper. Place eggs and sugar in a blender; cover and process until frothy. Add hazelnuts, flour and baking powder; cover and process 1 minute or until blended.

2. Transfer to prepared pan. Bake 20-25 minutes or until the top springs back when lightly touched. Cool in pan 10 minutes. Loosen sides from pan with a knife. Remove rim from pan. Invert cake onto a wire rack; carefully remove pan bottom and paper. Cool completely.

3. In a small bowl, combine the filling ingredients; beat until smooth. Using a long serrated knife, cut the cake horizontally in half. Place one cake layer on a serving plate; spread with filling. Top with remaining cake layer.

4. In a large bowl, beat cream until it begins to thicken. Add confectioners' sugar and vanilla; beat until soft peaks form. Spread whipped cream over top and sides of cake. Decorate as desired with shaved chocolate and hazelnuts. Refrigerate leftovers.

Browned Butter Apple Pie with Cheddar Crust

How do you make good old-fashioned apple pie even better? Enhance the crust with cheddar cheese and stir browned butter into the filling. Scrumptious!

—**KATHRYN CONRAD** MILWAUKEE, WI

PREP: 40 MIN. + CHILLING
BAKE: 45 MIN. + COOLING
MAKES: 8 SERVINGS

- 2½ cups all-purpose flour
- 3 tablespoons semolina flour
- ¾ teaspoon salt
- 14 tablespoons cold butter, cubed
- ½ cup shredded aged sharp cheddar cheese
- 10 to 12 tablespoons ice water

FILLING
- ¼ cup butter, cubed
- 8 large Honeycrisp apples, peeled and cut into ¾-inch pieces (about 12 cups)
- ⅓ cup sugar
- 3 tablespoons brown sugar
- 3 tablespoons all-purpose flour
- 1 egg
- 1 tablespoon water

1. Place the flours and salt in a food processor; pulse until blended. Add the cold butter; pulse until the butter is the size of peas. Add the cheddar cheese; pulse 1-2 times. Transfer flour mixture to a large bowl. Gradually add ice water to the flour mixture, tossing with a fork until the dough holds together when pressed. Divide dough in half. Shape each into a disk; wrap in plastic wrap. Refrigerate 30 minutes or overnight.

2. Preheat oven to 400°. For the filling, in a Dutch oven, melt the butter over medium heat. Heat 5-7 minutes or until golden brown, stirring constantly.

3. Stir in the apples, sugar and brown sugar; bring to a boil. Reduce the heat; simmer, covered, 6-8 minutes or until the apples are almost tender. Uncover; cook 4-6 minutes longer or until slightly thickened, stirring occasionally. Stir in flour. Transfer mixture to a large bowl; refrigerate until cool.

4. On a lightly floured surface, roll out half of the dough to fit a 9-in. deep-dish pie plate. Transfer the pastry to the pie plate; trim the pastry to ½ in. beyond the edge of the plate. Refrigerate 30 minutes.

5. Add the apple filling to the pastry. Roll remaining dough to a 12-in. circle; cut into eight wedges. Place the wedges over filling. Trim, seal and flute edges. In a small bowl, whisk egg with water; brush over pastry.

6. Bake 45-55 minutes or until crust is golden brown and filling is bubbly. Cover the edge loosely with foil during the last 15 minutes if needed to prevent overbrowning. Remove the foil. Cool on a wire rack.

Holiday Helper

If you need to cover the edge of a pie with foil during baking, try this easy method. Start with a square of foil big enough to cover your pie and cut a circle out of the center. Then lay the square on top of your pie and wrap the foil over the edges.

—**LORI H.** SPARKS, NV

Maple-Pecan Cream Pie

I love to bake using the real maple syrup I get from a local farm. Mixing ½ cup into the filling really enhances my pecan pie.

—DIANE NEMITZ LUDINGTON, MI

PREP: 25 MIN. • **BAKE:** 40 MIN. + COOLING
MAKES: 8 SERVINGS

    **Pastry for single-crust pie
      (9 inches)**
  2 **eggs, lightly beaten**
  1 **cup packed brown sugar**
  1 **cup (8 ounces) sour cream**
  ½ **cup heavy whipping cream**
  ½ **cup maple syrup**
  ¼ **cup all-purpose flour**
  1 **cup pecan halves**

1. Preheat oven to 450°. On a lightly floured surface, roll the pastry dough to a ⅛-in. thick circle; transfer to a 9-in. pie plate. Trim pastry to ½ in. beyond rim of plate; flute edge.
2. Line the pie pastry with a double thickness of foil. Fill with pie weights, dried beans or uncooked rice. Bake 8 minutes. Remove foil and weights; bake 5 minutes longer. Cool on a wire rack. Reduce oven setting to 325°.
3. In a large bowl, whisk eggs, brown sugar, sour cream, whipping cream, syrup and flour. Pour into pie shell. Bake 15-20 minutes or until filling begins to set.
4. Sprinkle the pecan halves over the pastry. Cover the edge loosely with foil. Bake 25-30 minutes longer or just until set (mixture will jiggle). Remove foil. Cool on a wire rack.

Chocolate Ginger Cake

Indulge in a dark, decadent cake that showcases seasonal flavor. I stir grated fresh ginger into the batter and sprinkle chopped crystallized ginger over the velvety ganache on top.

—AMBER EVANS BEAVERTON, OR

PREP: 40 MIN. • **BAKE:** 40 MIN. + COOLING
MAKES: 12 SERVINGS

  6 **ounces milk chocolate, cut into
     ½-inch pieces**
2⅓ **cups all-purpose flour**
  ½ **cup baking cocoa**
  1 **teaspoon ground cinnamon**
  ½ **teaspoon salt**

  ¼ **teaspoon ground cloves**
  1 **cup canola oil**
  1 **cup molasses**
  1 **cup sugar**
  1 **cup water**
1½ **teaspoons baking soda**
  3 **tablespoons grated fresh
     gingerroot**
  2 **eggs**
  2 **egg yolks**
GANACHE
  4 **ounces bittersweet chocolate,
     chopped**
  ½ **cup heavy whipping cream**
  2 **tablespoons chopped crystallized
     ginger**
    **Vanilla ice cream or sweetened
     whipped cream, optional**

1. Preheat oven to 350°. Grease a 9-in. springform pan. Place on a baking sheet.
2. Place the milk chocolate in a small bowl. In another bowl, whisk the flour, cocoa, cinnamon, salt and cloves; add 1 tablespoon flour mixture to the milk chocolate and toss to coat.

3. In a large bowl, beat oil, molasses and sugar until blended. In a small saucepan, bring the water to a boil; stir in the baking soda until dissolved, then ginger. Add to oil mixture; beat until blended. Gradually add the remaining flour mixture, beating on low speed just until moistened. In a small bowl, lightly beat eggs and egg yolks; stir into batter until combined.
4. Fold in the milk chocolate. Transfer to prepared pan. Bake 40-50 minutes or until toothpick inserted in center comes out clean. Cool on a wire rack 30 minutes.
5. Loosen sides from pan with a knife; remove the rim from pan. Cool cake completely on wire rack.
6. For the ganache, place chocolate in a small bowl. In a small saucepan, bring the cream just to a boil. Pour over the chocolate; let stand 2 minutes. Stir with a whisk until smooth; cool slightly, stirring occasionally. Pour over cake; sprinkle with the crystallized ginger. If desired, serve with ice cream.

Glazed Spiced Rum Pound Cakes

This favorite recipe makes two loaf-size desserts—perfect for sharing with your family, neighbors or friends.

—**CHRISTINE RUSSELL** LITTLETON, NH

PREP: 30 MIN. • **BAKE:** 45 MIN. + COOLING
MAKES: 2 LOAVES (8 SLICES EACH)

- 1 cup butter, softened
- 2 cups packed brown sugar
- 5 eggs
- ⅓ cup spiced rum
- 2 teaspoons vanilla extract
- 3½ cups all-purpose flour
- 2 teaspoons baking powder
- ½ teaspoon baking soda
- ½ teaspoon salt
- ½ cup 2% milk

GLAZE
- ½ cup sugar
- ¼ cup butter, cubed
- 2 teaspoons water
- 2 teaspoons spiced rum
- ½ cup chopped pecans, toasted

1. Preheat oven to 350°. Grease and flour two 9x5-in. loaf pans. In a large bowl, cream butter and brown sugar until light and fluffy. Add eggs, one at a time, beating well after each addition. Beat in the rum and vanilla. In another bowl, whisk the flour, baking powder, baking soda and salt; add to creamed mixture alternately with milk, beating well after each addition.

2. Spoon the batter into the prepared pans. Bake 45-50 minutes or until a toothpick inserted in center comes out clean. Cool in the pans 10 minutes before removing to wire racks to cool.

3. Meanwhile, in a small saucepan, combine the sugar, butter, water and rum. Bring to a boil. Remove from heat; drizzle over warm cakes. Sprinkle with pecans. Cool completely on wire racks.

NOTE *To toast nuts, bake in a shallow pan in a 350° oven for 5-10 minutes or cook in a skillet over low heat until lightly browned, stirring occasionally.*

Great Gramma's Steamed Pudding

I grew up in a large family of children, cousins, aunts, uncles and grandparents. Steamed pudding was always our special Christmas treat. It's yummy with the accompanying cream sauce.

—JOY JOHNSON CULBERTSON, MT

PREP: 25 MIN.
COOK: 1½ HOURS + STANDING
MAKES: 12 SERVINGS

- 2⅔ cups all-purpose flour
- 4 teaspoons baking soda
   Pinch salt
- 1 cup hot water
- ⅔ cup molasses
- 4 cups fresh or frozen cranberries
- ⅔ cup chopped walnuts, toasted

SAUCE

- 2 cups sugar
- 2 teaspoons all-purpose flour
- 1 cup heavy whipping cream
- 1 cup butter, cubed

1. Grease and flour a 10-in. fluted tube pan. In a large bowl, whisk flour, baking soda and salt. In another bowl, whisk hot water and molasses until blended. Add to the flour mixture; stir just until moistened. Fold in the cranberries and walnuts. Transfer to the prepared pan; cover with foil.

2. Place tube pan on a rack in a large roasting pan; add 2 in. of hot water. Bring water to a gentle boil; cover the pot and steam cake 1½ to 1¾ hours or until a toothpick inserted in center comes out clean; add additional water to pot as needed. Remove the pudding from pot; let stand 15 minutes before removing to a serving plate.

3. Meanwhile, in a large saucepan, mix the sugar and flour until blended; stir in cream. Add the butter; bring mixture to a rolling boil, stirring occasionally. Cool slightly. Serve with warm or room temperature pudding.

NOTE *To remove cakes easily, use solid shortening to grease plain and fluted tube pans.*

Limoncello Cream Pie

After a rich and hearty dinner, we like the cool refreshment of this frozen lemon pie. Limoncello brings a bit of sophistication to each smooth, creamy piece.

—JESSIE GREARSON-SAPAT FALMOUTH, ME

PREP: 20 MIN. + FREEZING
MAKES: 8 SERVINGS

- 1 quart vanilla ice cream, softened
- ⅓ cup lemon curd, divided
- 3 tablespoons limoncello
- 1 teaspoon grated lemon peel
- 1 graham cracker crust (9 inches)
- 6 ounces white baking chocolate, chopped
- 1 cup heavy whipping cream, divided
- ¼ cup marshmallow creme
   Grated lemon peel, optional

1. In a large bowl, combine ice cream, half of lemon curd and all of limoncello and peel. Spoon into the crust. Freeze, covered, several hours or overnight.

2. In a microwave, heat white baking chocolate with ¼ cup whipping cream at 70% power until melted; stir until smooth. Set aside to cool.

3. In a small bowl, beat the remaining whipping cream until soft peaks form. Beat in the marshmallow creme. Fold in the remaining curd. With a spatula, fold half of the cream mixture into the cooled chocolate mixture just until blended. Fold in the remaining cream mixture; spread or pipe over top of pie. Freeze, covered, 1 hour.

4. Remove from freezer 10 minutes before serving. If desired, top with peel.

Cinnamon-Spiced Pumpkin Flan

Pumpkin is one of my favorite ingredients. I thought of adding it to a traditional flan recipe for a holiday variation.
—**ALISHA RODRIGUES** TETONIA, ID

PREP: 20 MIN. • **BAKE:** 50 MIN. + CHILLING
MAKES: 12 SERVINGS

⅔ cup sugar
FLAN
2 cups half-and-half cream
6 egg yolks
1 egg
1 cup sugar
1 cup canned pumpkin
1 teaspoon ground cinnamon
1 teaspoon vanilla extract

1. Preheat oven to 325°. In a small heavy saucepan, spread sugar; cook, without stirring, over medium-low heat until it begins to melt. Gently drag melted sugar to center of pan so sugar melts evenly. Cook, without stirring, until the melted sugar turns a medium amber color, about 8 minutes. Quickly pour into an ungreased 9-in. deep-dish pie plate, tilting to coat bottom of plate.
2. In a large saucepan, heat the cream until bubbles form around side of pan; remove from the heat. In a large bowl, whisk egg yolks, egg, sugar, pumpkin, cinnamon and vanilla until blended. Slowly stir in the hot cream. Pour into the pie plate.
3. Place the pie plate in a larger baking pan. Place pan on oven rack; add very hot water to pan to within ½ in. of the top of pie plate. Bake 50-60 minutes or until the center is just set (mixture will jiggle). Immediately remove flan from water bath to a wire rack; cool 1 hour. Refrigerate until cold, about 5 hours or overnight.
4. Run a knife around the edge and invert onto a rimmed serving platter. Refrigerate leftovers.

Mint-Chocolate Bombe

Wow the yuletide crowd with a spectacular frozen dessert. You'll want to keep this ice cream treat in mind for summer, too!

—**MARY KISINGER** MEDICINE HAT, AB

PREP: 15 MIN. + FREEZING
MAKES: 12 SERVINGS

 1 **cup heavy whipping cream**
 ⅓ **cup sweetened condensed milk**
 3 **tablespoons green creme de menthe**
 2 **cups chocolate ice cream, softened if necessary**
 3 **cups vanilla ice cream, softened if necessary**
 20 **chocolate wafers, coarsely crushed**
   Chocolate syrup and chopped mint Andes candies, optional

1. Line a 1½-qt. bowl with plastic wrap. Place in the freezer 30 minutes. In a large bowl, beat the cream until it begins to thicken. Add the milk and creme de menthe; beat until soft peaks form. Quickly spread onto bottom and up sides of bowl to within ½ in. of top. Freeze 2 hours or until firm. Spread chocolate ice cream over mint layer. Freeze 1 hour or until firm.

2. Spoon the vanilla ice cream into ice cream shell, spreading to completely cover the top. Cover and freeze bombe overnight.

3. Invert the bombe onto a serving plate. Remove bowl and plastic wrap. Top with the crushed wafers. Cut into wedges. If desired, top with chocolate syrup and candies.

Chocolate Coconut Pie with Coconut Crust

Chewy coconut in both the fudgy filling and the homemade pastry crust makes this pie a real standout. For even more appeal, I mix in chopped almonds.

—**DARLENE BRENDEN** SALEM, OR

PREP: 35 MIN. + CHILLING
BAKE: 30 MIN. + COOLING
MAKES: 8 SERVINGS

 1 **cup all-purpose flour**
 ½ **cup flaked coconut**
 ⅓ **cup cold butter, cubed**
 ¼ **teaspoon coconut extract**
 3 **to 4 tablespoons 2% milk**

FILLING
 4 **ounces German sweet chocolate, chopped**
 ¼ **cup butter, melted**
 1 **can (14 ounces) sweetened condensed milk**
 ½ **cup 2% milk**
 2 **eggs**
 1 **teaspoon vanilla extract**
 ⅛ **teaspoon salt**
 1 **cup flaked coconut**
 ½ **cup chopped almonds**
   Whipped cream, optional

1. Place flour and coconut in a food processor; process until the coconut is finely chopped. Add the cold butter; pulse until the butter is the size of peas. While pulsing, add the coconut extract and just enough milk to form moist crumbs. Shape the dough into a disk; wrap in plastic wrap. Refrigerate 1 hour or overnight.

2. Preheat oven to 400°. On a lightly floured surface, roll the dough to a ⅛-in.-thick circle; transfer to a 9-in. pie plate. Trim pastry to ½ in. beyond rim of plate; flute edge.

3. Line unpricked pastry with a double thickness of foil. Fill with pie weights, dried beans or uncooked rice. Bake on a lower oven rack 10-15 minutes or until edges are light golden brown. Remove the foil and weights; bake 5-7 minutes longer or until bottom is golden brown. Cool on a wire rack. Reduce the oven setting to 350°.

4. For filling, in a large saucepan, melt the chocolate and butter over medium heat; cool slightly. Whisk in the milks, eggs, vanilla and salt. Pour into crust. Sprinkle with coconut and almonds.

5. Cover edge loosely with foil. Bake 30-35 minutes or until center is set. Remove the foil. Cool on a wire rack. If desired, serve with whipped cream.

Cherrimisu

Love Italian tiramisu? This super-simple variation dresses up a prepared angel food cake with festive red maraschino cherries and a luscious cream filling and frosting. I finish it all off with a dusting of baking cocoa for a decadent touch.

—KELLY BYLER GOSHEN, IN

START TO FINISH: 25 MIN.
MAKES: 12 SERVINGS

- 1 **jar (10 ounces) maraschino cherries**
- ½ **cup ricotta cheese**
- 4 **ounces cream cheese, softened**
- 2 **tablespoons confectioners' sugar**
- ¼ **teaspoon cherry extract**
- 1½ **cups heavy whipping cream**
- 1 **prepared angel food cake (8 to 10 ounces)**
- 1 **tablespoon baking cocoa**

1. Drain the maraschino cherries; reserving ¼ cup juice. In a large bowl, beat the ricotta cheese, cream cheese, confectioners' sugar and cherry extract until blended. Gradually beat in the heavy whipping cream and reserved maraschino cherry juice until stiff peaks form.

2. Using a long serrated knife, cut cake horizontally in half. Place one cake layer on a serving plate; spread with 1 cup whipped cream mixture. Arrange the maraschino cherries over the cream layer. Top with remaining cake layer. Frost the top and sides of cake with remaining cream mixture. Dust with baking cocoa.

Chocolate & Peppermint Ice Cream Roll

The popular pairing of chocolate and mint makes this a holiday favorite. Embellish the roll with a holly design...or simply sprinkle the entire top of the cake with confectioners' sugar.

—JILL EVELY WILMORE, KY

PREP: 40 MIN. • **BAKE:** 10 MIN. + FREEZING • **MAKES:** 10 SERVINGS

- 4 eggs, separated
- ½ cup all-purpose flour
- ¼ cup plus 2 tablespoons baking cocoa, divided
- ½ teaspoon baking powder
- ¼ teaspoon baking soda
- ⅛ teaspoon salt
- ¾ cup sugar, divided
- 3 tablespoons water
- 2 tablespoons canola oil
- 1 teaspoon vanilla extract
- 3 cups peppermint or vanilla ice cream, softened if necessary
  Confectioners' sugar
  Red Hots candies

1. Place the egg whites in large bowl; let stand at room temperature 30 minutes.

2. Meanwhile, preheat oven to 375°. Line the bottom of a greased 15x10x1-in. baking pan with parchment paper; grease paper. Sift flour, ¼ cup cocoa, baking powder, baking soda and salt together twice.

3. In another large bowl, beat the egg yolks until slightly thickened. Gradually add ¼ cup sugar, beating on high speed until thick and lemon-colored. Beat in water, oil and vanilla. Fold in flour mixture (batter will be thick).

4. With clean beaters, beat egg whites on medium until soft peaks form. Gradually add the remaining sugar, 1 tablespoon at a time, beating on high after each addition until the sugar is dissolved. Continue beating until soft glossy peaks form. Fold a fourth of the whites into batter, then fold in remaining whites. Transfer to prepared pan, spreading evenly.

5. Bake 8-10 minutes or until top springs back when lightly touched. Cool 5 minutes. Invert onto a tea towel dusted with the remaining cocoa. Gently peel off the paper. Roll up the cake in the towel jelly-roll style, starting with a short side. Cool completely on a wire rack.

6. Unroll cake; spread ice cream over cake to within ½ in. of the edges. Roll up again without towel. Place on a platter, seam side down. Freeze, covered, at least 2 hours or until firm; trim ends.

7. Arrange desired holly leaf cardboard cutouts on the cake roll; sprinkle with confectioners' sugar. Carefully remove the cutouts; top with Red Hots for berries.

Forming Leaves on Chocolate & Peppermint Ice Cream Roll

1. Cut holly leaves or other simple holiday shapes from sturdy paper or thin cardboard. Arrange the cutouts on top of the rolled cake. Spoon confectioners' sugar into a fine mesh strainer and gently tap the side of the strainer over the top of the cake.

2. Using tweezers or tongs, gently remove each paper or cardboard cutout. Be careful not to tip the cutouts too much while holding them over the cake so that the sugar on the cutouts doesn't fall on the cake.

Tangerine Chocolate Semifreddo

For a new frozen treat to serve my family, I came up with a citrusy chocolate version of classic Italian semifreddo.

—CLAIRE CRUCE ATLANTA, GA

PREP: 35 MIN. + FREEZING
MAKES: 6 SERVINGS

- 8 **egg yolks**
- ¾ **cup sugar, divided**
- 1 **tablespoon grated tangerine peel**
- 1 **tablespoon tangerine juice**
- ⅛ **teaspoon salt**
- ½ **cup semisweet chocolate chips, melted**
- 1 **teaspoon vanilla extract**
- 1 **cup heavy whipping cream**
  Sweetened whipped cream and baking cocoa

1. In top of a double boiler or metal bowl over simmering water, combine egg yolks, ½ cup sugar, tangerine peel, juice and salt. Beat on medium speed until mixture is thick, frothy and holds a ribbon and a thermometer reads 160°. Remove from heat; whisk in the melted chocolate and vanilla. Quickly transfer to a bowl; place in ice water and refrigerate 15 minutes or until completely cool, stirring occasionally.

2. In a large bowl, beat the cream until it begins to thicken. Add the remaining sugar; beat until stiff peaks form. Fold into cooled chocolate mixture. Pour into six freezer-safe dessert glasses or dishes. Freeze until firm, about 4 hours.

3. Just before serving, top with the sweetened whipped cream and dust with cocoa. Serve immediately.

Eggnog Eclairs

My mother's beautiful eclairs have a rich, creamy custard filling everyone loves.

—LAURINDA JOHNSTON BELCHERTOWN, MA

PREP: 55 MIN. + CHILLING
BAKE: 25 MIN. + COOLING
MAKES: ABOUT 1 DOZEN

- ¾ **cup sugar**
- ¼ **cup cornstarch**
- ½ **teaspoon salt**
- 2 **cups whole milk**
- 2 **egg yolks**
- 2 **tablespoons butter**
- 1 **teaspoon vanilla extract**
- ¼ **teaspoon ground nutmeg**

ECLAIRS

- 1 **cup water**
- ½ **cup butter, cubed**
- ¼ **teaspoon salt**
- 1 **cup all-purpose flour**
- 4 **eggs**

ASSEMBLY

- 1 **cup heavy whipping cream**
- 1 **cup confectioners' sugar**
- 1 **to 2 tablespoons whole milk**

1. In a small heavy saucepan, mix the sugar, cornstarch and salt. Whisk in the milk. Cook and stir over medium heat until thickened and bubbly. Reduce the heat to low; cook and stir 2 minutes longer. Remove from heat.

2. In a small bowl, whisk a small amount of the hot mixture into egg yolks; return all to the pan, whisking constantly. Bring to a gentle boil; cook and stir 2 minutes. Remove from the heat. Stir in the butter, vanilla and nutmeg. Cool 15 minutes, stirring occasionally. Transfer the custard to a bowl. Press plastic wrap onto the surface of custard. Refrigerate until cold, about 3 hours.

3. Preheat oven to 400°. In a large saucepan, bring the water, butter and salt to a rolling boil. Add the flour all at once and beat until blended. Cook over medium heat, stirring vigorously until the mixture pulls away from the sides of pan and forms a ball. Remove from heat; let stand 5 minutes.

4. Add the eggs, one at a time, beating well after each addition until smooth. Continue beating until the mixture is smooth and shiny. Transfer dough to a resealable plastic bag; cut a 1-in. hole in one corner of the plastic bag. Pipe 3-in. strips 3 in. apart on greased baking sheets.

5. Bake 10 minutes. Reduce the heat to 350°; bake 15-20 minutes longer or until puffed, very firm and golden brown. Pierce the side of each eclair with the tip of a knife. Cool completely on a wire rack.

6. To assemble, cut off the top third of each eclair. Pull out and discard the soft dough from inside the tops and bottoms of the eclairs. In a small bowl, beat the heavy whipping cream until stiff peaks form. Fold into cold custard. Spoon into the bottoms of the eclairs; replace the tops.

7. For the icing, in a small bowl, mix the confectioners' sugar and milk until smooth; spread over the eclairs. Serve immediately.

Pumpkin Cranberry Cheesecake

One Thanksgiving, I was eating pumpkin pie and decided to add some cranberry sauce to it. I enjoyed the combination so much, I experimented and came up with a two-tone, fall-flavored cheesecake that has berries on the bottom.

—JOHN ABRAHAM BOCA RATON, FL

PREP: 45 MIN. • **BAKE:** 70 MIN. + CHILLING
MAKES: 12 SERVINGS

- 1½ cups graham cracker crumbs
- ¾ cup ground pecans
- 2 tablespoons sugar
- ¼ cup butter, melted

CRANBERRY LAYER

- 1 package (12 ounces) fresh or frozen cranberries
- 1 cup sugar
- 2 tablespoons cornstarch
- 2 tablespoons water
- 4 teaspoons grated orange peel

FILLING

- 3 packages (8 ounces each) cream cheese, softened
- ¾ cup sugar
- ¾ cup packed brown sugar
- 1 can (15 ounces) solid-pack pumpkin
- 3 teaspoons vanilla extract
- 1 teaspoon ground cinnamon
- 4 eggs, lightly beaten

1. Preheat oven to 350°. Place a greased 9-in. springform pan on a double thickness of heavy-duty foil (about 18 in. square). Wrap the foil securely around the pan. Place pan on a baking sheet.

2. In a small bowl, mix the graham cracker crumbs, ground pecans and sugar; stir in the butter. Press onto the bottom and 2 in. up the sides of the prepared pan. Bake 15 minutes. Cool crust on a wire rack. Reduce the oven setting to 325°.

3. In a large saucepan, combine the cranberry layer ingredients. Bring to a boil, stirring to dissolve the sugar. Reduce the heat to medium; cook, uncovered, 8-10 minutes or until berries pop and mixture is slightly thickened, stirring occasionally. Remove from heat. Cool slightly. Gently spread into crust.

4. In a large bowl, beat the cream cheese, sugar and brown sugar until smooth. Beat in the pumpkin, vanilla and cinnamon. Add the eggs; beat on low speed just until blended. Pour over the cranberry layer. Place springform pan in a larger baking pan; add 1 in. of hot water to larger pan.

5. Bake 70-80 minutes or until center is just set and top appears dull. Remove springform pan from water bath. Cool cheesecake on wire rack for 10 minutes. Loosen the sides of pan with a knife; remove the foil. Cool 1 hour longer. Refrigerate overnight, covering when completely cooled. Remove rim of pan.

Chocolate Lover's Mousse Torte

PREP: 40 MIN. • **BAKE:** 15 MIN. + COOLING
MAKES: 12 SERVINGS

- 1 cup butter, softened
- 1 cup sugar
- 3 eggs
- 1½ teaspoons vanilla extract
- 2 cups all-purpose flour
- ⅔ cup baking cocoa
- 1 teaspoon baking powder
- ¼ teaspoon baking soda
- 1⅓ cups whole milk

FILLING

- 1 teaspoon unflavored gelatin
- 3 tablespoons cold water
- ⅓ cup confectioners' sugar
- 3 tablespoons baking cocoa
- 1 cup heavy whipping cream
- 1 teaspoon vanilla extract

1. Preheat oven to 350°. Line a greased 15x10x1-in. baking pan with waxed paper; grease paper.

2. In a large bowl, cream the butter and sugar until light and fluffy. Add the eggs, one at a time, beating well after each addition. Beat in the vanilla. In another bowl, whisk flour, baking cocoa, baking powder and baking soda; add to the creamed mixture alternately with milk, beating just until combined. Transfer to prepared pan.

3. Bake 15-20 minutes or until a toothpick inserted in center comes out clean. Cool 10 minutes before inverting onto a wire rack to cool completely. Carefully remove waxed paper.

4. In a small saucepan, sprinkle the unflavored gelatin over the cold water; let stand 1 minute. Heat and stir over low heat until gelatin is completely dissolved. Cool to room temperature.

5. Sift confectioners' sugar and baking cocoa together. In a large bowl, beat the heavy whipping cream until it begins to thicken. Beat in confectioners' sugar mixture and vanilla. While beating, gradually add the gelatin until stiff peaks form.

6. Trim the cake edges; cut crosswise into fourths. Place one cake layer on a serving plate; spread with ½ cup filling. Repeat the layers three times. Refrigerate until serving.

"With layer after luscious layer of creamy filling and cake, Chocolate Lover's Mousse Torte proves irresistible every time."

—**BRENDA FISHER** STELLA, MO

Ginger-Poached Pears

Here's a simply elegant choice for dessert. The fresh pear halves are roasted in a sweet sauce of ginger ale and honey.

—**HARRIET MILLSTONE** TORONTO, ON

PREP: 15 MIN. • **BAKE:** 25 MIN.
MAKES: 4 SERVINGS

- 4 **medium pears**
- ½ **cup ginger ale**
- ½ **cup honey**
- ½ **cup chopped crystallized ginger**
- ½ **cup chopped pecans, toasted**

1. Preheat oven to 375°. Core the pears from the bottom, leaving stems intact. Peel pears; cut in half vertically. Cut ¼ in. from the bottoms to level pears if necessary. Place in an ungreased 13x9-in. baking dish.

2. Place the ginger ale and honey in a small saucepan. Cook and stir until combined; spoon over pears. Bake, uncovered, 25-30 minutes or until tender, basting occasionally.

3. With a slotted spoon, remove pears to individual serving dishes. Transfer pan juices to a small saucepan; stir in ginger. Cook and stir over medium heat 5-8 minutes or until heated through. Spoon over pears; sprinkle with pecans.

Special Raspberry Torte

Raspberry preserves, a burst of lemon and a homemade buttercream frosting make this torte my mom's absolute favorite.

—**LORI LEE DANIELS** BEVERLY, WV

PREP: 45 MIN. + CHILLING
BAKE: 20 MIN. + COOLING
MAKES: 12 SERVINGS

- 5 **egg whites**
- ½ **cup butter, softened**
- ½ **cup shortening**
- 2 **cups sugar**
- 1 **teaspoon lemon extract**
- 3 **cups all-purpose flour**
- 2 **teaspoons baking powder**
- ½ **teaspoon baking soda**
- ⅛ **teaspoon salt**
- 1½ **cups buttermilk**

FROSTING
- ¾ **cup shortening**
- ⅓ **cup butter, softened**
- 4½ **cups confectioners' sugar**
- 1½ **teaspoons lemon extract**
- 5 **to 6 tablespoons 2% milk**
- 1 **jar (10 ounces) seedless raspberry preserves**
  Fresh raspberries

1. Place egg whites in a large bowl; let stand at room temperature 30 minutes. Preheat oven to 350°. Line bottoms of two greased 9-in. round baking pans with parchment paper; grease paper.

2. In a large bowl, cream the butter, shortening and sugar until light and fluffy. Beat in extract. In another bowl, whisk the flour, baking powder, baking soda and salt; add to creamed mixture alternately with buttermilk, beating well after each addition.

3. With clean beaters, beat egg whites on medium speed until stiff peaks form. Fold into cake batter.

4. Transfer to prepared pans. Bake 20-25 minutes or until a toothpick inserted in the center comes out clean and edges are golden. Cool in the pans 10 minutes before removing to wire racks; remove paper. Cool completely.

5. In a large bowl, beat the shortening and butter until combined. Beat in the confectioner's sugar alternately with extract and enough milk to reach a spreading consistency.

6. Using a long serrated knife, cut each cake horizontally in half. Place one cake layer on a serving plate; spread with half of the preserves. Top with another cake layer and ¾ cup frosting. Place third cake layer over frosting; spread with remaining preserves. Top with remaining cake layer.

7. Frost the top and sides of the cake with 1 cup frosting, forming a crumb coating. Refrigerate cake until frosting is set, about 30 minutes. Remove from refrigerator and cover with remaining frosting. Top with raspberries.

Festive Nut Cake

Any Christmas nutcracker would be proud! With four kinds of nuts—pecans, walnuts, almonds and cashews—this glazed cake is loaded with crunchy appeal.

—JEANNE KEMPER BAGDAD, KY

PREP: 40 MIN. • **BAKE:** 1 HOUR + COOLING
MAKES: 16 SERVINGS

- 2 **eggs, separated**
- 1 **cup butter, softened**
- 2 **cups sugar**
- 1 **teaspoon almond extract**
- 1 **teaspoon vanilla extract**
- 3 **cups all-purpose flour**
- 2 **teaspoons baking powder**
- 1 **teaspoon ground cinnamon**
- ½ **teaspoon salt**
- ½ **teaspoon baking soda**
- 1 **cup 2% milk**
- 1 **teaspoon cream of tartar**
- 1 **cup slivered almonds**
- 1 **cup each chopped cashews, pecans and walnuts**

TOPPING
- ½ **cup confectioners' sugar**
- 3 **to 4 teaspoons 2% milk**
  Additional slivered almonds, salted cashews, and pecan and walnut halves, toasted, optional

1. Place the egg whites in a small bowl; let stand at room temperature 30 minutes. Preheat oven to 325°. Grease and flour a 10-in. tube pan.
2. In a large bowl, cream the butter and sugar until light and fluffy. Add the egg yolks, one at a time, beating well after each addition. Beat in the extracts. In another bowl, whisk the flour, baking powder, cinnamon, salt and baking soda; add to the creamed mixture alternately with milk, beating well after each addition.
3. Add the cream of tartar to the egg whites; with clean beaters, beat on high speed until stiff peaks form. Fold into the batter with the almonds, cashews, pecans and walnuts.
4. Transfer cake batter to prepared pan. Bake 60-65 minutes or until a toothpick inserted in the center comes out clean. Cool in the pan 10 minutes before removing to a wire rack to cool completely.
5. For glaze, in a small bowl, mix the confectioners' sugar and enough milk to reach desired consistency. Drizzle over cake and, if desired, sprinkle with additional nuts.

White Chocolate Macadamia Bread Pudding

Cozy, comforting, indulgent...this luscious pudding represents just about everything I love about the Christmas season. For an extra-special presentation, scoop each serving into a martini glass.

—BARB MILLER OAKDALE, MN

PREP: 10 MIN. + STANDING
BAKE: 50 MIN. + STANDING
MAKES: 10 SERVINGS (1¼ CUPS SAUCE)

- 4 **eggs**
- 3 **cups heavy whipping cream**
- 1 **cup packed light brown sugar**
- 1 **cup 2% milk**
- 1 **teaspoon ground cinnamon**
- 1 **teaspoon vanilla extract**
- 6 **ounces white baking chocolate, chopped**
- ¾ **cup chopped macadamia nuts**
- 10 **cups cubed croissants or French bread**

SAUCE
- ½ **cup heavy whipping cream**
- 6 **ounces white baking chocolate, chopped**
- ¼ **cup hot caramel ice cream topping**

1. Preheat oven to 350°. In a large bowl, whisk eggs, heavy cream, brown sugar, milk, cinnamon and vanilla until blended. Stir in the baking chocolate and nuts. Gently stir in the croissants; let stand about 15 minutes or until the bread is softened.

2. Transfer bread mixture to a greased 13x9-in. baking dish. Bake, uncovered, 50-60 minutes or until puffed, golden and a knife inserted near the center comes out clean. Let stand 15 minutes before serving.

3. Meanwhile, in a small saucepan, combine cream, chocolate and caramel topping; bring to a boil. Reduce heat; simmer 1-3 minutes or until chocolate is melted, stirring occasionally. Serve with warm bread pudding.

STOCKING STUFFER GIFTS

Mocha Cookie Pretzels

Give the holidays a twist with chocolaty cookies shaped like pretzels. Wrap up a few and tuck them into the stockings of the coffee lovers on your list.

—*TASTE OF HOME* TEST KITCHEN

PREP: 1½ HOURS + CHILLING
BAKE: 10 MIN./BATCH
MAKES: 4 DOZEN

- ½ **cup butter, softened**
- ½ **cup sugar**
- 1 **egg**
- 2 **ounces white baking chocolate, melted and cooled**
- 1 **teaspoon vanilla extract**
- 2 **cups cake flour**
- ¼ **teaspoon salt**

GLAZE

- 1 **cup (6 ounces) semisweet chocolate chips**
- 1 **teaspoon shortening**
- 1 **teaspoon light corn syrup**
- 1 **cup confectioners' sugar**
- 3 **to 5 tablespoons hot brewed coffee**
- 2 **ounces white baking chocolate, chopped**
  Green colored sugar, optional

1. In a large bowl, cream butter and sugar until light and fluffy. Beat in egg. Beat in melted chocolate and vanilla. Combine flour and salt; gradually add to the creamed mixture and mix well. Cover and refrigerate for 1 hour or until dough is easy to handle.

2. Divide cookie dough into fourths; divide each portion into 12 pieces. Shape each into a 6-in. rope; twist into a pretzel shape. Place 1 in. apart on lightly greased baking sheets.

3. Bake at 400° for 7-9 minutes or until set. Remove to wire racks to cool.

4. For glaze, in a microwave, melt the semisweet chips, shortening and light corn syrup; stir until smooth. Stir in confectioners' sugar and enough coffee to achieve a glaze consistency. Dip the cookies in glaze; allow excess to drip off. Place on waxed paper until set.

5. In a microwave, melt white chocolate at 30% power; stir until smooth. Drizzle over the cookies. Decorate with green sugar if desired; let stand until set.

Sweet & Salty Popcorn

Need Christmas presents for teachers? Let your children help you make this yummy popcorn mix and package it to bring to school. Your kids will be proud of their homemade gift.

—DIANE SMITH PINE MOUNTAIN, GA

START TO FINISH: 25 MIN. • **MAKES:** 4 QUARTS

- 10 cups popped popcorn
- 1 cup broken miniature pretzels
- 1 cup candies of your choice, such as Almond Joy pieces or milk chocolate M&M's
- 1 cup chopped dried pineapple
- 10 ounces white candy coating, coarsely chopped

1. In a large bowl, combine popcorn, pretzels, candies and pineapple. In a microwave, melt the candy coating; stir until smooth. Pour over popcorn mixture; toss to coat.

2. Immediately spread onto waxed paper; let stand until set. Break into pieces. Store in airtight containers.

Chili Spiced Pecans

Fans of spicy food get a real kick out of crunchy pecans coated with a blend of hot sauce, chili powder, cumin and more. In just 10 minutes, I can get a big pan of them in the oven.

—JOYCE WELLING SWANTON, OH

PREP: 10 MIN. • **BAKE:** 15 MIN. + COOLING • **MAKES:** 3 CUPS

- 3 tablespoons olive oil
- 1 teaspoon garlic salt
- 1 teaspoon curry powder
- 1 teaspoon chili powder
- 1 teaspoon Worcestershire sauce
- ½ teaspoon ground cumin
- ½ teaspoon hot pepper sauce
- ¼ teaspoon ground ginger
- ¼ teaspoon ground cinnamon
- 3 cups pecan halves

1. In a large skillet, combine the first nine ingredients; cook and stir for 3 minutes. Remove from the heat. Stir in pecans and toss to coat.

2. Transfer the pecans to a greased 15x10x1-in. baking pan. Bake at 325° for 15-20 minutes or until lightly browned, stirring occasionally. Cool. Store in an airtight container.

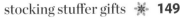

Ginger & Maple Macadamia Nut Cookies

These treats have a spicy ginger flavor that always reminds me of traditional German lebkuchen. Add colored sprinkles if you want a little extra sparkle for the season.

—THOMAS FAGLON SOMERSET, NJ

PREP: 45 MIN. + CHILLING
BAKE: 10 MIN./BATCH + COOLING
MAKES: ABOUT 7 DOZEN

- 1½ cups butter, softened
- ½ cup sugar
- ¾ cup maple syrup
- 4 cups all-purpose flour
- 3 teaspoons ground ginger
- 3 teaspoons ground cinnamon
- 1 teaspoon ground allspice
- ½ teaspoon ground cloves
- 1½ teaspoons salt
- 1½ teaspoons baking soda
- 1½ cups finely chopped macadamia nuts
- 24 ounces dark chocolate candy coating, melted
- ⅓ cup finely chopped crystallized ginger

1. In a large bowl, cream butter and sugar until light and fluffy. Gradually beat in syrup. In another bowl, whisk the flour, spices, salt and baking soda; gradually beat into creamed mixture. Stir in nuts.

2. Divide dough in half; shape each into a 12-in.-long roll. Wrap in plastic wrap; refrigerate 2 hours or until firm.

3. Preheat oven to 350°. Unwrap and cut dough crosswise into ¼-in. slices. Place 1 in. apart on ungreased baking sheets. Bake 8-10 minutes or until set. Cool on pans 2 minutes. Remove to wire racks to cool completely.

4. Dip each cookie halfway into melted candy coating; allow excess to drip off. Place on waxed paper-lined baking sheets; sprinkle with crystallized ginger. Refrigerate until set.

Winter Herb Tea Mix

When I pick fresh herbs from my garden, I dry some of them for tea. This soothing blend of mint, sage, rosemary and thyme warms you body and soul.

—SUE GRONHOLZ BEAVER DAM, WI

START TO FINISH: 10 MIN.
MAKES: 18 SERVINGS
(9 TABLESPOONS TEA MIX)

- 6 **tablespoons dried mint**
- 1 **tablespoon dried sage leaves**
- 1 **tablespoon dried rosemary, crushed**
- 1 **tablespoon dried thyme**

ADDITIONAL INGREDIENTS (FOR EACH SERVING)
- 1 **cup boiling water**
- 1 **teaspoon honey**
- 1 **lemon wedge**

In a small airtight container, combine the herbs. Store in a cool dry place for up to 6 months.

TO PREPARE TEA *Place 1½ teaspoons tea mix in a glass measuring cup. With the end of a wooden spoon handle, crush the mixture until aromas are released. Add the boiling water. Cover and steep for 10 minutes. Strain tea into a mug, discarding the herbs. Stir in the honey; serve with lemon.*

Texas-Style BBQ Sauce

In the South, barbecue is serious business! One of our family's favorite sauce recipes includes ketchup, yellow mustard, garlic, Worcestershire and apple cider vinegar.

—**SANDY KLOCINSKI** SUMMERVILLE, SC

START TO FINISH: 25 MIN.
MAKES: 1¾ CUPS

- 1 **tablespoon butter**
- 1 **small onion, chopped**
- 2 **garlic cloves, minced**
- 1 **cup ketchup**
- ¼ **cup packed brown sugar**
- ¼ **cup lemon juice**
- 2 **tablespoons apple cider vinegar**
- 2 **tablespoons tomato paste**
- 1 **tablespoon yellow mustard**
- 1 **tablespoon Worcestershire sauce**
- 2 **teaspoons chili powder**

1. In a large saucepan, heat butter over medium heat. Add onion; cook and stir 2-3 minutes or until tender. Add garlic; cook 1 minute longer.
2. Stir in the remaining ingredients; bring to a boil. Reduce heat; simmer, uncovered, 15-20 minutes to allow flavors to blend.

Peanut Butter Spread

For as long as I can remember, our church has served sandwiches featuring this fluffy, peanutty spread. It's great on toast as a quick breakfast or snack, too.

—**MAUDIE RABER** MILLERSBURG, OH

START TO FINISH: 10 MIN.
MAKES: 5 HALF-PINTS

- 2 **cups peanut butter**
- 1 **jar (7 ounces) marshmallow creme**
- 1 **cup dark corn syrup**
- 1 **cup light corn syrup**

In a large bowl, beat all ingredients until smooth. Place the spread in sterilized half-pint jars. Store at room temperature.

Lime Shortbread with Dried Cherries

My Aunt Mary loved shortbread, and I think my version with cherries and lime would do her proud. For a variation, substitute cranberries and grated orange peel.

—**ABIGAIL BOSTWICK** TOMAHAWK, WI

PREP: 25 MIN. + CHILLING
BAKE: 10 MIN./BATCH
MAKES: ABOUT 4½ DOZEN

- 1 **cup butter, softened**
- ¾ **cup confectioners' sugar**
- 1 **tablespoon grated lime peel**
- 2 **teaspoons vanilla extract**
- ½ **teaspoon almond extract**
- 2 **cups all-purpose flour**
- ¼ **teaspoon baking powder**
- ⅛ **teaspoon salt**
- ½ **cup chopped dried cherries**

1. In a large bowl, cream butter and confectioners' sugar until blended. Beat in the lime peel and extracts. In another bowl, mix flour, baking powder and salt; gradually beat into creamed mixture. Stir in cherries.
2. Divide dough in half; shape each portion into a 7-in.-long roll. Wrap in plastic wrap; refrigerate 3-4 hours or until firm.
3. Preheat oven to 350°. Unwrap and cut dough crosswise into ¼-in. slices. Place 2 in. apart on ungreased baking sheets. Bake 9-11 minutes or until the edges are golden brown. Remove from pans to wire racks to cool.

Chocolate Chai Snickerdoodles

What's better than classic snickerdoodles? Snickerdoodles featuring the flavors of chai and chocolate! Indulge with a cup of coffee, tea or hot cocoa.

—**KATHERINE WOLLGAST** FLORISSANT, MO

PREP: 30 MIN. • **BAKE:** 10 MIN./BATCH
MAKES: ABOUT 3 DOZEN

- 2¼ **cups sugar**
- 1 **teaspoon ground ginger**
- 1 **teaspoon ground cardamom**
- 1 **teaspoon ground cinnamon**
- ½ **teaspoon ground allspice**
- ¼ **teaspoon white pepper**
- 1 **cup butter, softened**
- 2 **eggs**

- 2 **teaspoons vanilla extract**
- 2¼ **cups all-purpose flour**
- ½ **cup baking cocoa**
- 2 **teaspoons cream of tartar**
- 1½ **teaspoons baking powder**
- ½ **teaspoon salt**

1. Preheat oven to 350°. In a large bowl, combine the first six ingredients. Remove ½ cup sugar mixture to a shallow dish.
2. Add the butter to the remaining sugar mixture; beat until light and fluffy. Beat in the eggs and vanilla. In another bowl, whisk the flour, baking cocoa, cream of tartar, baking powder and salt; gradually beat into the creamed mixture.
3. Shape the dough into 1½-in. balls. Roll in the reserved sugar mixture; place 2 in. apart on ungreased baking sheets. Flatten slightly with the bottom of a glass. Bake 10-12 minutes or until the edges are firm. Remove to wire racks to cool.

Mint Cocoa Mix

This yummy mix is my go-to holiday gift for relatives, friends, neighbors, teachers... just about everyone. It's so good, you'll want to make extra to keep at home!

—**LAVONNE HEGLAND** ST. MICHAEL, MN

START TO FINISH: 5 MIN.
MAKES: 53 SERVINGS (17⅔ CUPS TOTAL)

- 7½ **cups instant chocolate drink mix**
- 1 **package (25.6 ounces) nonfat dry milk powder**
- 2½ **cups confectioners' sugar**
- 1 **cup powdered nondairy creamer**
- 25 **peppermint candies, crushed**
- **ADDITIONAL INGREDIENT (FOR EACH SERVING)**
- 1 **cup milk**

In a large bowl, combine the first five ingredients. Store in an airtight container in a cool dry place for up to 6 months.
TO PREPARE HOT DRINK *Warm milk; stir in ⅓ cup mix until dissolved.*

Beer and Pretzel Caramels

Beer and pretzels just naturally go together. Combine them with ooey-gooey caramel, and you'll have a sure hit.

—TASTE OF HOME TEST KITCHEN

PREP: 1 HOUR + COOLING
COOK: 50 MIN. + STANDING
MAKES: ABOUT 3 POUNDS

- ⅓ cup sugar
- ½ teaspoon salt
- 2 cups miniature pretzels
- 1 tablespoon canola oil
- 1 tablespoon vanilla extract

CARAMELS

- 4 cups dark beer
- 1 teaspoon plus 1 cup butter, divided
- 3 cups sugar
- ⅔ cup corn syrup
- 2 cups heavy whipping cream, divided
- ⅓ cup water
- 1 teaspoon salt
- ½ teaspoon kosher salt

1. In a small bowl, combine sugar and salt; set aside. In a large bowl, combine the pretzels, oil and vanilla. Add the sugar mixture; toss to coat. Transfer to a 15x10x1-in. foil-lined baking pan coated with cooking spray.

2. Bake at 350° for 18-22 minutes, stirring occasionally. Cool completely. Coarsely chop the pretzels; set aside.

3. In a large saucepan, bring the beer to a boil; cook until reduced to ⅔ cup. Set aside to cool.

4. Meanwhile, line a 9-in.-square pan with foil; grease the foil with 1 teaspoon butter and set aside.

5. In a Dutch oven, combine sugar, corn syrup, ⅔ cup whipping cream, water, 1 teaspoon salt and remaining butter. Cook and stir over medium heat until a candy thermometer reads 238°, about 20 minutes. In a small bowl, combine reduced beer and remaining whipping cream; slowly stir into the sugar mixture.

6. Using a pastry brush dipped in cold water, wash down the sides of pan to eliminate sugar crystals. Cook, stirring constantly, until a candy thermometer reads 245° (firm-ball stage), about 30 minutes.

7. Remove from the heat. Pour into the prepared pan (do not scrape saucepan); sprinkle with the candied pretzels and kosher salt. Let stand until firm, about 5 hours or overnight.

8. Using the foil, lift the candy out of the pan. Discard the foil; cut candy into 1-in. squares using a buttered knife.

Wrap squares individually in waxed paper; twist the ends.

NOTE *We recommend that you test your candy thermometer before each use by bringing water to a boil; the thermometer should read 212°. Adjust your recipe temperature up or down based on your test.*

S'mores Candy

> "When I needed to save money by making my own gifts, I created S'mores Candy. The little sandwiches are fun for parties, too."
>
> —STEPHANIE TEWELL ELIZABETH, IL

PREP: 1 HOUR • **COOK:** 5 MIN. + STANDING
MAKES: 4 DOZEN

- 2 cups milk chocolate chips
- ½ cup heavy whipping cream
- 1 package (14.4 ounces) whole graham crackers, quartered
- 1 cup marshmallow creme
- 2 cartons (7 ounces each) milk chocolate for dipping
- 4 ounces white candy coating, coarsely chopped

1. Place the chips in a small bowl. In a small saucepan, bring cream just to a boil. Pour over chips; whisk until smooth. Cool, stirring occasionally, to room temperature or until mixture reaches a spreading consistency, about 10 minutes.

2. Spread the chocolate mixture over half of the graham crackers; spread marshmallow creme over remaining crackers and press together.

3. Melt dipping chocolate according to package directions; dip half of each cracker in the melted chocolate and allow excess to drip off. Place on waxed paper; let stand until set.

4. In a microwave, melt candy coating; stir until smooth. Drizzle over the tops; let stand until set. Store in an airtight container in the refrigerator.

Buffalo Wing Munch Mix

Store-bought snack mixes just can't beat this Buffalo wing version. Keep the recipe in mind not only for gift-giving, but also for snacking when the big game's on TV.
—**KERI THOMPSON** PLEASANT HILL, IA

START TO FINISH: 20 MIN.
MAKES: 3 QUARTS

- 4 **cups Corn Chex**
- 4 **cups Wheat Chex**
- 2 **cups cheddar-flavored snack crackers**
- 2 **cups potato sticks**
- 6 **tablespoons butter, melted**
- 2 **tablespoons hot pepper sauce**
- 1 **tablespoon Worcestershire sauce**
- 1 **envelope ranch salad dressing mix**
- ⅛ **teaspoon cayenne pepper**

1. In a large bowl, combine cereals, snack crackers and potato sticks. Combine the butter, hot sauce and Worcestershire. Drizzle over cereal mixture and toss to coat. Sprinkle with dressing mix and cayenne; toss to coat.
2. Microwave half of mixture on high for 2 minutes, stirring once. Spread onto waxed paper to cool. Repeat. Store in an airtight container.
NOTE *This recipe was tested in a 1,100-watt microwave.*

Holiday Helper

Want ideas for packaging your food gifts? Try these:

● Put snack mixes in inexpensive clear jars or cellophane bags tied with ribbon.

● Wash potato chip cans, coffee tins or shortening cans and fill them with cookies or candies.

● Wrap cookies in plastic wrap and tuck them in coffee mugs.

Homemade Candy Canes

Have you mastered homemade caramels and meringues? Why not try creating your own candy canes? They're a fun novelty gift and guaranteed to get friends and family asking, "How did you make those?"

—*TASTE OF HOME* TEST KITCHEN

PREP: 25 MIN. • **COOK:** 25 MIN.
MAKES: 16 CANES

- 1 **teaspoon butter**
- 1 **cup sugar**
- 1 **cup water**
- 1 **cup light corn syrup**
- ¼ **teaspoon cream of tartar**
- 1 **teaspoon peppermint or spearmint extract**
- 6 **drops red or green food coloring**

1. Grease two baking sheets with butter; set aside. In a large saucepan, bring the sugar, water, corn syrup and cream of tartar to a boil. Cook, without stirring, until a candy thermometer reads 280° (soft-crack stage).

2. Remove from the heat; stir in the extract and food coloring. Immediately pour onto prepared pans in eight 8-in. strips. Let stand just until cool enough to handle, about 1-2 minutes.

3. Working quickly, roll each candy strip into a 10-in. log. Cut each into two 5-in. lengths. Curve the top of each to form the cane handle. Cool completely. Store in an airtight container.

NOTE *We recommend that you test your candy thermometer before each use by bringing water to a boil; the thermometer should read 212°. Adjust your recipe temperature up or down based on your test.*

Soft Peppermint Candy

These goodies remind me of pulling taffy with my grandmother on Christmas Eve.

—**SUZETTE JURY** KEENE, CA

PREP: 1½ HOURS
COOK: 20 MIN. + COOLING
MAKES: 1¾ POUNDS

- 1 **tablespoon plus ¼ cup butter, cubed**
- 2 **cups light corn syrup**
- 1½ **cups sugar**
- 2 **teaspoons peppermint extract**
- ½ **teaspoon salt**
- 6 **drops red food coloring**

1. Grease a 15x10x1-in. pan with 1 tablespoon butter; set aside.

2. In a heavy, small saucepan, combine the corn syrup and sugar. Bring to a boil over medium heat. Add the remaining butter; stir until melted. Cook and stir until a candy thermometer reads 250° (hard-ball stage).

3. Remove from the heat; stir in the peppermint extract, salt and red food coloring. Pour the mixture into the prepared pan. Let stand for 5-10 minutes or until cool enough to handle. Divide into four portions.

4. With well-buttered fingers, quickly pull one portion of candy until firm but pliable (color will become light pink). Pull into a ½-in.-wide rope. Repeat with the remaining candy. Cut ropes into 1-in. pieces. Wrap each piece in waxed paper.

NOTE *We recommend that you test your candy thermometer before each use by bringing water to a boil; the thermometer should read 212°. Adjust your recipe temperature up or down based on your test.*

Peanutty Candy Bars

Family and friends will feel extra-special when you surprise them with homemade candy bars loaded with chocolate, oats, butterscotch and peanut butter. Bring some to the next school or church bake sale, too—they'll disappear in a flash. Just be ready to hand out the recipe!

—MARY SCHMITTINGER COLGATE, WI

PREP: 30 MIN. + CHILLING
MAKES: 2 DOZEN

- 4 cups quick-cooking oats
- 1 cup packed brown sugar
- ⅔ cup butter, melted
- ½ cup plus ⅔ cup peanut butter, divided
- ½ cup light corn syrup
- 1 teaspoon vanilla extract
- 1 package (11 ounces) butterscotch chips
- 1 cup (6 ounces) semisweet chocolate chips
- 1 cup chopped salted peanuts

1. In a large bowl, combine the oats, brown sugar, butter, ½ cup peanut butter, light corn syrup and vanilla. Press into a greased 13x9-in. baking pan. Bake at 375° for 12-14 minutes or until the mixture is bubbly around the edges.

2. In a microwave-safe bowl, melt the butterscotch chips and chocolate chips; stir until smooth. Stir in peanuts and remaining peanut butter; spread over oat mixture. Cool for 10 minutes; chill until set.

NOTE *Reduced-fat peanut butter is not recommended for this recipe.*

Holiday Helper

I wipe a bit of vegetable oil inside my measuring cup when I need to measure sticky ingredients like peanut butter or molasses for candy, cookies or other recipes. The measured ingredients slide right out instead off clinging to the cup—no scraping needed. Cleanup is a snap, too.

—**LYNN HAYES** ST. JOHN, NB

Homemade Crisp Crackers

These cheesy, crispy crackers are perfect to make ahead and keep on hand for drop-in guests. Let the holiday munching begin!
—*TASTE OF HOME* TEST KITCHEN

PREP: 20 MIN. + CHILLING • **BAKE:** 20 MIN./BATCH + COOLING
MAKES: 4 DOZEN

- 1¾ cups all-purpose flour
- ½ cup cornmeal
- ½ teaspoon baking soda
- ½ teaspoon sugar
- ½ teaspoon salt
- ½ teaspoon garlic powder
- ¼ teaspoon Italian seasoning
- ½ cup cold butter, cubed
- 1½ cups (6 ounces) shredded Colby-Monterey Jack cheese
- ½ cup plus 2 tablespoons cold water
- 2 tablespoons cider vinegar

1. In a large bowl, combine the first seven ingredients; cut in butter until crumbly. Stir in cheese. Gradually add cold water and cider vinegar, tossing with a fork until the dough forms a ball. Wrap in plastic wrap and refrigerate for 1 hour or until firm.
2. Divide into six portions. On a lightly floured surface, roll each portion into an 8-in. circle. Cut into eight wedges and place on greased baking sheets.
3. Bake at 375° for 17-20 minutes or until edges are lightly browned. Cool on wire racks. Store in an airtight container.

Cranberry-Nut Granola

I treat the fitness buffs I know to a powerhouse snack of crunchy granola packed with coconut, cranberries and three kinds of nuts.
—**MELANIE SCHREINER** LIVERPOOL, NY

PREP: 25 MIN. • **BAKE:** 20 MIN. + COOLING • **MAKES:** 18 CUPS

- 8 cups old-fashioned oats
- 1½ cups toasted wheat germ
- 1½ cups oat bran
- 1 cup sunflower kernels
- 1 cup coarsely chopped almonds
- 1 cup coarsely chopped pecans
- 1 cup coarsely chopped walnuts
- ¾ cup canola oil
- ½ cup packed brown sugar
- ½ cup honey
- ¼ cup maple syrup
- 3 teaspoons ground cinnamon
- 1½ teaspoons salt
- 3 teaspoons vanilla extract
- 2 cups dried cranberries
- ½ cup flaked coconut

1. In a large bowl, combine the first seven ingredients. In a small saucepan, combine the oil, brown sugar, honey, maple syrup, cinnamon and salt. Cook and stir over medium heat until brown sugar is dissolved. Remove from the heat; stir in vanilla. Pour over oat mixture; stir to coat.
2. Transfer to two parchment paper-lined 15x10x1-in. baking pans. Bake at 325° for 20-25 minutes or until crisp, stirring once. Cool completely on a wire rack. Stir in dried cranberries and coconut. Store in an airtight container.

Carrot Cake Jam

This unusual jam tastes almost as good as real-deal carrot cake. Bring on the bagels!

—**RACHELLE STRATTON** ROCK SPRINGS, WY

PREP: 45 MIN. • **PROCESS:** 5 MIN.
MAKES: 8 HALF-PINTS

- 1 can (20 ounces) unsweetened crushed pineapple, undrained
- 1½ cups shredded carrots
- 1½ cups chopped peeled ripe pears
- 3 tablespoons lemon juice
- 1 teaspoon ground cinnamon
- ¼ teaspoon ground cloves
- ¼ teaspoon ground nutmeg
- 1 package (1¾ ounces) powdered fruit pectin
- 6½ cups sugar

1. In a large saucepan, combine the first seven ingredients. Bring to a boil. Reduce the heat; cover and simmer 15-20 minutes or until the pears are tender, stirring occasionally. Stir in pectin. Bring to a full rolling boil over high heat, stirring constantly. Stir in the sugar; return to a full rolling boil. Boil and stir 1 minute.

2. Remove from the heat; skim off foam. Ladle the hot mixture into eight hot sterilized half-pint jars, leaving ¼-in. headspace. Remove air bubbles and adjust the headspace, if necessary, by adding hot mixture. Wipe the rims. Center the lids on jars; screw on bands until fingertip tight.

3. Place the jars into canner with simmering water, ensuring that they are completely covered with water. Bring to a boil; process for 5 minutes. Remove jars and cool.

NOTE *The processing time listed is for altitudes of 1,000 feet or less. Add 1 minute to the processing time for each 1,000 feet of additional altitude.*

AFTER-HOLIDAY
FEASTS

Fiesta Ham Soup

Ham it up! Savor every last morsel of that holiday meat in a chunky soup. Packed with potatoes, creamed corn, onion and chilies, this will warm your family from head to toe. A dollop of sour cream is the perfect finishing touch for each bowlful.

—**CATHY HASTIE** AUBURN, CA

PREP: 20 MIN. • **COOK:** 20 MIN.
MAKES: 8 SERVINGS (2 QUARTS)

- 2 **tablespoons butter**
- ½ **cup chopped onion**
- ¼ **cup chopped celery**
- 1½ **pounds potatoes (about 3 medium), peeled and cubed**
- 2 **cups cubed fully cooked ham**
- 1 **can (4 ounces) chopped green chilies**
- 2 **tablespoons dried parsley flakes**
- ⅛ **teaspoon pepper**
- 2 **cups chicken broth**
- 1 **can (14¾ ounces) cream-style corn**
- 1 **cup 2% milk**
- 1 **cup (4 ounces) shredded cheddar cheese**
  Sour cream, optional

1. In a large saucepan, heat the butter over medium heat. Add the onion and celery; cook and stir 3-4 minutes or until onion is tender. Add the potatoes, ham, green chilies, parsley and pepper; cook and stir 1 minute.

2. Stir in the chicken broth; bring to a boil. Reduce the heat; simmer, covered, 15-20 minutes or until the potatoes are tender.

3. Stir in the corn, milk and cheddar cheese; heat through. If desired, serve with sour cream.

Holiday Helper

I like to finely chop my leftover ham and add mayonnaise, pickle relish, onion, salt and pepper for a speedy ham salad. It's good in sandwiches for lunch or spread on crackers as a snack. You could also substitute cooked turkey or chicken for the ham.

—**KAREN GENTRY** SOMERSET, KY

After-Christmas Empanadas

Refrigerated pie pastry is the secret to these delicious empanadas. They're so easy to prepare! Even better, they can be assembled in advance. We pop them in the freezer to keep on hand for a quick dinner on busy nights. Simply follow the freezer directions at the end of the recipe.

—**CHERYL MARINACCIO** WEBSTER, NY

PREP: 30 MIN. • **BAKE:** 15 MIN.
MAKES: ABOUT 1½ DOZEN

- 1 cup cubed cooked turkey
- ½ cup cooked stuffing
- 2 tablespoons whole-berry cranberry sauce
- 2 tablespoons turkey gravy
- 2 packages (14.1 ounces each) refrigerated pie pastry
- 1 egg
- 1 tablespoon water
  Rubbed sage, optional
  Additional turkey gravy or whole-berry cranberry sauce, optional

1. Preheat oven to 400°. In a small bowl, combine the turkey, stuffing, cranberry sauce and gravy.

2. On a lightly floured surface, unroll one pastry. Roll out into a 12-in. circle. Cut with a floured 4-in. biscuit cutter. Repeat with remaining pastry.

3. In a small bowl, whisk the egg with the water; brush over the edges of the pastry circles. Place 1 tablespoon turkey filling on one side. Fold dough over the filling. Press the edges with a fork to seal.

4. Place 2 in. apart on greased baking sheets. Brush tops with remaining egg mixture; sprinkle with sage if desired. Bake 12-15 minutes or until golden brown. Serve warm with gravy or cranberry sauce if desired.

FREEZE OPTION *Freeze the cooled pastries in resealable plastic freezer bags. To use, reheat the pastries on a greased baking sheet in a preheated 400° oven 8-10 minutes or until lightly browned and heated through.*

Cranberry-Banana Smoothies

Cranberry sauce makes a tongue-tingling ingredient for smoothies. This five-minute version is guaranteed to start off your day in an energizing way. Don't have a frozen banana? No problem—just use a regular banana and add more ice.

—**GINA FENSLER** CINCINNATI, OH

START TO FINISH: 5 MIN.
MAKES: 2 SERVINGS

- 1 large banana, peeled, quartered and frozen
- ⅔ cup whole-berry cranberry sauce
- ½ cup fat-free vanilla yogurt
- ½ cup ice cubes

Place all ingredients in a blender; cover and process until smooth. Serve immediately.

Stuffing & Sausage Strata

We are major stuffing fans, and we love it in this hearty sausage strata. Fresh fruit on the side makes a complete breakfast.

—ELIZABETH RAY CORONA, CA

PREP: 20 MIN. + CHILLING
BAKE: 1 HOUR + STANDING
MAKES: 12 SERVINGS

- **1 pound Italian turkey sausage links, casings removed**
- **½ cup sliced fresh mushrooms**
- **6 cups cooked stuffing**
- **2 cups (8 ounces) shredded sharp cheddar cheese**
- **10 eggs**
- **3 cups 2% milk**
- **1 teaspoon salt**

1. In a large skillet, cook the Italian turkey sausage and mushrooms over medium heat 6-8 minutes or until no longer pink, breaking the sausage into crumbles; drain.

2. In a greased 13x9-in. baking dish, layer half of each of the following: cooked stuffing, sharp cheddar cheese and turkey sausage mixture. Repeat the layers. In a large bowl, whisk the eggs, milk and salt until blended. Pour over the layers. Refrigerate the strata, covered, overnight.

3. Preheat oven to 325°. Remove the strata from refrigerator while the oven heats. Bake, uncovered, 1-1¼ hours or until a knife inserted near the center comes out clean. Let stand 10 minutes before serving.

Thanksgiving Wontons

Get creative with your holiday bird and turn the extra meat into wonton appetizers. The little fried triangles are so yummy served warm and always disappear in a flash at parties.

—**SARAH GILBERT** BEAVERTON, OR

START TO FINISH: 25 MIN. • **MAKES:** 3 DOZEN

- 1½ cups finely chopped cooked turkey breast
- ⅔ cup dried cranberries, finely chopped
- ⅓ cup whipped cream cheese
- ⅓ cup jellied cranberry sauce
- 36 wonton wrappers
- Oil for deep-fat frying

1. In a small bowl, combine turkey, cranberries, cream cheese and cranberry sauce. Place 1 tablespoon filling in center of a wonton wrapper. (Cover remaining wrappers with a damp paper towel until ready to use.) Moisten edges with water. Fold one corner diagonally over filling to form a triangle; press edges to seal. Repeat with remaining filling and wonton wrappers.

2. In an electric skillet, heat oil to 375°. Fry wontons, a few at a time, 30-60 seconds on each side or until golden brown. Drain on paper towels. Serve warm.

Gobbler Cakes

I watched a chef make crab cakes and decided to try it with turkey and stuffing. Now my kids request the patties year-round, so I buy the ingredients whenever I don't have leftovers.

—**SUZEE KREBS** BRIELLE, NJ

PREP: 25 MIN. • **COOK:** 10 MIN./BATCH • **MAKES:** 4 SERVINGS

- 1 egg
- 2 cups cooked stuffing
- 1¼ cups finely chopped cooked turkey
- ½ cup dried cranberries
- ¼ cup mayonnaise
- ½ cup crushed cornflakes
- 1 tablespoon canola oil
- Cranberry sauce and turkey gravy, optional

1. In a large bowl, mix egg, stuffing, turkey, cranberries and mayonnaise. Shape into eight ½-in.-thick patties. Coat with crushed cornflakes.

2. In a large skillet, heat the oil over medium heat. Add the patties in batches; cook 3-4 minutes on each side or until golden brown. Serve warm, with cranberry sauce and turkey gravy if desired.

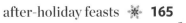

Day-After-Thanksgiving Cookies

Bummed the holiday is over? Cheer up with fresh-baked cookies. I've used jellied and whole-berry cranberry sauce, and the pumpkin can be canned or cooked.

—**HEATHER BATES** ATHENS, ME

PREP: 25 MIN. + CHILLING
BAKE: 15 MIN./BATCH
MAKES: ABOUT 6 DOZEN

- 1 **cup butter, softened**
- 1 **cup sugar**
- 1 **cup packed brown sugar**
- ¾ **cup canned pumpkin pie filling**
- ½ **cup whole-berry cranberry sauce**
- 1 **egg**
- 2 **teaspoons vanilla extract**
- 2½ **cups all-purpose flour**
- 1½ **cups quick-cooking oats**
- 2 **teaspoons ground cinnamon**
- 1 **teaspoon baking soda**
- ½ **teaspoon salt**
- ½ **teaspoon ground nutmeg**
- ¼ **teaspoon ground cloves**
- 1 **cup white baking chips**
- 1 **cup (6 ounces) semisweet chocolate chips**

1. In a large bowl, cream butter and sugars until light and fluffy. Beat in pie filling, cranberry sauce, egg and vanilla. In another bowl, whisk the flour, oats, cinnamon, baking soda, salt, nutmeg and cloves; gradually beat into creamed mixture. Stir in the chips. Refrigerate, covered, 2 hours or until firm.

2. Preheat oven to 350°. Drop dough by rounded tablespoonfuls 2 in. apart onto ungreased baking sheets. Bake 15-18 minutes or until edges are golden brown. Cool on the pans 5 minutes. Remove to wire racks to cool.

Holiday Helper

When I crave mashed potato cakes but am short on time, I mix the spuds with seasoned bread crumbs and form patties. Then I roll the cakes in more crumbs and brown them on both sides.

—**ANGELINA R.** AKRON, OH

Crispy Mashed Potato Cakes

Mashed potato cakes are a nice alternative to the usual hash browns—try 'em and see!

—**JERI PSIKAL** NORMAN, OK

PREP: 15 MIN. + CHILLING • **BAKE:** 35 MIN.
MAKES: ABOUT 1½ DOZEN

- 3 **cups mashed potatoes (with added milk and butter)**
- 1 **cup biscuit/baking mix**
- 1 **cup cooked stuffing**
- 2 **eggs, lightly beaten**
- 1 **cup French-fried onions, crushed**
- ¾ **cup dry bread crumbs**

1. In a large bowl, mix the mashed potatoes, baking mix, cooked stuffing and eggs until blended. Refrigerate, covered, 30 minutes.

2. Preheat oven to 400°. In a shallow bowl, mix the French-fried onions and dry bread crumbs. Shape ¼ cupfuls of the potato mixture into ¾-in.-thick patties. Dip patties in crumb mixture, patting to help coating adhere.

3. Transfer the coated patties to two greased 15x10x1-in. baking pans. Bake 35-40 minutes or until golden brown, turning once. Let stand 5 minutes before serving.

Carrot-Cranberry Spice Cake

Every slice of this special dessert bursts with seasonal flavors, from bits of carrot to nutmeg and cloves. Baking the cake in a fluted tube pan gives it a beautiful shape, and a sprinkling of confectioners' sugar is all you need for an elegant finishing touch. What a way to eat leftovers!
—**ELIZABETH KING** DULUTH, MN

PREP: 20 MIN. • **BAKE:** 50 MIN. + COOLING
MAKES: 12 SERVINGS

- 4 **eggs**
- 1 **cup sugar**
- 1 **cup packed brown sugar**
- 1 **cup canola oil**
- 1 **cup whole-berry cranberry sauce**
- 3 **cups all-purpose flour**
- 2 **teaspoons baking powder**
- 1 **teaspoon baking soda**
- ½ **teaspoon salt**
- ½ **teaspoon ground nutmeg**
- ½ **teaspoon ground cloves**
- 1 **cup grated carrots (about 2 medium)**
- 1 **tablespoon confectioners' sugar**

1. Preheat oven to 350°. Grease and flour a 10-in. fluted tube pan.

2. In a large bowl, beat the eggs, sugar, brown sugar, oil and cranberry sauce until well blended. In another bowl, whisk the flour, baking powder, baking soda, salt, nutmeg and cloves; gradually beat into the cranberry mixture. Stir in the carrots.

3. Transfer the cake batter to the prepared pan. Bake 50-60 minutes or until a toothpick inserted in the center comes out clean. Cool in the pan 10 minutes before removing to a wire rack to cool completely. Sprinkle with the confectioners' sugar.

NOTE *To remove cakes easily, use solid shortening to grease plain and fluted tube pans.*

Holiday Stromboli

Turn what's left of your fancy dinner into a casual meal the next day. With convenient ready-made pizza dough, I roll everything into a golden-brown stromboli and slice up servings. My family can't get enough!

—**ALIA SLATTON** BOULDER, CO

PREP: 15 MIN. • **BAKE:** 20 MIN.
MAKES: 6 SERVINGS

- 1 tube (13.8 ounces) refrigerated pizza crust
- 1 cup mashed potatoes (with added milk and butter), warmed
- 2 cups shredded cooked turkey
- 1 cup cooked stuffing
- 1 cup whole-berry cranberry sauce
- ¼ teaspoon salt
- ⅛ teaspoon pepper
- 1 tablespoon butter, melted

1. Preheat oven to 400°. On a lightly floured surface, unroll pizza dough and pat into a 13x10-in. rectangle. Spread the mashed potatoes to within ½ in. of the edges. Layer with turkey, stuffing and cranberry sauce; sprinkle with salt and pepper.

2. Roll up jelly-roll style, starting with a long side; pinch seam to seal and tuck ends under. Place on a greased baking sheet, seam side down. Brush with butter. Bake 20-25 minutes or until golden brown.

Spinach & Turkey Turnovers

These flaky pockets formed with puff pastry can make not only a terrific main course, but also a substantial appetizer. We dip them into a tangy sauce of orange juice, grated peel and cranberries.

—**ANJLI SABHARWAL** MARLBORO, NJ

PREP: 25 MIN. • **BAKE:** 15 MIN.
MAKES: 8 SERVINGS

- 1½ teaspoons olive oil
- 2 green onions, chopped
- 1 garlic clove, minced
- ½ teaspoon dried rosemary, crushed
- ¼ teaspoon dried thyme
- 1 cup cubed cooked turkey
- 1 package (10 ounces) frozen chopped spinach, thawed and squeezed dry
- ½ cup shredded Monterey Jack cheese
- ¼ cup turkey gravy
- ¼ teaspoon salt
- ¼ teaspoon pepper
- 1 package (17.3 ounces) frozen puff pastry, thawed
- 1 egg, lightly beaten
- 1 tablespoon water

SAUCE
- 1 cup whole-berry cranberry sauce
- ¼ cup orange juice
- 1 tablespoon grated orange peel

1. Preheat oven to 400°. In a large skillet, heat oil over medium-high heat. Add green onions, garlic, rosemary and thyme; cook and stir 1 minute. Remove from heat. Stir in the turkey, spinach, Monterey Jack cheese, turkey gravy, salt and pepper.

2. Unfold puff pastry; cut each sheet into four squares. Transfer to greased baking sheets. Spoon turkey mixture onto the center of each square.

3. In a small bowl, whisk the egg and water; brush over the edges of pastry. Fold one corner of dough diagonally over filling, forming triangles; press the edges with a fork to seal. Brush the tops with egg mixture. Bake 12-14 minutes or until golden brown.

4. Meanwhile, in a small saucepan, combine sauce and orange juice. Bring to a boil; cook and stir 3-4 minutes or until slightly thickened. Stir in orange peel. Serve with turnovers.

Turkey-Stuffed Acorn Squash

After yuletide celebrations, relax with this fuss-free meal. It's easy to fix as much or as little as necessary to clean out the fridge.

—**CINDY ROMBERG** MISSISSAUGA, ON

PREP: 10 MIN. • **BAKE:** 55 MIN.
MAKES: 4 SERVINGS

- **2 medium acorn squash (about 1½ pounds each)**
- **1 small onion, finely chopped**
- **2 cups cubed cooked turkey**
- **2 cups cooked stuffing**
- **½ cup whole-berry cranberry sauce**
- **⅓ cup white wine or chicken broth**
- **½ teaspoon salt**

1. Preheat oven to 350°. Cut each squash lengthwise in half; remove and discard seeds. Using a sharp knife, cut a thin slice from the bottom of each half to allow them to lie flat. Place in a shallow roasting pan, hollow side down; add ¼ in. of hot water. Bake, uncovered, 30 minutes.

2. Meanwhile, place onion in a large microwave-safe bowl; microwave, covered, on high for 1-2 minutes or until tender. Stir in turkey, stuffing, cranberry sauce and wine.

3. Carefully remove squash from roasting pan; drain water. Return squash to pan, hollow side up; sprinkle with salt. Spoon turkey mixture into squash cavities. Bake, uncovered, 25-30 minutes longer or until heated through and squash is easily pierced with a fork.

Baked Egg & Stuffing Cups

Christmas stuffing the next morning? Yes! I simply break an egg in the middle of each individual-size cup and pop them into the oven for a hearty, satisfying breakfast.

—**KAREN DEAVER** BABYLON, NY

PREP: 10 MIN. • **BAKE:** 25 MIN.
MAKES: 4 SERVINGS

- 1 cup cooked stuffing
- 4 eggs
- ¼ teaspoon salt
- ¼ teaspoon pepper
  Minced fresh sage, optional

1. Preheat oven to 325°. Press the cooked stuffing into four greased 4-oz. ramekins, forming wells in the centers. Break and slip an egg into center of each; sprinkle with salt and pepper.

2. Place ramekins on a baking sheet. Bake 25-30 minutes or until the egg whites are completely set and the egg yolks begin to thicken but are not hard. If desired, sprinkle with sage.

Greens and Beans Turkey Soup

On blustery winter evenings, a steaming bowl of soup tastes better than just about anything. This recipe uses a turkey carcass to make the flavorful stock.

—**SUSAN ALBERT** JONESBURG, MO

PREP: 15 MIN. • **COOK:** 2 HOURS 20 MIN.
MAKES: 10 SERVINGS (2½ QUARTS)

- 1 leftover turkey carcass (from a 12-pound turkey)
- 9 cups water
- 2 celery ribs, cut into ½-inch pieces
- 1 medium onion, cut into chunks
- 1 can (15½ ounces) great northern beans, rinsed and drained
- 1 package (10 ounces) frozen chopped spinach, thawed and squeezed dry
- 3 tablespoons chopped onion
- 2 teaspoons chicken bouillon granules
- 1 teaspoon salt
- ¼ teaspoon pepper

1. Place turkey carcass in a stockpot; add water, celery and onion. Slowly bring to a boil. Reduce heat; simmer, covered, 2 hours.

2. Remove the carcass and cool. Strain the broth through a cheesecloth-lined colander; discard the vegetables. Skim the fat. Remove the meat from bones and cut into bite-size pieces; discard the bones. Return the broth and meat to the pot.

3. Add the beans, spinach, onion, bouillon, salt and pepper. Bring to a boil. Reduce the heat; simmer, covered, 10 minutes.

Holiday Helper

To prepare a tasty turkey soup with my holiday leftovers, I saute onion and green pepper in oil, then add chicken broth. I puree the leftover mashed potatoes and vegetables, then stir that into the broth with the chopped turkey. We love it!

—**MARION S.** CHICAGO, IL

Turkey Croquettes with Cranberry Salsa

Instead of serving another round of the same holiday dinner, we transform it into a totally different meal. These yummy little croquettes fried to a golden brown are fun to eat. To make them even better, we add a tangy cranberry-apple salsa that gets a kick from jalapeno peppers.

—**JACQUE CAPURRO** ANCHORAGE, AK

PREP: 30 MIN. + CHILLING
COOK: 5 MIN./BATCH
MAKES: 16 CROQUETTES (2 CUPS SALSA)

- 2 **tablespoons butter**
- ⅓ **cup chopped onion**
- ¼ **cup all-purpose flour**
- ¼ **cup 2% milk**
- ¼ **cup chicken broth**
- 2 **cups finely chopped cooked turkey**
- ½ **cup mashed sweet potato**
- ½ **teaspoon salt**
- ¼ **teaspoon pepper**
- ⅛ **teaspoon cayenne pepper**

CRANBERRY SALSA

- ¾ **cup chopped tart apple**
- 1 **tablespoon lemon juice**
- ½ **cup chopped cranberries**
- 2 **jalapeno peppers, seeded and chopped**
- 2 **green onions, chopped**
- 3 **tablespoons golden raisins, chopped**
- 1 **tablespoon honey**

CROQUETTES

- 2 **eggs**
- 1 **tablespoon water**
- ½ **cup all-purpose flour**
- ½ **cup dry bread crumbs**
  Oil for deep-fat frying

1. In a large saucepan, heat the butter over medium heat. Add onion; cook and stir 3-4 minutes or until tender.

2. Stir in the flour until blended. Gradually add the milk and chicken broth. Bring to a boil; cook and stir 2 minutes or until thickened. Remove from the heat; stir in turkey, mashed sweet potato, salt, pepper and cayenne pepper. Refrigerate, covered, 2 hours or until firm.

3. Meanwhile, in a small bowl, toss the chopped apple with lemon juice. Stir in the remaining cranberry salsa ingredients. Refrigerate, covered, at least 1 hour.

4. For the croquettes, in a shallow bowl, beat the eggs and water. Place the flour and dry bread crumbs in separate shallow bowls. Shape turkey mixture into 1½-in. balls. Roll in flour; shake off excess. Roll in egg mixture, then in bread crumbs, patting to help the coating adhere.

5. In an electric skillet or deep-fat fryer, heat oil to 375°. Fry croquettes, a few at a time, 1-2 minutes on each side or until golden brown. Drain on paper towels. Serve with salsa.
NOTE *Wear disposable gloves when cutting hot peppers; the oils can burn skin. Avoid touching your face.*

Meat Lover's Bread Salad

Growing up, we often visited a sandwich shop in Nebraska. The amazing creations inspired my salad of bread and cold cuts, ideal for meat lovers everywhere.

—MOLLY ATHERTON KANSAS CITY, MO

PREP: 25 MIN. + CHILLING
MAKES: 12 SERVINGS (2 CUPS EACH)

1½ cups canola oil
⅔ cup tarragon vinegar

1 teaspoon salt
1 teaspoon dried oregano
½ teaspoon pepper
½ pound fully cooked ham, chopped
½ pound cooked turkey, chopped
½ pound cooked roast beef, chopped
½ pound thinly sliced hard salami
½ pound sliced pepperoni
1 medium head iceberg lettuce, torn
2 medium tomatoes, seeded and chopped

2 to 3 Italian rolls, cubed
2 cups (8 ounces) shredded part-skim mozzarella cheese

1. Place the first five ingredients in a jar with a tight-fitting lid; shake well. Refrigerate 1 hour.

2. Just before serving, in a large bowl, combine the meats, lettuce, tomatoes, cubed rolls and cheese. Shake dressing again; pour over salad and toss to coat.

Thanksgiving Stuffed Shells

Love pasta? Stuff extra turkey, dressing and sweet potatoes into jumbo shells. Served with gravy, this dinner is a nice change of pace and really delicious.

—**ROBIN HAAS** CRANSTON, RI

PREP: 25 MIN. • **BAKE:** 15 MIN.
MAKES: 8 SERVINGS

- 24 **uncooked jumbo pasta shells**
- 1 **cup (4 ounces) shredded part-skim mozzarella cheese**
- 1 **cup cubed cooked turkey**
- 1 **cup cooked stuffing**
- 4 **green onions, chopped**
- 1 **cup mashed sweet potatoes**
- ¼ **teaspoon chili powder, optional**
- ½ **cup grated Parmesan cheese**
- 1 **cup turkey gravy, warmed**

1. Preheat oven to 350°. Cook pasta shells according to package directions for al dente.
2. Meanwhile, in a large bowl, mix mozzarella cheese, turkey, stuffing and green onions. In a small bowl, mix sweet potatoes and, if desired, chili powder.
3. Drain pasta shells; fill each with 2 tablespoons stuffing mixture and 2 teaspoons sweet potato mixture. Arrange in a greased 11x7-in. baking dish; sprinkle with Parmesan cheese. Bake, covered, 15-20 minutes or until heated through. Serve with gravy.

Cranberry Eggnog Muffins

START TO FINISH: 30 MIN.
MAKES: 1 DOZEN

- 2 **cups all-purpose flour**
- ¾ **cup sugar**
- 3 **teaspoons baking powder**
- ½ **teaspoon salt**
- ¼ **teaspoon ground cinnamon**
- 1 **egg**
- 1 **cup eggnog**
- ¼ **cup butter, melted**
- ¾ **cup whole-berry cranberry sauce**

1. Preheat oven to 400°. In a large bowl, whisk the first five ingredients. In another bowl, whisk egg, eggnog and melted butter until blended. Add to flour mixture; stir just until moistened.
2. Spoon 1 tablespoon batter in bottom of each of 12 greased or paper-lined muffin cups. Drop 1 teaspoon cranberry sauce into the center of each; top with the remaining batter and cranberry sauce. Cut through the batter with a knife to swirl.
3. Bake 15-18 minutes or until a toothpick inserted in center comes out clean. Cool 5 minutes before removing from pan to a wire rack. Serve warm.

"Warm and soft from the oven, tender Cranberry Eggnog Muffins will make you want to enjoy them all year long.*"*

—**NANCY MOCK** COLCHESTER, VT

Sweet Potato Dumplings with Caramel Sauce

When family stays over during the holidays, I make sweet potato dumplings, eggs and bacon for breakfast. Later, I serve extra dumplings for dessert. They're so good with caramel sauce and ice cream.

—MARY LEVERETTE COLUMBIA, SC

PREP: 40 MIN. • **BAKE:** 30 MIN.
MAKES: 10 SERVINGS

- 2 tubes (12 ounces each) refrigerated buttermilk biscuits
- 1½ cups mashed sweet potatoes
- 1½ teaspoons ground cinnamon, divided
- 1 cup sugar
- 1 cup packed brown sugar
- 1 cup water
- ½ cup butter, cubed
  Vanilla ice cream, optional

1. Preheat oven to 350°. Roll out each buttermilk biscuit into a 3-in. circle. In a small bowl, mix the mashed sweet potatoes and ¾ teaspoon cinnamon. Place 1 tablespoon sweet potato mixture on one side of each dough circle. Fold the dough over the filling. Press the edges with a fork to seal. Transfer the dumplings to a greased 13x9-in. baking pan, overlapping slightly.

2. In a small heavy saucepan, combine the sugar, brown sugar, water, butter and remaining cinnamon. Bring to a boil; cook and stir 2-3 minutes or until the sugar is dissolved.

3. Pour the sauce over the dumplings. Bake, uncovered, 30-35 minutes or until golden brown. If desired, serve with vanilla ice cream.

Holiday Helper

Sweet potato biscuits are one of my favorite treats. So I make large batches of mashed sweet potatoes and put 2-cup portions into heavy-duty freezer bags. When I want to whip up some biscuits in a hurry, I just thaw the potatoes in the microwave.

—MARCIA P. GREENSBORO, MD

Monte Cristo Casserole with Raspberry Sauce

My husband is a big fan of the traditional ham and cheese sandwich known as the Monte Cristo. I did some experimenting in the kitchen and came up with a new version that features the same flavors but bakes in a casserole dish. Try this recipe the next time you're hosting brunch.

—**MARY STEINER** PARKVILLE, MD

PREP: 20 MIN. + CHILLING
BAKE: 30 MIN. + STANDING
MAKES: 12 SERVINGS (1¾ CUPS SAUCE)

- 1 loaf (1 pound) day-old Italian bread, cut into 1-inch slices
- 2 tablespoons Dijon mustard
- ½ pound sliced deli ham
- ½ pound sliced Swiss cheese
- ½ pound sliced deli turkey
- 6 eggs
- 1½ cups milk
- 2 teaspoons sugar
- 2 teaspoons vanilla extract

TOPPING
- ½ cup packed brown sugar
- ¼ cup butter, softened
- ½ teaspoon ground cinnamon

RASPBERRY SAUCE
- ⅓ cup sugar
- 1 tablespoon cornstarch
- ¼ cup cold water
- ¼ cup lemon juice
- ¼ cup maple syrup
- 2 cups fresh or frozen raspberries

1. Line a greased 13x9-in. baking dish with half of the bread. Spread the Dijon mustard over the bread. Layer with the ham, cheese, turkey and remaining bread (dish will be full).

2. In a large bowl, whisk eggs, milk, sugar and vanilla; pour over the top. Refrigerate, covered, overnight.

3. Preheat oven to 375°. Remove the casserole from refrigerator while oven heats. In a small bowl, mix the topping ingredients; sprinkle over casserole. Bake, uncovered, 30-40 minutes or until golden brown.

4. Meanwhile, in a small saucepan, combine the sugar and cornstarch. Stir in the cold water, lemon juice and maple syrup until smooth. Add the raspberries. Bring to a boil; cook and stir until thickened, about 2 minutes. Cool slightly.

5. Let casserole stand 10 minutes before cutting. Serve with sauce.

Turkey Nacho Dip

Want to spice up the Christmas season? Here's a zesty Mexican-style snack that will please kids and adults alike.

—**GAYLE LEWIS** WINSTON, OR

START TO FINISH: 10 MIN.
MAKES: ABOUT 2 CUPS

- 1 can (10¾ ounces) condensed cheddar cheese soup, undiluted
- ¾ cup salsa
- 1 cup cubed cooked turkey or chicken
  Tortilla chips

In a small saucepan, combine the cheddar cheese soup and salsa. Bring to a boil. Reduce the heat; stir in the turkey. Heat through. Serve dip warm with tortilla chips.

Eggnog Bread Pudding with Cranberries

Everyone likes this Christmasy bread pudding loaded with dried cranberries and crunchy glazed pecans—my parents especially. The comforting dessert will use the last few cups of eggnog in your refrigerator and any leftover dinner rolls you may have from a holiday meal.

—EMILY HOBBS SPRINGFIELD, MO

PREP: 15 MIN. + STANDING • **BAKE:** 35 MIN.
MAKES: 9 SERVINGS

- 4 **eggs**
- 2 **cups eggnog**
- 6 **cups cubed soft dinner rolls**
- ¾ **cup finely chopped glazed pecans**
- ½ **cup dried cranberries**

1. Preheat oven to 375°. In a large bowl, whisk the eggs and eggnog until blended. Stir in the cubed soft dinner rolls, pecans and dried cranberries; let stand about 15 minutes or until bread is softened.

2. Transfer bread pudding mixture to a greased 8-in.-square baking dish. Bake 35-40 minutes or until puffed, golden and a knife inserted near the center of the pudding comes out clean. Serve warm.

DECK THE HALLS

Monogrammed Burlap Runner

Transform a piece of plain burlap fabric into a decorative family heirloom using standard sewing and art supplies. You'll want to display this rustic yet refined table runner not only at Christmastime, but also during the rest of the year.

FINISHED SIZE

Varies.

MATERIALS

Burlap, cut to length of table plus 30 in. (15-in. drop at each end)
Fabric paint
Purchased clear stencils of choice (or make your own—see Note)
Painter's tape
Stiff stencil brush
Small scissors or seam ripper

NOTE

To make your own stencil, use a blank clear stencil (available at craft stores and online) and follow the directions at right. Before stenciling the runner, stencil on a fabric scrap to determine how much paint and pressure to apply. If using the same stencil in reverse for symmetrical designs, wash and dry it completely before reusing it on the runner.

DIRECTIONS

MAKING STENCIL (OPTIONAL)

1. To make your own stencil for this project, choose a monogram or other simple shape from a book or other source. Print or photocopy the design to transfer it to a sheet of paper, enlarging or reducing the design to the desired size as needed.

2. Use painter's tape to secure the paper design to a cutting mat. Tape a clear blank stencil on top. Cut out the design from stencil with a craft knife, using a clear ruler or straight-edge guide as needed and applying even pressure for a clean stencil edge.

TABLE RUNNER

1. To trim the burlap to the desired width for table runner, find a thread at desired width and pull out the thread using small scissors or seam ripper. Cut crosswise threads.

2. Make 1/2-in. fringe along all edges of the runner by gently removing a few edge threads.

3. Lay the runner flat on a large work table. Using tape, secure runner above and below stenciling area.

4. Position the monogram stencil in the center of the runner, about 12 in. from 1 short end. Tape in place.

5. Daub paint onto the burlap using stiff stencil brush, working the paint into the fabric. When paint is dry, carefully remove stencil.

6. Continue stenciling each short end of runner in the same way as desired, using 1 stencil at a time and securing each with tape. Allow paint to dry before removing each stencil.

Cutting Monogrammed Burlap Runner

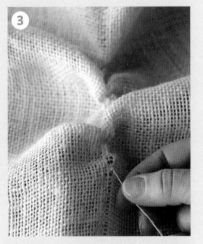

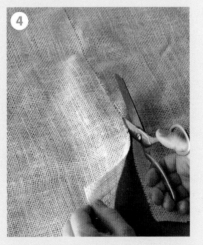

1. Determine the desired width of runner and choose a thread at the edge of desired width.

2. Using a seam ripper or small scissors, pull the chosen thread to remove.

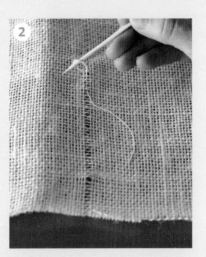

3. Continue pulling out the thread, creating a line in the burlap at the desired edge of width.

4. Using a small scissors, cut the crosswise threads along the thread line.

Cinnamon Applesauce Ornaments

Although not edible, these wonderfully fragrant ornaments show fabulous taste! The directions here make a batch of about 60 cinnamon-scented cutouts.

FINISHED SIZE
Varies.

MATERIALS
1 cup applesauce
Approximately 3/4 cup ground cinnamon
2 Tbsp. ground cloves
1 Tbsp. nutmeg
1 Tbsp. ground allspice
1½-in. cookie cutters of choice
Red or green heavy thread for hangers
Straw or wooden skewer
Parchment paper-lined baking sheets

DIRECTIONS
1. In a large bowl, combine the applesauce and spices; mix well until a stiff dough forms, adding additional cinnamon if needed.

2. On a board dusted with additional cinnamon, roll out each portion of dough to 1/4-in. thickness. Cut into shapes using 1½-in. cookie cutters dipped in cinnamon. Reroll scraps. Place cutouts on lined baking sheets. Using straw or skewer, make a small hole in top of each.

3. Bake at 200° for 20 to 30 minutes. Remove cutouts to paper towels to dry and cool completely.

4. Cut a 6-in. length of thread for each ornament. String a piece through each hole; tie the ends to form a loop.

Snowflake Doormat

It's snow easy! Use spray paint and masking tape to turn an inexpensive coir mat into a welcoming decoration at your door.

FINISHED SIZE
Varies.

MATERIALS
Plain coir doormat of choice
Blue spray paint
Masking tape in ¾-, 1- and 2-in. widths
Drop cloth or newspaper to protect work surface

DIRECTIONS

1. Protect work surface with drop cloth or newspaper, covering enough area so that there will be several inches of covered work surface all the way around mat. Place mat in center of work surface, right side up.

2. Attach pieces of masking tape to mat, creating snowflakes of various shapes and sizes as desired.

3. Spray-paint across entire taped side of mat in smooth, continuous strokes. To ensure even coverage, begin each stroke a few inches to 1 side of the mat on the work surface, spray across mat and end the stroke a few inches on the other side of mat.

4. In the same way, apply additional coats of paint as needed to achieve the desired color saturation, waiting 1 to 2 minutes between coats.

5. After applying the final coat, wait several minutes before removing tape. Let mat dry completely before use.

Decoupaged Silhouette Plates

Arrange these charming home accents on a wall with adhesive plate hangers.

FINISHED SIZE
Varies.

MATERIALS
White plates of various sizes
Scrapbook or other decorative paper
Decoupage glue
Clear matte varnish spray
Cookie cutters or other design templates
Paintbrush
Craft knife or scissors
Cutting mat

NOTE
Decoupaged plates are not food-safe and are for decorative use only.

DIRECTIONS

1. Clean and dry plates thoroughly.

2. Trace cookie cutter shapes or other design templates separately onto the wrong side of desired scrapbook paper. Cut out paper shapes.

3. With paintbrush, apply a thin coat of decoupage glue over the entire face of a plate, using even strokes.

4. Carefully position a paper cutout where desired on the plate.

5. Using paintbrush, apply a thin coat of decoupage glue over paper cutout to seal. Let dry. Apply another thin coat of decoupage glue over the entire face of the plate, using even strokes.

6. Add desired paper designs to the remaining plates the same as before. Let dry completely.

7. Spray the plates with a thin coat of clear varnish. Let plates dry completely before displaying.

Clothespin Card Display

This colorful but simple wall plaque lets Christmas cards take center stage. After the holidays, paint it a neutral color for a year-round mail or note holder.

FINISHED SIZE
Excluding cards, display measures about 24 in. high x 7 in. wide.

MATERIALS
**Pine signboard plaque or wood plank—
   24x4-in. or size of choice (see Note)**
Twelve 2¾-in. wood clothespins
Washi tape
Red acrylic craft paint
Paintbrush
Sawtooth hanger
Glue gun

NOTE
Look for pine signboards at craft stores or online. If using a wood plank from a home improvement store, sand the plank with medium-grit and then fine-grit sandpaper before painting.

DIRECTIONS
1. Paint wood board with red acrylic craft paint. Let dry.
2. Attach the sawtooth hanger to the back of the wood board, positioning the sawtooth hanger about 2 in. from 1 short end of board so that the board will hang vertically.
3. Cover a flat side of each clothespin with washi tape. Trim tape if needed.
4. Lay the board vertically in front of you with painted side up and hanger at the top. Place a clothespin horizontally on left-hand side of signboard about 2 in. from the bottom, positioning the clothespin so that the handle overlaps about ¾ in. of board and the clip end faces out. Glue clothespin in place.
5. Glue 5 more clothespins to the left-hand side of board in same way, spacing them about 4 in. apart.
6. Glue remaining clothespins to the right-hand side of board in same way, starting 2 in. from the top. Let dry.

'Twas the night before Christmas

Christmas Stocking Holder

Put your best foot forward for the holidays with this yuletide sign. Drawer pulls become handy hangers for your family's stockings so they're ready for treats on Christmas Eve.

FINISHED SIZE
Excluding stockings, holder measures 24 in. wide x 8 in. high.

MATERIALS
2-ft. length of 1x8 pine (see Note)
2 wood corner trim pieces
4 drawer pulls of choice
Two 20 lb. sawtooth hangers
Coarse-grit and fine-grit sandpaper
Wood glue
Dust-free rag
Acrylic craft paints—brown and white
Paintbrushes
Sharpie gold oil-based paint pen
Computer printout or photocopy of holiday phrase of choice
Drill
Orbit sander (optional)

NOTE
Some lumber departments in home improvement stores will cut lumber pieces for little or no charge.

DIRECTIONS
1. Sand all surfaces and edges of board with coarse-grit sandpaper or orbit sander. Wipe board with dust-free rag. Sand again with fine-grit sandpaper and wipe clean.
2. Glue wood corner trim pieces to the top corners on front of board. Let dry.
3. Daub brown paint on a paintbrush and blot off excess on paper towel (do not thin paint with water). Apply a thin layer of paint to sides of board. In same way, add random patches of paint across front of board. Let dry.
4. With a clean dry paintbrush, cover board with a thin layer white paint, following the wood grain and allowing brown patches to show through in random spots to create an aged look. Wipe paint with paper towel periodically to ensure that brush strokes are visible.
5. Lay paper printout or photocopy of phrase face down on work surface and pencil in the area behind phrase. Cut out phrase and center right side up on board, about 2½ in. from the top. Trace over each letter with pencil.
6. Remove paper and draw over tracings with gold paint pen. Let dry.
7. For drawer pulls, drill 4 holes evenly spaced across the board, positioning holes about 2½ in. from the bottom of board. Attach drawer pulls.
8. Attach sawtooth hangers to back of board. Hang stocking holder as desired.

Cozy Sweater Stocking

Wondering what to do with that old sweater or thrift-shop find? Use it to sew a simple but heartwarming holiday stocking.

FINISHED SIZE
Excluding loop, stocking measures about 18 in. long. x 10 in. wide.

MATERIALS
Pattern on page 186
Sweater of choice (see Note)
Coordinating all-purpose thread
Standard sewing supplies

NOTE
If your sweater is 100% wool, felt it first to prevent the stocking from stretching out of shape. To felt, machine-wash in hot water and dry on hot cycle. Repeat 2-3 times until the weave tightens.

DIRECTIONS
1. Trace enlarged pattern onto tracing paper and cut out. Position pattern on sweater so that the ribbing is at the top edge to form cuff. Pin pattern in place. Cut around pattern through both layers of sweater. Transfer seam allowance on pattern to fabric using chalk or water-soluble marking pen.
2. With right sides of sweater pieces together, stitch pieces together along outside edge, leaving the top edge open. Clip curves close to stitching if necessary. Turn right side out. (Ribbing at top of stocking will form cuff.)
3. For the loop, cut a 1x6-in. rectangle from the remaining sweater fabric. Fold the rectangle in half lengthwise, right sides together. Sew along the long edge, using a ¼-in. seam allowance. Leave short edges open. Turn right side out.
4. Fold loop in half; sew raw edges together. Sew short edge to inside back seam of stocking, about 1 in. from cuff edge.

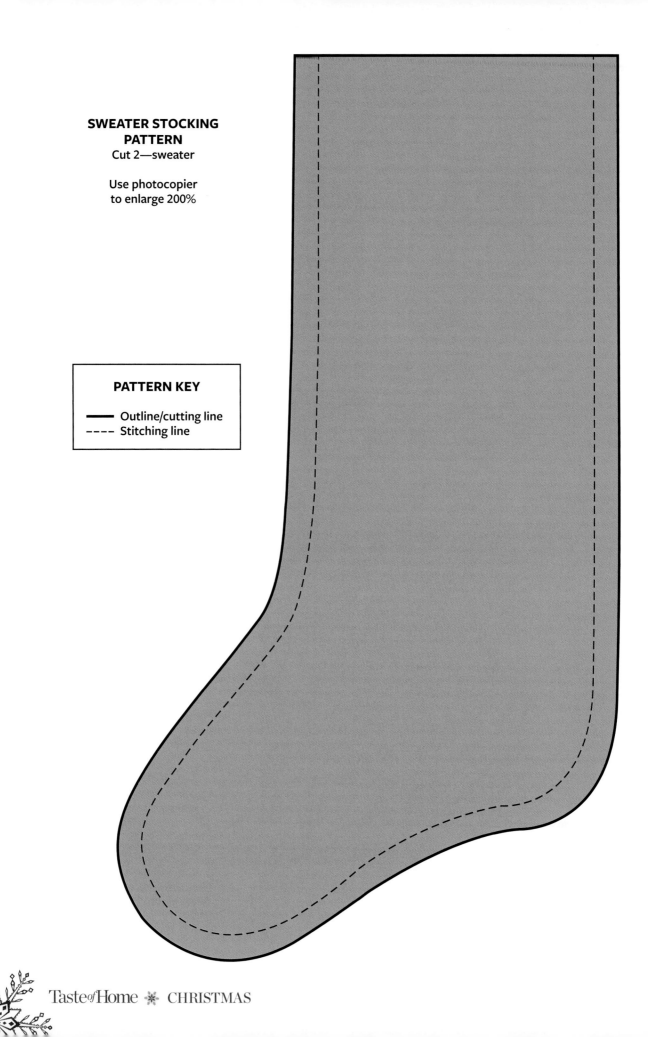

SWEATER STOCKING PATTERN
Cut 2—sweater

Use photocopier
to enlarge 200%

PATTERN KEY

⎯⎯ Outline/cutting line
- - - - Stitching line

Mercury Glass Candle Holders

Mirror-like spray paint, water and white vinegar are all you'll need to produce the effect of 19th-century distressed mercury glass on inexpensive containers.

FINISHED SIZE
Varies.

MATERIALS
Glass vases or candle holders of choice
Krylon Looking Glass Mirror-Like spray paint
White vinegar
Clean empty spray bottle with misting valve
Drop cloth

NOTE
The directions here follow the spray paint manufacturer's recommendation for painting glass containers. If you're short on time and want a quicker project, try this simple alternative: Spray the glass (inside or outside) with a light mist of water, then quickly apply a coat of spray paint and let dry. The results are similar to, though not as authentic-looking as, the method below that uses vinegar and multiple paint layers.

DIRECTIONS
1. Place the drop cloth over a work surface in a well-ventilated area. Wash and dry the glass vase or candle holder thoroughly.
2. Mix a solution of 1 part vinegar to 1 part water. Fill the squirt bottle with the solution.
3. Shake can of spray paint vigorously for 3-5 minutes.
4. Paint the inside of the glass vase or candle holder as follows: Hold the can close to the glass (no more than 12 in. away) and spray with quick short bursts, working quickly and shaking the can occasionally as you work. Rotate the vase or candle holder as you work until the inside is covered in a thin coat of paint.
5. Let coating dry for 1-2 minutes. Apply a second coat the same as before.
6. Continue adding coats of paint in the same way, letting the paint dry for 1-2 minutes between coats. Apply up to 5 coats if desired.
7. Spray a light mist of the vinegar solution onto the painted area of the glass. Let sit for about 1 minute.
8. Mist a paper towel with the vinegar solution. Gently rub the paper towel over the painted area in small circles, breaking up some of the surface paint. Vary your speed and pressure to mimic the texture of aged mercury glass.
9. Shake can of spray paint vigorously and spray on a final thin coat. Let dry completely.

Burlap Ribbon Wreath

The homespun look of burlap combines with a vibrant red hue and shimmering gold metallic accents to create a festive wreath for Christmastime.

FINISHED SIZE
Wreath measures about 23 in. across.

MATERIALS
18-in. wire wreath frame
Spool of 6-in.-wide red burlap ribbon
¼ yd. of gold metallic burlap
12-in. purchased lightweight monogram letter (or size of choice)
Gold glitter spray paint or spray adhesive and extra-fine gold craft glitter
Newspaper
Floral wire
Stapler

DIRECTIONS
WREATH WITH LETTER
1. Cover the work surface with newspaper; place monogram letter on newspaper. Either spray the letter with gold glitter spray paint or apply spray adhesive to the letter and sprinkle it with extra-fine gold craft glitter while still wet. Let dry.
2. Secure one end of the 6-in.-wide red burlap ribbon to the innermost part of the wire wreath frame with floral wire.
3. Push the burlap ribbon through to make a loose loop, about 3 in., on wire wreath frame.
4. Continue pulling the burlap ribbon through the wreath frame openings in loose 3-in. loops (the loops should resemble waves).
5. Flip wreath over, twist the burlap ribbon several times and push burlap ribbon through the inner section of the wire frame.
6. Flip the wreath to the front and continue weaving the burlap ribbon, alternating inside and outside of the wire frame openings. Flip the wreath to the back; twist the same as before. Continue weaving in the same way until wire frame is completely covered. Cut off any excess burlap ribbon and secure the end of ribbon with floral wire at the back of wreath.

7. Twist a length of floral wire into a loop at one end. Staple the wire loop to the top back of the monogram letter. Twist the straight end of the wire piece into wire frame near the top, tucking the wire under the folds of burlap to conceal wire.

THREE-TIERED BOW
1. From red burlap ribbon, cut a 2x6-in. strip and a 4x20-in. strip.
2. From gold metallic burlap, cut a 2½x15-in. strip and a 6x30-in. strip.
3. Make a loop with the 6x30-in. strip of gold metallic burlap; overlap the ends and staple them together. In the same way, make a second loop with the 4x20-in. strip of red burlap and a third loop with the 2½x15-in. strip of gold metallic burlap.
4. Layer the loops with the largest on the bottom and the smallest on top, positioning the stapled seams at the center back. Cinch the loops together in the center with floral wire. Cover the center wire with the 2x6-in. strip of red burlap; staple the burlap ends in back to secure.
5. Use floral wire to attach completed three-tiered bow to the wreath.

Starry Swirl Bowl

The sky's the limit when you use simple clay shapes to embellish a plain bowl. Designed by Sandy Rollinger, of Apollo, Pennsylvania, this decorative container is perfect for filling with ornaments.

FINISHED SIZE

Bowl shown has a 10-in. diameter.

MATERIALS

Patterns on this page
Smooth clear glass bowl of choice
(Sandy used a 10-in.-diameter bowl)
Glass cleaner and soft cloth
White oven-bake clay
Clay roller
Plastic mat
Pearl white powdered pigment
Swirl pattern rubber stamp or texture sheet
Clay oven and foil-lined baking tray
Craft knife
Craft glue
Frosted glass finish
Newspaper
Clear flat-back beads

DIRECTIONS

1. Clean outside of bowl with glass cleaner and cloth. Place bowl upside down on foil-lined baking tray.

2. Trace patterns separately onto tracing paper with pencil and cut out.

3. Condition the clay and roll out to a ¼-in. thickness. Apply powdered pigment over clay. Press stamp or texture sheet onto clay to make impressions and remove.

4. Use craft knife and patterns to cut 5 large stars and 5 small stars from clay. Use your fingers to gently curve tips of each star. Press each star onto outer sides of bowl where desired.

5. Following clay manufacturer's instructions, bake bowl at 275° for 10 minutes. Let cool. Pop each star off of bowl and set stars aside.

6. Clean outside of bowl with glass cleaner and soft cloth. Place bowl upside down on newspaper-covered surface. Following manufacturer's instructions, spray entire outside of bowl with frosted glass finish. Let dry. Repeat until desired look is achieved.

7. Apply a small amount of glue to the back of each star and glue to outside of bowl where desired. Let dry.

8. Apply a thin bead of glue to outside of bowl. Roll a tiny amount of unbaked clay on tip of a toothpick and use to pick up a bead. Place bead over glue.

9. Add beads around outside of bowl in the same way, creating swirl designs next to clay stars. Let dry.

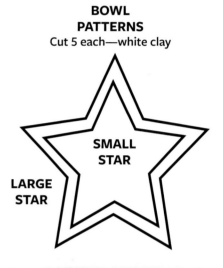

BOWL PATTERNS
Cut 5 each—white clay

SMALL STAR

LARGE STAR

Gold Leaf Glass Vases

FInish a table, mantel or shelf with the rich look of gold leaf. These vases make stunning holders for floral arrangements or candles.

FINISHED SIZE
Varies.

MATERIALS
Glass vases of choice
Gold leaf foil sheets
Gold leaf adhesive
Gold leaf sealer

2 medium-width soft bristle or foam brushes
Small soft bristle brush
Masking or painter's tape (optional)

DIRECTIONS (FOR EACH)
1. Clean and dry vase thoroughly. Gently tear off pieces of gold foil from sheets, varying the sizes and shapes for visual interest.
2. If desired, use tape to mark off an edge on outside of vase. Coat the rest of vase exterior with adhesive, using a bristle or foam brush.
3. Let vase sit for about 20 minutes or until the coating is sticky but not completely dry.
4. Working quickly, apply gold foil pieces using your fingers or another clean foam brush, overlapping pieces at random as desired to add texture. Pat and press pieces until adhered.
5. Remove excess bits with a small dry brush. Carefully remove any tape.
6. Spray vase with sealer and let dry completely.

Gift-Wrapped Clock

Is it Christmastime yet? This finished-in-minutes project lets you customize the look of a simple clock using wrapping paper to coordinate with your holiday decor.

FINISHED SIZE
Wrapped clock measures about 12 in. square.

MATERIALS
Clock kit of choice
12-in. square of canvas stretched over wood frame
Wrapping paper of choice
Packing tape or other sturdy tape
Cutting mat
Craft knife or matte knife

DIRECTIONS
1. Measure a piece of wrapping paper to cover the front of the square canvas frame, allowing at least 1½ in. of extra paper on all sides of frame. Cut out wrapping paper piece.
2. Cover canvas frame carefully and evenly with wrapping paper as if wrapping a gift, keeping the sides neat. Secure paper on back with tape.
3. Using craft or matte knife, cut a small slit in the center of the wrapped canvas, making the slit just big enough for the clock mechanism to fit through.
4. Finish assembling the clock according to the clock kit manufacturer's directions.

Beaded Sequin Ornaments

These intricate ornaments may take a bit of extra time to create, but the results will be cherished decorations year after year.

FINISHED SIZE
Excluding hanger, ornament measures about 2½ in. across.

MATERIALS (FOR ONE)
2-in. foam ball
Loose sequins
4.5g seed beads
About 200 sequin pins
½-in. screw eye
Craft glue
⅛-in.-wide ribbon for hanging

DIRECTIONS (FOR ONE)
1. Lay sequins on work surface with concave side down.
2. With a pin, pick up a seed bead and then a sequin. Push the pin into the foam ball.
3. In the same way, pick up another bead and sequin, then push pin into the ball beside the first pin so that the sequins overlap slightly. In the same way, continue adding pinned beads and sequins to the ball in a row, working around the circumference of the ball.
4. Continue adding rows in same way, slightly overlapping the previous row with the next row.
5. When ball is completely covered, apply glue to the tip of the screw eye and push into the top of the ornament. Let dry completely.
6. Thread ribbon through screw eye and tie for hanger.

Granny Circle Ornaments

Baby's first Christmas will be extra-special when you trim a pint-size tree with soft and cozy crocheted ornaments. Created by Melina Martin Gingras, of Milwaukee, Wisconsin, these adorable granny circles bring back old-fashioned charm.

FINISHED SIZE

Excluding hanger, each ornament measures about 4 in. across.

MATERIALS (FOR ONE)

3 skeins Baby Bee Sweet Delight (4 oz./115 g/340 yd./54% acrylic; 36% polyamide; 10% rayon) in colors of choice (A, B and C)
Size E/4 (3.50mm) crochet hook (or size needed to obtain correct gauge)
4-in. embroidery hoop
Tapestry or yarn needle

GAUGE

16 sc and 20 rows = 4 in. When checking gauge, be sure granny circle will fit inside the 4-in. embroidery hoop before joining with the hoop.

DIRECTIONS (FOR ONE)

1. With A, ch 6. Join with sl st.
2. Rnd 1: Ch 3, 2 dc in loop,* ch 2, 3 dc; rep from * 4 times, ch 1. Join with sl st in top of ch 3. Fasten off A.
3. Rnd 2: Join B in any ch-2 sp with a sl st. Ch 3, 2 dc, *ch 2, 3 dc in next ch-2 sp; rep from * 4 times, ch 1. Join with sl st in top of ch 3. Fasten off B.
4. Rnd 3: Join A in any ch-2 sp with a sl st. Ch 3, 2 dc, ch 1, 3 dc in same ch-2 space, *[ch 2, 3 dc, ch 1, 3 dc] in next ch-2 sp; rep from * 4 times, ch 1. Join with sl st in top of ch 3. Fasten off A.
5. Rnd 4: Join C in any ch-2 sp with a sl st. [Ch 3, 2 dc] in same ch-2 sp, *3 dc in next ch 1 sp, ch 2, 3 dc in next ch-2 sp; rep from * 5 times, 3 dc in next ch-1 sp. Join with sl st in top of ch 3. Fasten off.
6. Join A in any ch-2 sp with a sl st. Ch 1, *3 sc around the 4-in. embroidery hoop and ch 2 sp, 3 sc around hoop into second dc of next cluster; rep from * around. Join to first sc around hoop with sl st.
7. Weave in all ends with tapestry or yarn needle.

Baby Stocking Ornaments

After making her Granny Circle Ornaments (at left), Melina Martin Gingras kept on crocheting and came up with miniature Christmas stockings. They're perfect for hanging on a little one's first tree. Want more ideas? For older recipients, use the cute socks to hold small gifts.

FINISHED SIZE

Excluding hanger, each ornament measures about 4½ in. long.

MATERIALS (FOR ONE)

2 skeins Baby Bee Sweet Delight (4 oz./115 g/340 yd./54% acrylic; 36% polyamide; 10% rayon) in colors of choice (A and B)
Size G/6 (4.25mm) crochet hook (or size needed to obtain correct gauge)
Tapestry or yarn needle

GAUGE

16 sc and 20 rows = 4 in.

DIRECTIONS (FOR ONE)

BEGINNING

With A, ch 19. Join with sl st.

LEG (WORKED IN ROUNDS)

Rnds 1-7: Ch 1. Sc in next 19 sts. Join.

HEEL (WORKED IN ROWS)

1. Row 1 (RS): Join B in same space of the join from previous rnd. Ch 1. Sc in next 9 sc. Turn.
2. Rows 2-4: Ch 1. Sc in next 9 sc. Turn.
3. Row 5: Ch 1. Sc in next 4 sc. Sc2tog, 1 sc. Turn.
4. Row 6: Ch 1. Sc in next sc. Sc2tog, 1 sc. Turn.
5. Row 7: Ch 1. Sc in next 2 sc. Sc2tog, 1 sc. Turn.
6. Row 8: Ch 1. Sc in next 4 sc. Sc2tog, 1 sc. Turn.
7. Break B.

GUSSET/FOOT (WORKED IN ROUNDS)

1. Rnd 1: With RS facing, join A where the right side of the heel meets A. Ch 1. Sc in next 10 sc, 6 sc up the left side of the heel, 6 sc across the top of the heel, 6 sc down the right side of the heel. Join. (28 sc)
2. Rnd 2: Pm at beginning of rnd. Ch 1. Sc in next 9 sc, pm, sc2tog, 15 sc, sc2tog. Join. (26 sc)
3. Rnds 3-5: Ch 1, sc to marker, mm up 1 row, sc2tog, sc to next marker, mm up 1 row, sc2tog. Join. (20 sc)
4. Break A.

TOE

Join B in same space of join from previous rnd. Ch 1, 20 sc. Do not join. 2 sc, sc2tog, sc2tog, 5 sc, sc2tog, sc2tog, 7 sc, sc2tog, sc2tog, 3 sc, sc2tog, sc2tog, 5 sc, sc2tog, sc2tog, 1 sc, sc2tog, sc2tog. Sl st toe closed.

CUFF

1. Join B to top of leg with sl st.
2. Rnds 1-7: Ch 1, sc in next 19 sc. Join.
3. Rnd 8: Ch 1, * 5 sc in next sc, 1 sc in next 2 sc; rep from * to end of rnd. Join.
4. Break B.
5. Fold the cuff down on RS. Join B at the fold. Ch 20. Fasten off the yarn in a small loop to create a hanger for tree ornament.
6. Weave in all ends with tapestry or yarn needle.

ABBREVIATIONS

ch	chain	sc	single crochet
dc	double crochet	sc2tog	single crochet
mm	move marker		2 together
pm	place marker		(decrease)
rep	repeat	sl st	slip stitch
rnd(s)	round(s)	sp	space
RS	right side	st(s)	stitch(es)

Magnolia Leaf Wreath

Translucent, feathery leaves make a lovely yuletide wreath. Give yourself an afternoon to create enough layers for a full effect.

FINISHED SIZE
Wreath measures about 16½ in. across.

MATERIALS
12-in. foam wreath form
About 200 magnolia skeleton leaves
¼ yd. natural burlap, cut into 2-in. strips
3-in. length of ¼-in. or ½-in. ribbon
2 straight pins
Glue gun
Decoupage glue
Fine white glitter
Foam stencil brush

DIRECTIONS
1. Cover work surface with waxed paper. Use brush to daub 5 leaves with decoupage glue. On a clean sheet of waxed paper, pour glitter over leaves. Shake off excess glitter; let dry.
2. Wrap wreath form tightly with burlap strips, using glue gun to secure.
3. Using glue gun to glue 2 leaves at a time and placing leaf tips to the left, glue stalks of plain leaves to the form's inner rim. Moving toward outer rim, glue 3 more pairs about 1 in. apart at stalks. Add another row of leaves about 2 in. to the right of first row. Continue adding rows, moving counterclockwise around form. Repeat once.
4. Add single leaves to fill in wreath as desired. If leaves become bent, gently reshape with your fingertips.
5. With glue gun, glue stalks of glitter leaves to wreath as desired.
6. Loop ribbon for hanger; attach ends to back of wreath with glue gun and pins.

Simple Stocking Pillowcase

Want to dress up an accent pillow for the holidays? It's easy to do using basic sewing supplies and printed fabric appliques.

FINISHED SIZE
Varies.

MATERIALS
Pillow of choice
Simple stocking and cuff designs
  of choice for templates (see Note)
1 yd. plain linen or muslin (or amount
  needed to cover desired pillow)
Fabric scraps in seasonal colors and
  patterns of choice
Coordinating all-purpose thread
Fusible web
Standard sewing supplies

NOTE
To create a simple stocking template and a separate cuff template for the stocking and cuff appliques, use a basic stocking design from a child's coloring book or other source.

DIRECTIONS
1. From plain linen or muslin, cut a front panel measuring 1 in. larger than the pillow on all sides, a back panel measuring 1 in. wider than the pillow and half the pillow's length, and a second back panel measuring 1 in. wider than the pillow and 4 in. shorter than the pillow's length.
2. On 1 long raw edge of a back panel, fold a ¼-in. seam to wrong side and press. Fold and press again. Pin. Repeat with the second back panel.
3. Using desired stocking template and cuff template, cut 3 stockings and 3 cuffs from desired fabric scraps.
4. Following the web manufacturer's directions, attach fusible web to each fabric stocking.
5. Place each fabric stocking right side up on the front panel and fuse in place following manufacturer's directions. Let cool. In same way, fuse the fabric cuffs to front panel so that each cuff slightly overlaps the top of a stocking.
6. Using a medium zigzag stitch, sew along the edges of stockings and cuffs.
7. With right sides together, line up the long raw edge of the longer back panel with the long top raw edge of the front panel.
8. With back facing up, place the short back panel wrong side up on top of the longer back panel, lining up the short panel's long raw edge with the bottom raw edge of front. Pin all edges.
9. Sew along the outer edges using a ¼-in. seam. Press seams open.
10. Turn pillowcase right side out and insert pillow.

Stenciled Peace Sign

This painting technique produces an aged, vintage look when you rub through the red paint layer with sandpaper. Stand this sign of the season next to your front door.

FINISHED SIZE
Varies.

MATERIALS
New or repurposed wood plank (see Note)
Latex paint—red for main color, yellow for contrasting color and antique white for lettering
Letter stencils of choice to spell "PEACE"
Painter's tape
2 bristle paintbrushes
Foam paintbrush
Sandpaper

NOTE
If your wood plank has knots or other character traits, highlight them by sanding those areas more vigorously.

DIRECTIONS
1. If necessary, clean the wood plank by wiping with a damp cloth; let dry.
2. Using broad strokes and following the wood grain, generously apply 1 coat of contrasting-color paint to plank with bristle paintbrush. Let dry. Apply a second coat in the same way and let dry.
3. Apply 2-3 coats of the main-color paint the same as before, letting each coat dry before applying the next coat.
4. When the plank is completely dry, place letter stencils in center of plank to spell "PEACE" and tape in place.
5. Using the foam brush, daub the lettering-color paint along the stencils. Let dry. Apply a second coat and let dry completely. Remove stencils.
6. Create a distressed look by lightly sanding the corners and edges of sign, following the wood grain and applying more or less pressure as needed to reveal desired amount of undercoat. Sand lightly over letters.

Hunter's Star Quilt

Love quilting? Using seasonal fabrics and this traditional pattern from Gayla Cox of Littleton, Colorado, you can stitch a classic hunter's star design that will warm your family for years to come.

FINISHED SIZE

Quilt measures 78 in. long x 54 in. wide.

MATERIALS

2½ yds. of 44-in.-wide white 100% cotton fabric

2½ yds. of 44-in.-wide print 100% cotton fabric

2¼ yds. of 44-in.-wide red 100% cotton fabric for binding

2¼ yds. of 60-in.-wide turquoise 100% cotton fabric for backing (or enough 44-in.-wide fabric to piece together a 56x80-in. piece)

Coordinating all-purpose thread

56x80-in. piece of quilt batting

Quilter's marking pen or pencil

Quilter's ruler

3½-in. square of see-through template plastic

Standard sewing supplies

Rotary cutter and mat (optional)

Safety pins (optional)

DIRECTIONS

GENERAL DIRECTIONS

Do all stitching with right sides together, edges even, coordinating thread and a ¼-in. seam allowance. Press seams toward the darker fabric whenever possible.

CUTTING FABRICS

1. Prewash fabrics without using fabric softeners, washing each color separately. If water is discolored, wash again until rinse water runs clear. Dry and press all fabrics.

2. Fold white and print fabrics in half crosswise with wrong sides together and selvages even. Smooth out wrinkles so fabrics lie flat.

3. Either use a water-soluble marking pen and ruler to mark the fabrics before cutting them with scissors or cut the fabrics with rotary cutting tools. From each of the white and print fabrics, cut four 6½x44-in. strips and one 42-in. square. From each 6½-in. strip, cut six 6½-in. squares, creating a total of 24 squares of each fabric.

4. From red fabric, cut two 8x80-in. strips and two 8x50-in. strips for the binding.

HALF-TRIANGLE SQUARES

1. On wrong side of the 42-in. square of white fabric, use quilter's ruler and marking pen or pencil to mark a grid of 4-in. squares, 10 squares wide x 10 squares high, then mark a diagonal line through all squares as shown in Fig. 1a below left.

2. With right sides together, lay the matching-size piece of print fabric behind the marked white fabric. With all-purpose thread, accurately stitch ¼ in. from each side of all the marked diagonal lines as shown by the dashed lines in Fig. 1b.

3. Cut out squares on the marked lines. Cut squares in half diagonally on marked lines. Press each piece open to make a half-triangle square.

4. Mark a diagonal line down the center of plastic square. Center plastic on top of a half-triangle square so the diagonal line matches the seam. Either trim off the excess with a rotary cutter or mark the square, remove plastic and trim with scissors. Trim all half-triangle squares. (There will be extras.)

HUNTER'S STAR BLOCK

Sew 4 half-triangle squares together as shown in Fig. 2a. Make 24 blocks. Assemble 4 of the blocks as shown in Fig. 2b for a hunter's star block. Make 6 hunter's star blocks.

REVERSE HUNTER'S STAR BLOCK

Sew 4 half-triangle squares together as shown in Fig. 3a on page 198. Make 24 blocks. Assemble 4 of the blocks as shown in Fig. 3b for a reverse hunter's star block. Make a total of 6 reverse hunter's star blocks.

4-PATCH BLOCK

Sew the 6½-in. squares together as shown in Fig. 4. Make 12 blocks.

QUILT TOP

Lay out all pieces as shown in the Assembly Diagram. Sew the pieces together in rows, then sew the rows together, carefully matching seams.

(Continued on next page)

FIG. 1A
Draw a grid of 4-in. squares

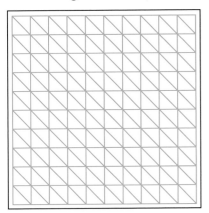

FIG. 1B
Stitch ¼ in. from each side of diagonal lines

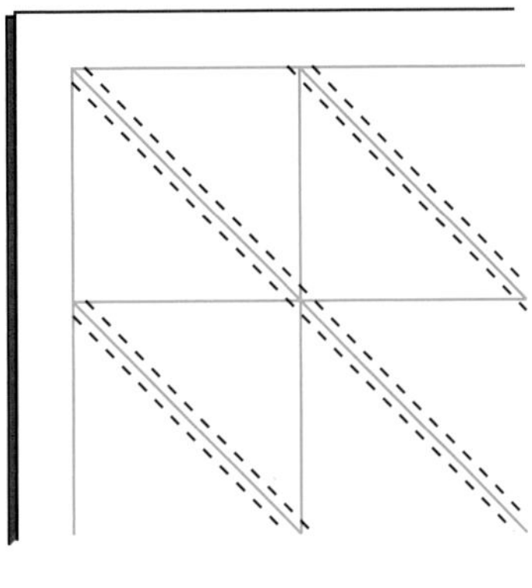

FIG. 2A
Assemble 24 blocks

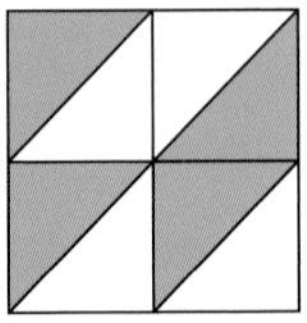

FIG. 2B
Assemble 6 stars

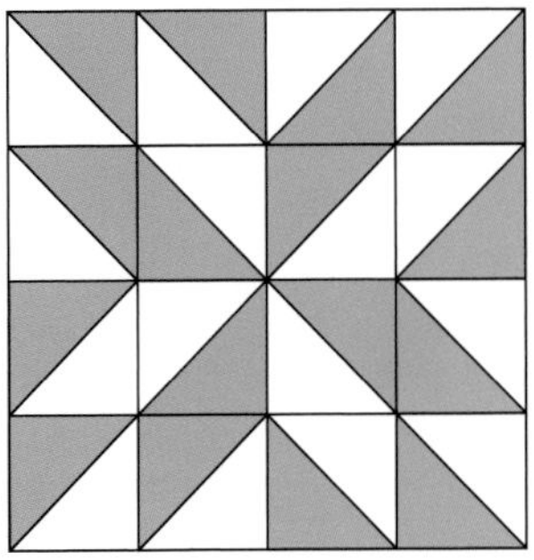

QUILTING

1. Smooth out backing fabric wrong side up on a flat surface. Center batting over backing; smooth out. Center the quilt top over batting, right side up, smoothing out all wrinkles.

2. Baste through all 3 layers, stitching from the center to the corners, then horizontally and vertically every 4 in. until the entire top is held together. If desired, use safety pins to pin-baste all layers of the quilt together, avoiding the seams.

3. Either hand-quilt as desired or thread machine, set a medium-long straight stitch and stitch-in-the-ditch of all seams where print fabric meets white fabric.

4. Trim batting and backing to extend 3 in. beyond the quilt top all around. Remove basting or safety pins.

BINDING

1. With wrong sides together and long raw edges matching, fold each red strip in half lengthwise and press in the fold.

2. With right sides together, match the long raw edges of a 50-in. red strip to the top raw edge of quilt top and sew together with a ¼-in. seam through all thicknesses. Trim ends even with the quilt top (not the batting).

3. Sew a 50-in. red strip to the bottom raw edge of quilt top in the same way, trimming as before.

4. Center and sew an 80-in. red strip to the left-hand edge of the quilt top, leaving the excess fabric on each end to be turned under later.

5. Sew remaining 80-in. red strip to right-hand side of quilt top in same way.

FINISHING

Turn all binding strips to the back of the quilt along the edge of the batting and backing pieces. Hand-stitch to back of quilt, folding under the excess fabric at each end of 80-in. strips.

ASSEMBLY DIAGRAM

FIG. 3A
Assemble 24 blocks

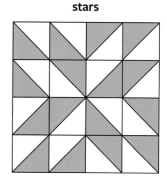

FIG. 3B
Assemble 6 reverse stars

FIG. 4
Assemble 12 four-patch blocks

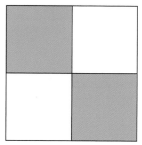

Quick Embroidered Ornaments

Timeless motifs mark these trims, based on a design from Elizabeth DeCroos, of Cambridge, Ontario.

FINISHED SIZE

Excluding hanger, each ornament measures about 3⅜ in. across.

MATERIALS

Charts on this page (see Note)
Three 4-in. squares of white 22-count Aida cloth
Size 5 pearl cotton in colors shown on charts or contrasting colors of choice
Three 3-in. embroidery hoops
Size 26 tapestry needle
Craft knife
Length of ribbon of choice for each ornament for hanging

NOTE

On the charts, each line represents one set of fabric threads and each square represents one hole. Charts are not to scale.

DIRECTIONS

1. Zigzag or overcast the edges of Aida cloth squares to prevent fraying. Fold each square in half lengthwise, then fold it in half again crosswise to determine the center and mark this point.

2. For each ornament, center an Aida cloth square in an embroidery hoop.

3. To find the center of charts, draw lines across each chart, connecting opposite arrows. Begin stitching at this point of desired chart so design will be centered, working straight stitches as shown on the chart. To begin, leave about a 1-in. tail of pearl cotton on back of work and hold it in place while working the first few stitches around it.

4. To end stitching, run needle under a few neighboring stitches in back before clipping pearl cotton close to work.

5. Trim excess Aida cloth with craft knife. Tie ribbon around screw of each ornament to hang.

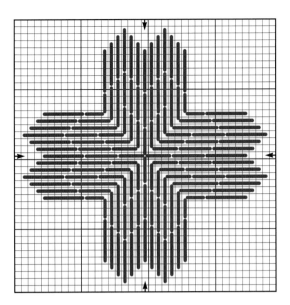

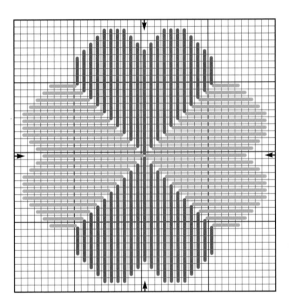

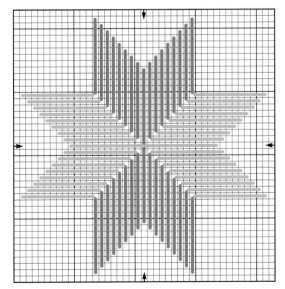

3-in. length of artificial green holly garland
12-in. length of 19-gauge craft wire
¼-in. domed furniture plug
Drill with ¼-in. bit
Sandpaper
Foam plate or palette
Acrylic craft paints—black, blush, flesh, gold and white
Small flat paintbrush
Black fine-line marker
White textured doll hair or white yarn
Glue gun
Standard sewing supplies

NOTE
Depending on the size of your potato masher handle, the opening of the hat may need to be made larger or smaller. Also, the beard may need to be made longer or shorter.

DIRECTIONS
GENERAL DIRECTIONS
Keep paper towels and a container of water handy to clean paintbrush. Place small dabs of each paint color onto the foam plate or palette as needed. Add coats of paint as needed for complete coverage. Let paint dry after every application.

WOOD PIECES
1. Measure 2¼ in. down from the end of the potato masher handle and drill an ⅛-in.-deep hole into side of handle for the nose.
2. If the top of handle does not have a hole, drill a hole through top of handle. Sand handle.
3. Glue domed furniture plug into the hole for nose. Let dry.
4. Use flesh paint to paint the potato masher handle and domed furniture plug. Let dry.
5. Use gold paint to paint the wood star. When dry, outline the front of star with black marker.

Santa Napkin Holder
You say potato, but Irene Wegener, of Corning, New York, says craft project! She turned an old masher into a folksy Santa napkin holder—and guaranteed conversation piece—for the holidays.

FINISHED SIZE
Napkin holder shown measures 14 in. high x 5½ in. wide.

MATERIALS
Pattern on this page
Wire potato masher with wooden handle
3x15-in. strip of red-and-green plaid fabric for hat
All-purpose thread to coordinate with fabric
1x4-in. piece of cotton quilt batting
½-in. wood star

HAT PATTERN
Trace 1—tracing paper
Cut 1 as directed in instructions

Grain

Leave open

Use photocopier to enlarge pattern 200%

HAIR/BEARD

1. Cut a 4-in. length of doll hair or yarn and hold it between your middle and ring fingers. Wrap additional yarn around all 4 fingers 8 times. Cut yarn. Tie off in center with the 4-in. piece. Cut through loops at opposite sides. Glue the center of bundle to the top of handle for hair. Let dry.

2. Create a bundle for beard in same way, wrapping around your fingers 20 times instead of 8. Set aside.

HAT

1. Trace enlarged hat pattern onto tracing paper with pencil and cut out.

2. Fold plaid fabric in half lengthwise with right sides together. Pin the hat pattern to the fabric with grain lines matching. Sew around hat, leaving opening where shown on pattern. Remove pattern. Trim excess fabric, leaving a narrow seam outside the stitching. Turn hat inside out.

3. Insert 1 end of wire through the hole in top of handle and twist the end back around the wire to secure, leaving about 10 in. of wire extending from top of handle.

4. Slip hat over end of wire and glue bottom edge of hat to top of handle.

5. Wrap batting around bottom of hat, positioning the ends of batting in back. Glue to secure.

6. Glue the gold star to the tip of hat.

7. Glue circle of holly garland to the cuff of hat. Let dry.

8. Shape end of hat as desired.

FINISHING

1. Dip end of paintbrush handle into black paint. Add 2 small dots to the face for eyes.

2. Dip brush into blush paint and wipe excess paint onto paper towel. Using a nearly dry paintbrush and a circular motion, add the cheeks and a bit of color to the nose.

3. Dip a toothpick into white paint and add a tiny dot to each eye.

4. Use black marker to add eyebrows.

5. Glue the center of the beard below Santa's nose. When dry, cut ends of beard to shape as desired.

6. Stand potato masher on flat surface and place desired napkins in the base.

Musical Candles

Enjoy carols by candlelight! Decorate traditional or flameless pillar candles, whichever variety you prefer.

FINISHED SIZE

Varies.

MATERIALS

Real or flameless candles of choice
Scrapbook paper or card stock with music print
Flexible tape measure
Decoupage glue
Sponge brush
Ribbon and other embellishments of choice (optional)

DIRECTIONS (FOR EACH)

1. Use the flexible tape measure to measure the circumference and height of candle, add ½ in. to circumference and make note of the measurements. Cut a piece of paper or card stock using the noted numbers for the dimensions.

2. Use sponge brush to apply a coat of decoupage glue to the back of the paper or card stock piece.

3. Wrap the glue side of paper or card stock around the candle, matching the height of the paper or card stock piece with the height of the candle. Slightly overlap paper or card stock at the seam.

4. To remove air bubbles, either gently roll covered candle on a flat surface or use your hands to flatten the paper or card stock toward the seam. Let dry.

5. If desired, add a coat of decoupage glue to the exterior of the paper or card stock to seal.

6. If desired, attach ribbon or other embellishments to wrapped candle, being sure to position them far enough away from the wick and flame area.

Gift Wrapping Station

Our craft editors picked up this TV armoire for $33 at a local thrift shop. Look for an inexpensive piece of your own, then follow these directions to transform it into the perfect spot for wrapping gifts—during the holiday season or any time at all.

FINISHED SIZE
Varies.

MATERIALS
TV armoire or large cabinet of choice
Pegboard cut to dimensions of armoire backing
Pegboard organizer kit or single pegboard hooks
Dowels, buckets and crates of varying diameters and sizes
Coarse- and medium-grit sandpaper
Latex primer and paint of choice
Foam board
Cork squares or panels
Fabric for covering bulletin board
Fabric ribbon
Quick-drying fabric glue
Wood glue
Small finish nails
Hammer
Paintbrush and roller
Craft knife
Glue gun
Nail gun
Power sander (optional)
Needle-nose pliers (optional)

NOTE
Use the glue gun for all gluing unless the directions state otherwise. See the box at right for additional ways of filling and decorating the armoire.

DIRECTIONS
1. Pry off the armoire backing with hammer claw or needle-nose pliers; discard backing.
2. Sand the armoire by hand or with a power sander using coarse-grit and then medium-grit sandpaper. Wipe all surfaces clean.
3. Apply 1 coat of primer with the roller and paintbrush where needed. Let dry. Cover with 2-3 coats of paint, letting each coat dry completely before applying the next coat.

(Continued on next page)

Finishing Gift Wrapping Station

Hang dowels and spool racks on pegboard to hold spools and rolls.

Use hooks to hang small buckets for storing tags and decorations.

Attach fabric-covered bulletin boards for cards and notes.

Create simple door pulls using large jingle bells and tassels.

4. Sand pegboard with medium-grit sandpaper; wipe clean.

5. Paint pegboard using roller. Apply 2-3 coats, letting each coat dry before applying the next coat.

6. Attach pegboard to inside back of armoire using nail gun (have a helper hold the board in place).

7. For bulletin boards, measure recessed panels on inside of armoire doors. Use craft knife to cut matching pieces of foam board and cork to fit recessed areas. Position each cork piece on top of a foam board piece and glue together. Let dry.

8. Center 1 assembled board, cork side down, on wrong side of fabric. Trim fabric, leaving a 1-in. border around the edge. Run a thin bead of glue along back of 1 long side of board close to the edge. Pull fabric taut and over the line of glue to secure. Repeat on the opposite side and then remaining sides, folding in corners as if wrapping a gift.

9. Cover remaining boards with fabric the same as before.

10. Glue bulletin boards to inside of armoire doors with wood glue. To set glue, gently tap a finish nail through cork, slightly piercing the door at corners of bulletin board without driving the nail too far into the wood (have a helper hold the door steady). Let glue set overnight. Gently remove nails.

11. To create a holder for cards or notes, cut 2 pieces of fabric ribbon and place them over a bulletin board to form an X. (Trim ends even to the angle of board.) Glue in place 1 piece at a time at the corners only using quick-drying fabric glue.

12. For ribbon trims, run a continuous length of ribbon around entire edge of each bulletin board, making corner folds at the turns. Glue in place along all edges and at corners. If armoire has inside shelves, glue ribbon to the edges of each shelf, folding over the edges to make neat ends.

13. Arrange pegboard kit hardware or hooks, buckets, dowels and crates inside armoire as desired.

Tiered Plate Centerpiece

This charming table topper is easy to make with secondhand items and costs a lot less than buying a similar ready-made centerpiece. Add ornaments, pinecones, greenery—you name it!

FINISHED SIZE
Varies.

MATERIALS
3 plates of choice—small, medium and large
2 candlesticks
Gold spray paint
Glue gun

NOTE
To disassemble the tiers later if desired, put centerpiece in the freezer. The parts will pop apart when the glue freezes.

DIRECTIONS
1. Paint candlesticks with spray paint and let dry.

2. Apply glue to the base of 1 candlestick and position the base in the center of the large plate. Let dry.

3. Glue around the top rim of the same candlestick and center the bottom of the medium plate on top of it. Let dry.

4. Apply glue to the base of the remaining candlestick and position the base in the center of the medium plate. Let dry.

5. Glue around the top rim of the top candlestick and center the bottom of the small plate on top of it. Let dry.

GIFTS TO GIVE

Roll-Up Travel Makeup Organizer

In Salisbury, Maryland, Penny Sperry came up with this practical project to make things super simple when traveling. With plenty of stitched pockets, the convenient fabric organizer will keep your favorite makeup bottles, brushes or tools in one spot and can easily tuck into a handbag or suitcase. Or use this roll-up carrier to manage your craft supplies, such as crochet hooks, for quick access any time at all.

FINISHED SIZE

Secured with elastic loop, rolled-up travel makeup organizer measures about 12 in. long x 3¾ in. wide. Open travel makeup organizer measures about 13 in. long x 12 in. wide.

MATERIALS

- ⅔ yd. cotton fabric for outer shell and makeup brush pocket
- ½ yd. cotton fabric for lining
- ½ yd. fusible fleece
- Ponytail elastic
- Coordinating all-purpose thread
- Rotary cutter or fabric scissors
- Quilter's ruler
- Soluble fabric marker
- Iron
- Sewing pins
- Tape measure
- Sewing machine

DIRECTIONS

CUTTING

1. From the fabric for the outer shell and pocket, cut one 14x13-in. outer piece and one 9x13-in. pocket piece.
2. From the lining fabric, cut a 14x13-in. piece.
3. From the fusible fleece, cut a 13½x12½-in. piece.

ASSEMBLY

1. Following the manufacturer's instructions, fuse the fleece to the center of the lining fabric's wrong side.
2. Fold the pocket fabric piece in half lengthwise and iron to crease. If desired, topstitch 18 in. along the folded edge.
3. Line up the pocket piece along all 3 raw edges on the lining piece. Place tape measure horizontally across the top of the pocket. Measure and pin at the following intervals: 1¾ in., 1½ in., 1 in., 2 in., 2 in., 1 in. and 1½ in. Mark these lines vertically with the soluble fabric marker. Stitch along the vertical lines, forming sections.
4. Lay ponytail elastic at the top right side of the pocket, overlapping slightly; pinch the outer edge of the elastic band and pin to pocket.
5. Place outer fabric piece right sides together with the lining/pocket piece and pin all the way around, making sure to leave a 2½-in. opening on the left-hand side just above the pocket. Re-pin the ponytail elastic so it is between the lining and outer fabric.
6. Stitch ¼ in. all the way around, beginning at the top of the unpinned section and finishing at the bottom of unpinned section. Snip all 4 corners and turn right side out. Iron flat and topstitch ⅛ in. all the way around.
7. Fold top edge of the fabric down to the top of pocket, overlapping slightly. Iron closed. If desired, topstitch ⅛ in. along folded edge.
8. Fold the left side of closed makeup organizer to the center and then fold again. Hand-stitch the button to the center of this section. Loop elastic over the button to close.

Silver Chain Earrings

Have you heard? It's a cinch to assemble a pair of elegant earrings for yourself or a friend using a few basic jewelry-making tools. Just follow the directions for this dangling chain design from Sarah Farley, of Menomonee Falls, Wisconsin.

FINISHED SIZE

Excluding the hook, each earring is about 2¾ in. long.

MATERIALs

Two silver French earring hooks
Two 4mm clear crystals
Two small silver cone caps
Two 36-in. lengths of silver chain
Two 3-in. lengths of fine silver wire
Wire cutters
Round-nose pliers
Needle-nose pliers

DIRECTIONS

GENERAL DIRECTIONS

Refer to the photo at right as a guide while making the earrings as directed in the directions that follow.

CUTTING

1. Using the wire cutters, cut one 36-in. length of silver chain into the following lengths, in the order listed: 1⁷/₁₆ in., 1¹¹/₁₆ in., 1³/₁₆ in., 1⅞ in., ½ in., 1¼ in., 2 in., 1⅝ in., 1¾ in., ¾ in., 1¹¹/₁₆ in., 2¹/₁₆ in., 1⅞ in., ¾ in., 1⅜ in., 1⅝ in., 1⅜ in., 1⅛ in., ⅞ in., 2 in., ⅞ in., 1⅛ in. and 1¾ in.
2. Repeat with the remaining 36-in. length of chain, keeping the two sets of cut chain pieces separate.

ASSEMBLY (FOR EACH EARRING)

1. Bend one 3-in. length of fine wire about an inch from an end so it resembles a check mark. String one set of cut chain pieces in order onto the short end of the 3-in. wire.
2. Bend the wire piece at the crease, bringing the two ends together. Using the needle-nose pliers, wrap the short end 3-4 times around the long end of wire. Cut off the excess from the short end with wire cutters.
3. String one cone cap and then one 4mm clear crystal onto the remaining long end of wire.

4. Using the needle-nose pliers, bend the wire end at a right angle, leaving a small amount of space above the clear crystal. Place round-nose pliers about ¼ in. from the crease and bend the wire to make a loop. While holding the loop with the round-nose pliers, use needle-nose pliers to wrap the excess wire around stem 3-4 times, making the crystal and cone fit tightly. Cut off the excess with wire cutters.
5. Using needle-nose pliers, pull the loop on a silver French earring hook slightly open. Slip the loop of the newly formed earring onto the French hook loop. Using needle-nose pliers, close the French hook loop to secure the earring on hook.
6. Repeat earring assembly to create the second earring.

Crocheted Toy Balls

Designer Tamara Kelly, of Bettendorf, Iowa, stitched these cute-as-can-be playthings you can make for little ones on your list.

FINISHED SIZE

Each ball measures about 3½ in. across.

MATERIALS

4 skeins Lion Brand Modern Baby (Light worsted/3; 50% acrylic, 50% nylon; 173 yds./158 m; 2.6 oz./75 g), 1 each of Grey (A), Orange (B), Chartreuse (C) and Turquoise (D)
1 F/3.75mm hook
Polyester stuffing

NOTE

Weave in ends as needed. Begin stuffing ball after Rnd 24. Use tail at the end to cinch the bottom closed.

DIRECTIONS

STRIPED BALL

1. Rnd 1: With A, ch 2, in 2nd ch from hook, sc 6; join with a sl st. (6 sts)
2. Rnd 2: Ch 1, 2 sc in each st around; join. (12 sts)
3. Rnd 3: Ch 1, *sc in next st, 2 sc in next st; rep from * around, join. (18 sts)
4. Rnd 4: Ch 1, *2 sc in next st, sc in next 2 sts; rep from * around, join. (24 sts)
5. Rnd 5: Ch 1, sc in first 2 sts, *2 sc in next st, sc in next 3 sts; rep from * until 2 sts remain, 2 sc in next st, sc in last st, join. (30 sts)
6. Rnd 6: Ch 1, *2 sc in next st, sc in next 4 sts; rep from * around, join. (36 sts)
7. Rnd 7: Ch 1, *sc in next 5 sts, 2 sc in next st; rep from * around, join. (42 sts)
8. Rnd 8: Ch 1, sc in first 3 sts, *2 sc in next st, sc in next 7 sts; rep from * until 7 sts remain, 2 sc in next st, sc in last 6 sts, join. (47 sts)
9. Rnd 9: Ch 1, *2 sc in next st, sc in next 8 sts; rep from * until 2 sts remain, sc in last 2 sts, join. (52 sts)
10. Rnd 10: Ch 1, *sc in next 12 sts, 2 sc in next st; rep from * around, join. (56 sts)
11. Rnd 11: Ch 1, sc in first 6 sts, *2 sc in next st, sc in next 13 sts; rep from * until 8 sts remain, 2 sc in next st, sc in last 7 sts, join. (60 sts)
12. Rnd 12: Ch 1, *2 sc in next st, sc in next 14 sts; rep from * around, join and finish off. (64 sts)
13. Rnd 13: With B, join to blo of any st of previous rnd, ch 1, sc in blo of each st around; join and finish off. (64 sts)
14. Rnd 14: With C, join to blo of any st of previous rnd, ch 1, sc in blo of each st around; join and finish off. (64 sts)
15. Rnd 15: With Color D, join to blo of any st of previous rnd, ch 1, sc in blo of each st around; join and finish off. (64 sts)
16. Rnds 16-18: Rep Rnds 13-15.
17. Rnd 19: With A, join to blo of any st of previous rnd, ch 1, sc in blo of each st around; join. (64 sts)
18. Rnd 20: Ch 1, working rnd in blo, *sc2tog, sc in next 14 sts; rep from * around, join. (60 sts)
19. Rnd 21: Ch 1, sc in first 6 sts, *sc2tog, sc in next 13 sts; rep from * until 8 sts remain, sc2tog, sc in last 7 sts, join. (56 sts)
20. Rnd 22: Ch 1, *sc in next 12 sts, sc2tog; rep from * around, join. (52 sts)
21. Rnd 23: Ch 1, *sc2tog, sc in next 8 sts; rep from * until 2 sts remain, sc in last 2 sts, join. (47 sts)
22. Rnd 24: Ch 1, sc in first 3 sts, *sc2tog, sc in next 7 sts; rep from * until 8 sts remain, sc2tog, sc in last 6 sts, join. (42 sts)
23. Rnd 25: Ch 1, *sc in next 5 sts, sc2tog; rep from * around, join. (36 sts)
24. Rnd 26: Ch 1, *sc2tog, sc in next 4 sts; rep from * around, join. (30 sts)
25. Rnd 27: Ch 1, sc in first 2 sts, *sc2tog, sc in next 3 sts; rep from * until 3 sts remain, sc2tog, sc in last st, join. (24 sts)
26. Rnd 28: Ch 1, *sc2tog, sc in next 2 sts; rep from * around, join. (18 sts)
27. Rnd 29: Ch 1, *sc in next st, sc2tog; rep from * around, join. (12 sts)
28. Rnd 30: Ch 1, sc2tog around, join and finish off. (6 sts)

COLOR-BLOCK BALL

1. Rnds 1-12: Rep Rnds 1-12 of Striped Ball directions.
2. Rnd 13: With B, join to any st of previous rnd, ch 4, skip next 2 sts, hdc in next 2 sts, *ch 2, skip next 2 sts, hdc in next 2 sts; rep from * around working last hdc in same st as the join, join with sl st in ch-4 sp. (32 hdc)
3. Rnd 14: Ch 1, *hdc in next 2 missed sts of Rnd 12, enclosing ch-2 from previous rnd; ch 2, skip next 2 sts; rep from * around, join to first hdc of rnd and finish off. (32 hdc)
4. Rnd 15: With C, join to first st of previous rnd, ch 4, skip next 2 sts, hdc in next 2 sts, enclosing ch-2 from previous rnd, *ch 2, skip next 2 sts, hdc in next 2 sts; rep from * around, join with sl st in ch-4 sp. (32 hdc)
5. Rnd 16: Rep Rnd 14.
6. Rnd 17: With D, rep Rnd 15.
7. Rnd 18: Rep Rnd 14.
8. Rnd 19: With A, join any st of previous rnd, ch 1, sc in each st of previous rnd and each skipped st of rnd before that; join. (64 sts)
9. Rnd 20: Ch 1, *sc2tog, sc in next 14 sts; rep from * around, join. (60 sts)
10. Rnds 21-30: Rep Rnds 21-30 of Striped Ball directions.

ZIGZAG BALL

1. Rnds 1-12: Rep Rnds 1-12 of Striped Ball directions.
2. Rnd 13: With B, join to any st of previous rnd, ch 1, *sc in next 2 sts, sc3tog, sc in next 2 sts, 3 sc in next st (3-sc group made); rep from * around, join and finish off. (64 sts)
3. Rnd 14: With C, join to center st of any 3-sc group, ch 1, *3 sc in next st, sc in next 2 sts, sc3tog, sc in next 2 sts; rep from * around, join and finish off. (64 sts)
4. Rnd 15: With D, rep Rnd 14.
5. Rnd 16: With B, rep Rnd 14.
6. Rnds 17-18: Rep Rnds 14-15.
7. Rnds 19-30: Rep Rnds 19-30 of Color-Block Ball directions.

ABBREVIATIONS

blo	back loop only
ch	chain
hdc	half double crochet
rep	repeat
rnd	round
sc	single crochet
sc2tog	single crochet 2 together (decrease)
sc3tog	single crochet 3 together (decrease)
sl st	slip stitch
sp	space
st(s)	stitch(es)

Pinecone Fire Starters

What a festive way to get a fire going!
Set a pinecone on your kindling and light
a single scale. Gather your own pinecones
(let them dry) or buy a bag at a craft store.
If you like, pretreat them with the additives
listed below to produce colored flames.
(Be sure to burn only one color at a time.)

FINISHED SIZE
Varies.

MATERIALS
Dry natural pinecones
Clear candle wax
Candle dye colors of choice
Tall tin can and metal tongs
Foil-lined baking sheet
Flame color additives (optional)—
    1 cup table salt (yellow flame)
    1 cup borax (yellow-green flame)
    1 cup salt substitute with potassium
    (violet flame) or 1 cup Epsom salts
    (white flame)

DIRECTIONS
PRETREATMENT FOR
COLORING FLAMES (OPTIONAL)
Fill a bucket with ½ gallon hot water.
Mix in 1 additive. Soak the pinecones
in the solution for 8 hours. Remove;
let pinecones dry until fully opened.
Dip in wax as directed below.

WAX COATING
Melt the clear candle wax in a double
boiler over low heat and mix in desired
candle dye. Remove from heat; pour
into tall tin can, leaving space near top.
With tongs, dip each pinecone into the
melted wax until completely covered,
then place on foil-lined baking sheet to
stand until wax sets.

Chunky Silver Bracelet

Cinching a silver chain creates the base of
this eye-catching accent from Sarah Farley,
of Menomonee Falls, Wisconsin. Beads
add a pretty hint of light blue.

FINISHED SIZE
Open bracelet measures about 8 in. long x
¾ in. wide.

MATERIALS
12-in. length of beading wire
    (or desired length of bracelet
    plus 4 in.)
Beading needle
78-in. length of small open-loop silver
    chain
24 silver head pins
Twenty-four 6mm beads (Sarah used
    a combination of clear, frosted, light
    blue and ice blue beads)
2 silver clam clasps
Silver toggle clasp with jump rings
Round-nose pliers
Chain-nose pliers
Wire cutters
G-S Hypo cement or jewelry glue

DIRECTIONS
1. Thread needle with beading wire
and tie the wire ends in a knot close to
the end. Use wire cutters to trim excess
wire close to knot.
2. Thread the unknotted end of wire
through the hole in one end of a clam
shell until the knot rests inside shell.
Add a drop of glue to secure. When dry,
use the chain-nose pliers to close and
secure clam clasp.
3. Thread the needle through every
other loop on the silver chain, drawing
up the loops close to each other.
4. Thread remaining clam clasp onto
wire. Tie a knot as close as possible to
chain, making bracelet about 7 in. long
or desired length. Add a drop of glue
to secure. When dry, use chain-nose
pliers to close and secure clam clasp.
5. Insert a head pin in a bead. Attach
the bead to chain where desired, using
round-nose pliers to make a loop close
to the top of the bead. Trim excess.
Repeat to add remaining beads.
6. Attach the toggle clasps to the clam
clasps at the opposite ends of bracelet.

DIY Gift Wrap

Give Christmas gifts a charming handmade touch with your own wrap made with kraft paper and paint. Have fun using a variety of household items as stamps.

FINISHED SIZE
Varies.

MATERIALS
Kraft paper roll
Items to be used for stamping (see Note)—cushioning wrap, corrugated cardboard, a pencil eraser, a wine bottle cork, rubber bands and a small wood block
Craft paints of choice
Paint palette or cardboard
Foam pouncers
Large and small craft knives
Cutting mat

NOTE
Many ordinary household items may be used as stamps for this project. Feel free to experiment with any on-hand items you like. Practice stamping on scrap paper or cardboard to master the technique before stamping on kraft paper.

DIRECTIONS
STAMPS
1. For Christmas trees, use the large craft knife to cut triangles of varying sizes from corrugated cardboard.
2. For snowflakes, use the small craft knife to cut 4 small triangles from the top of wine cork, evenly spacing them around cork to create a snowflake shape on top of cork.
3. For a graphic line design, wrap the small wood block with desired number of rubber bands.

GIFT WRAP
1. Spread craft paint of desired color on palette or piece of cardboard.
2. Using foam pouncer, apply paint to the desired stamp, being careful to coat only the raised areas of the design with paint.
3. Firmly press stamp onto the kraft paper and lift. Continue stamping to cover the desired amount of paper roll.
4. Let wrapping paper dry completely before using.

Ruffle Apron

Fashion this adorable apron using a simple pattern, standard sewing supplies and a colorful combination of fabrics.

FINISHED SIZE

Apron measures about 29 in. from top of bodice to bottom of skirt.

MATERIALS

Pattern on page 214
44-in.-wide fabric—¾ yd. of fabric A
  (for the bodice and pocket), ¾ yd.
  of fabric B (for the skirt) and 1 yd.
  of fabric C (for the straps)
2- or 2½-in. button
Coordinating all-purpose thread
Disappearing fabric marker
Standard sewing supplies

NOTE

All seams are ¼ in. unless the directions state otherwise.

DIRECTIONS

1. Wash, dry and press all fabrics.
2. From fabric A, cut bodice using enlarged bodice pattern.
3. From fabric A, cut a 7x6-in. rectangle for pocket.
4. From fabric B, cut an 18-in. square for skirt.
5. From fabric C, cut two 43x6½-in. strips for waist ties, one 30x6-in. strip for shoulder strap, one 18x4-in. strip for waistband and three 18x5-in. strips for ruffle.
6. Fold the shoulder strap in half lengthwise, right sides together. Press. Fold again lengthwise to mark center with a dot at the crease on a short raw edge. Open back up to single fold. Draw a line across the strip 2 in. from center point; mark a dot on the line at raw edge and at folded edge.
7. Beginning at the unmarked edge and leaving short edge open, sew long raw edges together. Pivot at first dot, sew on the angle to center dot, pivot again and sew on the angle to third dot (at folded edge).
8. Trim the fabric to ¼ in. from the seam. Turn right side out. Fold the raw edges inside ¼ in. Press. Slipstitch the pressed edges together. Press entire shoulder strap.

9. Sew 2 waist ties in the same way as shoulder strap.
10. Attach ruffle strips together using French seams as follows: Bring 2 ruffle strips wrong sides together and sew along a short raw edge. Trim to ⅛ in. from seam. Fold at seam, right sides together, and sew along the short edge again, encasing the first seam. Open and press the seam to one side. Attach third ruffle strip in same way to make one long strip. See Figs. 1-3 below.
11. Sew a double ¼-in. seam on a long edge of the ruffle.
12. Set machine to longest stitch. Leave a long tail of thread. Slowly stitch long raw edge of ruffle. Do not backstitch. When complete, leave a long thread tail at the end. Do not backstitch.
13. Lay the ruffle flat and mark center. Gently tug raw-edge thread at one end, gathering up fabric as you go. At center, turn the piece and tug the thread from the other side. Keep tugging the thread and gathering the fabric until the ruffle measures 18 in. Even out the gathers if needed.

14. Pin the raw gathered edge of ruffle to a raw edge of the skirt, wrong sides together. Sew together with a French seam the same as before.
15. Sew double ¼-in. seams along skirt sides and along sides and top of bodice.
16. Pin the bottom edge of the bodice to the top edge of the waistband, wrong sides together. Sew together with a French seam.
17. Pin top edge of skirt to bottom edge of waistband, wrong sides together. Sew together with a French seam.
18. Sew each straight edge of waist ties to apron sides at waistband.
19. Sew straight edge of shoulder strap to top right corner of bodice.
20. Make a buttonhole near the tip of the shoulder strap. Sew button to top left corner of bodice.
21. Sew a double ¼-in. seam along a short edge of pocket. Press under a ¼-in. seam on remaining 3 sides. Pin pocket to the desired position on skirt, with double-seamed edge at top. Sew pocket to skirt at sides and bottom, leaving top edge open. Press.

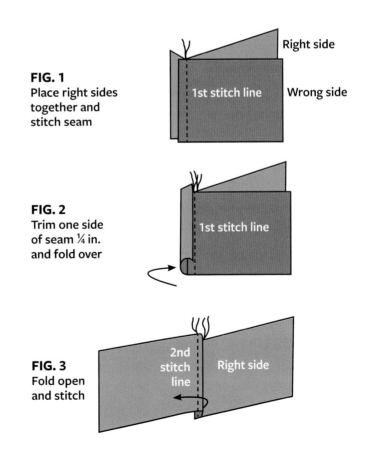

FIG. 1
Place right sides together and stitch seam

Right side
1st stitch line
Wrong side

FIG. 2
Trim one side of seam ¼ in. and fold over

1st stitch line

FIG. 3
Fold open and stitch

2nd stitch line
Right side

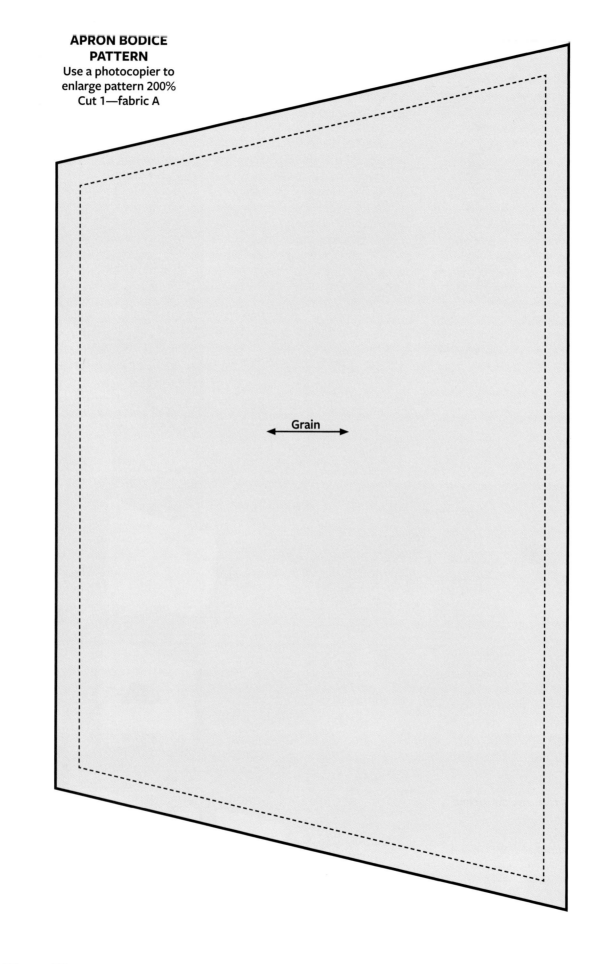

**APRON BODICE
PATTERN**
Use a photocopier to
enlarge pattern 200%
Cut 1—fabric A

Grain

Button Tree Tags

Here's a smart use for scraps! Gather extra card stock, cardboard, buttons and other supplies for DIY gift tags. If you don't have the exact items this project calls for, improvise with what's on hand.

FINISHED SIZE
Varies.

MATERIALS
Burlap-covered card stock (see Note)
Thin cardboard
Assorted round buttons
Assorted star-shaped buttons
Jute twine
Glue gun
Craft knife
Self-healing cutting mat

NOTE
If you don't have burlap card stock, substitute fabric or scrapbook paper instead.

DIRECTIONS
1. For each gift tag, cut 1 matching triangle from each of cardboard and burlap card stock, creating triangles that have 2 long sides of equal length and 1 side that measures half the length of a long side. Glue 1 card stock triangle to each cardboard triangle with edges matching.
2. Glue round buttons to each card stock triangle as desired to resemble Christmas tree ornaments.
3. For each tag, cut a 6-in. piece of jute twine. Thread each piece through a star-shaped button so that the button is in the center of the twine. Glue a threaded star-shaped button to the top of each tree. Let dry.
4. Write message on back of each tag and tie to package.

Birdseed Outdoor Ornaments

Whether you plan to surprise a bird enthusiast or you want to attract more birds to your own backyard, wing it with these simple birdseed cakes. Don't have heart-shaped cookie cutters? Substitute any simple shapes you like.

FINISHED SIZE
Varies.

MATERIALS
Twine, string or ribbon
Unflavored gelatin powder (such as Knox)
Birdseed
Waxed paper
Heart-shaped cookie cutters
Baking sheet (optional)

DIRECTIONS
1. For each cake, cut a 12- or 18-in. length of twine, string or ribbon. Loop and tie the ends in a knot. Set aside.
2. Mix ½ oz. unflavored gelatin (2 packages of Knox) with ½ cup boiling water. Stir well to dissolve gelatin completely.
3. Add about 1½ cups birdseed to gelatin solution. Mix well. If mixture is still watery, add more birdseed until it has a stiff but sticky consistency.
4. Line baking sheet or countertop with waxed paper. Place cookie cutters 1 in. apart on paper.
5. Fill each cookie cutter half full of birdseed mixture. Place knotted end of hanging loop on top center of mixture. Fill cookie cutter with more birdseed mixture on top of loop. Firmly press mixture with back of spoon to pack in place.
6. After several hours, gently unmold each cake onto fresh waxed paper. Let dry, flipping periodically, for 72 hours or until completely hardened. Hang as desired.

Canning Lid Coasters

Transform ordinary canning lids and bands into decorative coasters for the Christmas season or all winter long. Your family and friends will find them both fun and functional.

FINISHED SIZE
Each coaster measures about 3½ in. across.

MATERIALS
Wide-mouth canning band and lid for each coaster
Red spray paint
Cork disk for each coaster
Reindeer stamp or seasonal stamp and permanent ink of choice
Super glue
Craft knife

DIRECTIONS
1. Paint the wide-mouth canning bands and lids with red spray paint. Let dry.
2. Use a lid to trace a circle onto a cork disk for each coaster. Cut out cork circles.
3. Stamp each cork circle with permanent ink, centering the stamped design on the circle. Let dry.
4. Glue each lid to a band. Glue cork with stamped side up to each lid inside band, pressing firmly so cork stays flat. Let dry.

Solid Perfume Lockets

Whether your gift recipient is a preteen or adult, she's sure to love this delightfully secret but convenient cache of perfume. The lightly floral scent will appeal to just about everyone. Try searching thrift shops for unusual vintage lockets.

FINISHED SIZE
Varies.

MATERIALS (FOR FOUR)
4 lockets (see Note)
10 drops bergamot essential oil
10 drops jasmine essential oil
½ tablespoon sweet almond oil
½ tablespoon beeswax pellets
Small microwave-safe bowl
Dropper

NOTE
Make sure each locket has a shallow indentation inside that will hold the solid perfume.

DIRECTIONS (FOR FOUR)
1. Combine the beeswax and sweet almond oil in the bowl and microwave for about 2 minutes or until melted.
2. Add essential oils, swirl gently and microwave for another 20 seconds. Using dropper, immediately fill the bottom half of each locket.
3. If the wax begins to harden, melt it again in microwave, then continue filling lockets. When lockets are filled, let wax harden completely.

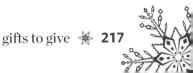

Japanese Four-Hole Bound Books

A traditional Japanese binding technique is the secret behind these beautiful books. You're likely to have many of the materials this project calls for on hand.

FINISHED SIZE
Each book measures 8½ in. long x 5½ in. wide.

MATERIALS (FOR ONE)
10 sheets of plain standard-size copy paper, cut in half crosswise
2 sheets of 5½x8½-in. decorative paper for covers
Waxed linen thread, embroidery floss or twine
Binder clip
Large-eye long needle (such as a sail needle or upholsterer's pin)
Thumbtack or awl
Craft knife
Self-healing cutting mat

NOTE
When sewing, keep the thread taut and neat around the spine.

DIRECTIONS (FOR ONE)
MAKING PAGES
1. Set aside 1 piece of copy paper to use for template.
2. Lay 1 decorative sheet of paper, right side down, on work surface. Stack the remaining copy paper pages on top. Place remaining decorative sheet, right side up, on top of stack.
3. On template paper, draw a line 1 in. from a short edge. Fold template in half lengthwise 3 times and unfold.
4. Draw dots along the line at the intersections of the first, third, fifth and seventh creases. With the template right side up and the dots on the left, label the dots 1, 2, 3 and 4, starting from the bottom.
5. Place template on top of the stack. Hold everything together with a binder clip opposite the dotted side.
6. On cutting mat, press a thumbtack or awl through each dot. Flip book and press again through the holes to widen. With book stack right side up, use a pencil to lightly label the holes 1, 2, 3 and 4 the same as for the template.

SEWING SPINE
1. Cut a length of thread measuring about 33 in. and thread the needle.
2. With stacked paper right side up, bring needle up from the back of book through hole 2, leaving a 2- to 3-in. tail at back. Wrap thread around spine and bring thread up through hole 2.
3. Bring thread through hole 1. Wrap thread around spine and bring back through hole 1. Wrap around book base and bring back down through hole 1.
4. Bring thread up through hole 2 and back down through hole 3.

5. Bring thread up through hole 4. Wrap thread around spine and bring back up through hole 4. Wrap thread around head of book and bring back up through hole 4.
6. Bring thread through hole 3. Wrap thread around spine and bring back down through hole 3.
7. Bring thread up through hole 2. On front, loop thread around cross-stitch between holes 1 and 2.
8. Bring thread down through hole 2. Cut thread; tie ends with a double knot at back of book near hole 2. Trim ends.

Pincushion & Notions Jar

Want to treat an avid seamstress? A little fabric and stuffing on the lid of an ordinary mason jar create a soft spot for pins, while the clear container underneath provides storage for small notions.

FINISHED SIZE
Varies.

MATERIALS
Canning jar with screw band and sealer lid
Cardboard
Compass
Fabric scrap
Polyester stuffing
Glue gun
Ribbon (optional)

DIRECTIONS
1. Trace the lid of canning jar onto cardboard. Cut out circle and set aside.
2. Using the compass and drawing on the wrong side of the fabric, draw a circle with a diameter that is 2 in. longer than the lid diameter. Cut out fabric circle and set aside.
3. Form a handful of stuffing into a ball. Center it between the cardboard circle and the wrong side of fabric circle. Push fabric through the band until cardboard edge touches the interior band rim and fabric is tightly stretched over stuffing.
4. Fold the excess fabric over cardboard edge and adhere to cardboard with glue gun.
5. Glue top of sealer lid to cardboard and fabric back. Push firmly in place until glue dries.
6. Glue ribbon to outer edge of band if desired. Let dry.

Santa Hat Card

Cap off your holiday mail with this well-suited greeting from Sandy Rollinger, of Apollo, Pennsylvania. She used simple shapes and cute details to make a quick but cheery Christmas card.

FINISHED SIZE
Card measures 7 in. wide x 5 in. high.

MATERIALS
5x7-in. blank white card with envelope
Scraps of card stock—red, green, dark green, white and gold
5x7-in. rectangle of holiday patterned paper
1¼-in. holly leaf paper punch
Miniature white pompom
5-7mm red rhinestone
Tacky craft glue
Paper trimmer (optional)

DIRECTIONS
1. With edges matching, glue holiday patterned paper on front of card.
2. Cut a 5x2-in. strip of gold card stock. Glue strip vertically on front of card so that the left-hand edge of strip is about 1 in. from left-hand edge of card.
3. Cut a 5x1½-in. strip of green card stock. Glue green strip centered on gold strip.
4. From red card stock, cut a 3½-in.-high x 1-in.-wide triangle for hat. Glue centered on green strip.
5. From white card stock, cut a 1¾x½-in. strip for hat brim. Glue centered along bottom of hat.
6. Punch 3 holly leaves from the dark green card stock. If desired, trim leaves to create different sizes. Glue leaves to top left-hand side of hat brim so that the leaves overlap onto hat and background.
7. Glue red rhinestone to the center of leaves for the berry. Glue white pompom to top of hat. Let dry.

Block-Printed Cards

How charming—a handwritten note on a handmade card. Use the technique of block printing and have fun experimenting.

FINISHED SIZE
Varies.

MATERIALS
Tracing paper
Card stock or decorative paper and envelopes
Block printing ink (water soluble)
Linoleum or other printing block (such as Soft-Kut or Speedy-Carve)
Linoleum cutting tools in various sizes
Rigid plastic sheet for rolling surface
Palette knife
Brayer (rolling tool)
Block printing baren (optional)

NOTE
If your craft store does not carry all the supplies for this project, look for them at art supply stores.

DIRECTIONS
CARVING BLOCK
1. Draw a simple design freehand or choose a shape from a child's book or other source. Using a soft pencil, trace desired design onto tracing paper. Lay traced design face down onto printing block. Transfer design by rubbing the back of paper with a spoon, making sure image doesn't shift.
2. Decide where you want ink to show in the print (carved areas will not hold ink). Carve out the desired areas using linoleum cutting tools, carving away from you for safety.
3. When carved design is complete, use cutting tool with a large blade to cut the outer edge from block. Clear shavings. If needed, run block under lukewarm water and pat dry.
4. Place a dollop of ink on plastic sheet and even out ink with palette knife. With light pressure, use brayer to roll the ink in several directions. When ink resembles the texture of an orange peel, roll the brayer in a single direction to coat the roller.
5. With block design face up on your work surface, roll inked brayer in one direction over block to cover the design evenly.

PRINTING CARDS
1. If the block is large or the carved design is intricate, keep the block ink side up on work surface, lay a piece of test paper or card stock on top of block and use the baren to exert even pressure on the paper for a uniform impression. If the block is small and looks more like a stamp, firmly press the block ink side down onto test paper or card stock, being careful not to shift the block.
2. Inspect the test design. If needed, carve out additional areas on block or add more ink, then test again.
3. When satisfied with design, block-print desired paper or card stock. Let dry. Fold paper or card stock to form cards.

Gold Reindeer Trim

A plain plastic reindeer from a craft store, toy shop or discount store becomes an elegant holiday accent when you add gold paint and a few other items. Hang this decoration from a wine bottle as a hostess gift or stuff it into a stocking. You may want to make extras to hang on your own Christmas tree!

FINISHED SIZE
Varies.

MATERIALS
Small plastic reindeer
Gold spray paint
18-gauge aluminum wire
Ribbon of choice for hanging
Glue gun
Wire cutters
Round-nose pliers

DIRECTIONS
1. Cut a 1½-in. length of 18-gauge aluminum wire. Bend the wire piece into a loop with pliers.
2. Using the glue gun, glue the wire loop to the middle of the reindeer's back.
3. When glue is dry, paint entire reindeer with gold spray paint and let dry.
4. Thread ribbon through wire loop on reindeer. Knot ends of ribbon to create a loop for hanging. Hang reindeer on tree or attach to a gift box.

Faux Mosaic Box

Fooling the eye with easy-to-make crafts that appear complicated is one of Loretta Mateik's specialties. In Petaluma, California, she embellished a plain papier-mache gift box—available in craft stores—with beads to resemble a mosaic. Place a Christmas present inside, and your recipient can save the container to use as a decoration.

FINISHED SIZE

Gift box shown measures about 4¼ in. across x 2½ in. high.

MATERIALS

Round papier-mache box with lid (Loretta used a papier-mache box measuring 4¼ in. across x 2 in. high including the lid)
Twenty-one 6mm square green glass beads for tree design
Three 8mm round brown glass beads for trunk design
Palette or foam plate
Acrylic craft paints—holly green and white
Paintbrushes—large flat and liner
Textured snow medium
Small palette knife or plastic knife
Tissue paper of choice (optional)

DIRECTIONS
GENERAL DIRECTIONS

Keep paper towels and a container of water handy to clean paintbrushes. Place dabs of each color of paint on palette or foam plate as needed. Add coats of paint as needed for complete coverage. Let paint dry after every application. Refer to the photo above as a guide while painting as directed in the instructions that follow.

PAINTING

1. Use the flat brush and holly green to paint the outer side edges of the lid and the outside of entire box bottom.
2. Use palette or plastic knife to apply a thick layer of textured snow medium to top of lid. While snow medium is still wet and with the holes of beads facing up, press the green beads into snow medium to form a triangular shape for the tree. With the holes facing to the side, press brown beads below the tree for trunk. Use the knife to shape the snow around beads as desired. Let dry.
3. Use the liner and white to paint spiral shapes on sides of box bottom.
4. Dip the end of a paintbrush handle into white and add a dot to the side of box bottom. Repeat to add dots around bottom. Let box dry completely. Line with tissue paper if desired.

Chunky Basket Weave Cowl

Cozy up in chilly winter weather with this fashionable knit cowl from Melina Martin Gingras, of Milwaukee, Wisconsin.

FINISHED SIZE
Knit cowl measures about 6 in. wide x 30 in. around.

MATERIALS
2 skeins Bernat Alpaca (each 70% acrylic, 30% alpaca; 120 yd.; 3.5 oz./100 g) or similar bulky-weight yarn
One 29-in. US 11 circular needle (or size needed to obtain correct gauge)
Stitch marker
Tapestry needle

GAUGE
Working in stockinette stitch, 3.75 sts = 1 in.

DIRECTIONS
1. Cast on 114 sts. Place stitch marker and join in rnd, being careful not to twist sts.
2. Rnd 1: k.
3. Rnd 2: p.
4. Rnd 3: k.
5. Rnd 4: p.
6. Rnds 5-6: k.
7. Rnds 7-10: *p4, k2; rep from * to end of rnd.
8. Rnds 11-12: k.
9. Rnds 13-16: p1, *k2, p4; rep from * to last 5 sts, k2, p3.
10. Rnds 17-28: Work rnds 5-16.
11. Rnds 29-36: Work rnds 5-12.
12. Finishing: Work rnds 2-4. Bind off loosely in k.
13. Weave in all ends with tapestry needle. Lightly steam to block.

ABBREVIATIONS

k	knit
p	purl
rep	repeat
rnd(s)	round(s)
st(s)	stitch(es)
*	repeat from this symbol

Stamped Metal Pet Tag

From Wilmington, Delaware, designer Shannon Bushong shares her idea for creating some seriously cute pet tags.

FINISHED SIZE
Stamped tag measures about 1½ in. across.

MATERIALS
Blank metal circular tag, about 1½ in. across (sterling silver, aluminum, stainless steel or copper)
Metal letter stamps
Flat-headed hammer for stamping metal
Metal or steel bench block
Extra fine-tip black marker
Fine sandpaper
Metal hole punch
Beads and metal charms of choice
Metal head pins (for beads and charms)
Masking tape
Wire cutters
Long-nose pliers
Small key ring

DIRECTIONS
1. Place the metal tag on bench block and secure in place with masking tape.
2. Lightly mark where you will stamp each letter of the name on the metal tag, starting with the center letter and working to the left and right so that the name will be centered.
3. Place metal stamp so that the head of the stamp is completely flush with the metal tag. Strike the stamp once with the hammer. Repeat if needed, making sure not to move the stamp from its original position. Continue stamping all letters.
4. Using the black marker, color in the impressions of all stamped letters on the metal tag.
5. Using fine sandpaper, gently sand the tag to give it a polished look.
6. Punch a hole in the tag and attach tag to key ring.
7. Place desired beads or charms on a head pin. Use wire cutters to cut off any excess length of head pin. With pliers, curve remaining end of head pin and attach securely to the key ring.
8. If desired, add additional beads or charms to head pins and attach to the key ring the same as before. Attach key ring to metal ring on pet collar.

Catnip Mouse Toy

Furry felines (and their owners) will think this toy is the cat's meow! Choose colorful fabrics for extra fun. No sewing machine is needed—simple hand-stitching will do.

FINISHED SIZE

Excluding tail, mouse toy measures about 3½ in. long x 2½ in. high.

MATERIALS (FOR ONE)

4¼-in. circle of fabric
Coordinating felt for ears
Coordinating all-purpose thread
5-in. length of jute twine
Black six-strand embroidery floss
Dried catnip
Hand-sewing needle
Embroidery needle

DIRECTIONS (FOR ONE)

1. Fold the fabric circle in half, right sides together.

2. Sew along the raw edge of fabric, using a ¼-in. seam allowance and leaving a 1½-in. opening at one end.

3. Turn fabric body right side out. Fill with catnip.

4. Insert ½ in. of twine piece into the opening, leaving a 4½-in. tail. Fold in fabric edges and sew opening closed. Sew through twine 3-4 times to secure.

5. Separate strands of floss and cut six 4-in. strands. Thread embroidery needle and run floss through the tip of mouse's head for whiskers. Knot floss on either side of head. Separate strands and trim to desired length.

6. Thread embroidery needle with 2 strands of floss. On each side of head, backstitch several times about ½ in. above the whiskers to form the eyes.

7. To make ears, cut 2 felt half-ovals measuring ½ in. across the straight edge and 1 in. at highest point of curve. Pinch each ear at the center of straight edge and sew to the top of body about 1 in. behind the eyes.

Beaded Snowflakes

Just like Mother Nature herself, you can easily create beautiful one-of-a-kind snowflakes. Simply string coordinating small beads onto premade wire forms available at craft and bead stores. Once you start, it's hard to stop!

FINISHED SIZE
Excluding hanging loop, each beaded snowflake measures about 4½ in. across.

MATERIALS (FOR ONE)
Snowflake ornament wire form (such as a 4½-in. Beadsmith form)
Assorted beads in various colors and sizes of your choice
Wire cutters
Needle-nose pliers or jewelry glue
6-in. length of monofilament thread

DIRECTIONS (FOR ONE)
1. On your work surface, arrange beads in pattern desired for snowflake, positioning smaller beads at the center. When pleased with the arrangement, slip desired beads for one spoke on a spoke of the wire snowflake form.
2. Either glue the last bead onto the beaded wire spoke and let it dry, or leave a small section of unbeaded wire at the end of the beaded spoke and use the needle-nose pliers to make a very small loop at the end of the wire to secure the beads in place. See Fig. 1 below.
3. Use wire cutters to trim away any excess wire at the end of the beaded spoke.
4. Add the desired beads to the remaining wire spokes of snowflake form in the same way.
5. Insert one end of monofilament thread through the wire loop or bead at the end of one spoke.
6. Tie monofilament thread to desired gift for a package trim or tie the ends of thread together to form a loop for hanging on a tree.

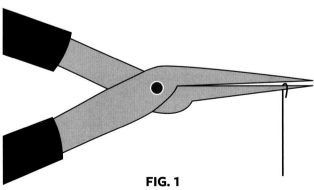

FIG. 1
Looping ends of wire

Solid Lotion Bars

With the calming scent of lavender, these luxurious moisturizing soaps are perfect additions to spa baskets. Follow the directions here to make about ten 1½-oz. lotion bars.

FINISHED SIZE
Varies.

MATERIALS
2 oz. shea butter
2 oz. cocoa butter
4 oz. grape seed oil
4 oz. beeswax
2 Tbsp. lavender essential oil or other essential oil (optional)
Microwave-safe bowl
Double boiler
Flexible silicone molds
Resealable plastic bags or lidded containers of choice

DIRECTIONS
1. Combine butters and grape seed oil in bowl. Microwave, stirring every 30 seconds, until completely liquefied.
2. In a double boiler on the stovetop, melt beeswax over low heat. Stir continually until completely liquefied.
3. Combine melted ingredients; add essential oil if desired and stir thoroughly. Pour into molds. Let harden for 2 hours or until cool and solid.
4. Remove from the molds. Store bars in lidded containers or resealable bags away from moisture.

Raw Sugar Scrub

Exfoliate and moisturize dry winter skin with this gentle treatment. For gifts, place the soothing sugar scrub into small lidded glass jars and tie a spoon to each with pretty ribbon.

FINISHED SIZE
Directions yield about 20 oz. of sugar scrub.

MATERIALS
½ cup coconut oil
2½ cups raw washed sugar
2 Tbsp. grape seed oil
20–30 drops lavender essential oil or other essential oil (optional)
Microwave-safe bowl
Lidded glass jars or other lidded containers of choice

DIRECTIONS
1. Microwave coconut oil in bowl, stirring every 30 seconds until completely liquefied.
2. Add the sugar, grape seed oil and, if desired, lavender essential oil to the melted coconut oil. Stir thoroughly (mixture will have a coarse, sticky texture).
3. Place sugar scrub into lidded glass jars or desired lidded containers. Shake scrub gently before each use. Store away from moisture.

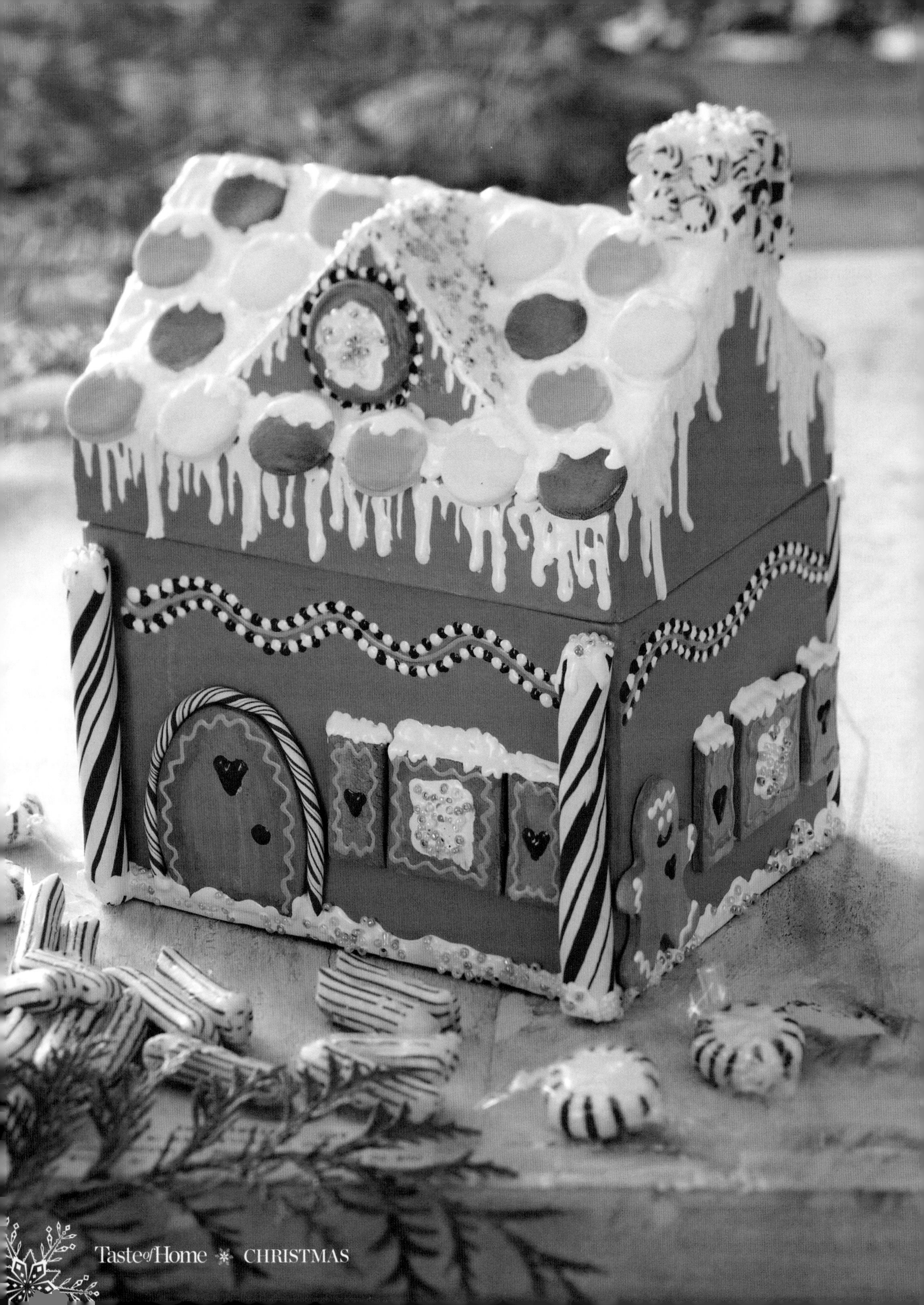

Gingerbread House Recipe Box

Love gingerbread houses? Why stop at the kind that's edible? Here's a creative and useful variation designed by Sandy Rollinger, of Apollo, Pennsylvania. Tuck a bundle of your favorite holiday recipe cards inside the box before giving it to the cook on your Christmas list.

FINISHED SIZE

Box measures about 7½ in. high x 5¾ in. wide x 3¾ in. deep.

MATERIALS

7½-in.-high x 5¾-in.-wide x 3¾-in.-deep papier-mache house-shaped box
Oven-bake polymer clay—red and white
Clay roller
Clay slicer
Plastic mat for rolling clay
Foam plate or palette
Acrylic craft paints—green, yellow, brown and pink
Paintbrushes—No. 12 shader and ¾-in. wash
Dimensional paints—two bottles of white and one bottle each of red and pink
Circle cutters—1 in. and ¾ in.
Multicolored seed beads
1½-in.-long gingerbread man cookie cutter
Foil-covered baking sheet
Craft glue
Recipe cards

DIRECTIONS

GENERAL DIRECTIONS

Keep paper towels and water handy to clean paintbrushes. Place dabs of each paint color on the foam plate or palette as needed. Add coats of paint as needed for complete coverage. Let the paint dry after every application. Refer to the photo at left as a guide while assembling house as directed in the instructions that follow.

CLAY

1. Condition each color of polymer clay and roll each to a ⅛-in. thickness on plastic mat.
2. From the white polymer clay, cut 32 circles using ¾-in. circle cutter for the shingles on the roof. Use 1-in. circle cutter to cut a circle for the dormer window and use the cookie cutter to cut 2 gingerbread men.
3. Also from white polymer clay, cut a 2-in.-high x 1½-in.-wide rounded door and cut eight 1-in. squares. Cut four of the squares in half for shutters, leaving four squares for windows.
4. Roll a ½-in.-thick x 5-in.-long log of white clay. Roll a same-size log of red clay and place the two logs side by side. Twist and roll them together to form a spiral pattern that resembles a peppermint stick. Continue to roll log to a ½-in. thickness. Cut log in half crosswise. Trim each piece as needed to fit against the front corners of house.
5. Repeat to make 2 more peppermint sticks for the back corners of house.
6. Roll a ½-in.-thick x 3-in.-long log of white clay. Roll a same-size log of red clay and place the logs side by side. Twist and roll them together to form a spiral pattern as before. Continue to roll the log to a ¼-in. thickness. Use clay slicer to cut thirty ¼-in.-thick disks for peppermint candies on the sides of the chimney.
7. Roll the remaining portion of log to make a ⅛-in.-thick log. Cut one piece to form trim around door.
8. Place all clay shapes on foil-lined baking sheet. Shape the door trim to fit around the door, but do not let the trim touch the edges of the door. Bake clay shapes at 275° for about 30 minutes. Let the clay shapes cool in the oven before removing.

PAINTING

1. Remove lid from house box. Use wash brush and brown to paint entire outside of box and lid.
2. Use shader and brown to paint the clay gingerbread men, door, windows, and shutters.
3. For the shingles, use the shader to paint 12 of the ¾-in. clay circles green, 10 circles yellow and 10 circles pink.
4. Use pencil to draw a wavy line around the house about 1 in. down from top. Use pink dimensional paint to paint over the line.
5. Use red and white dimensional paints to add dots in alternating colors along both sides of pink line.

6. Glue door, windows, shutters, peppermint stick corner pieces and gingerbread men to house.
7. Glue the painted shingles to the top of the roof, leaving about ¼ in. between shingles.
8. Glue the peppermint candy pieces to the sides of chimney, leaving a small space between pieces. Let dry.
9. Use pink dimensional paint to add wavy lines around the door, windows and shutters.
10. Use red dimensional paint to add a mouth and heart to each gingerbread man. Add a small heart to each shutter and the door. Add a small dot to door for doorknob.
11. Use white dimensional paint to add 2 tiny dots to each gingerbread man for eyes. Add wavy lines to the arms, legs and head.
12. Use white dimensional paint to cover the roof of the dormer. While paint is still wet, sprinkle roof of dormer with seed beads.
13. Add white dimensional paint to the center of each window and sprinkle on beads as before. In the same way, add white dimensional paint and beads to the bottom edge of house, to the top of chimney and to the tops of peppermint sticks at corners.
14. Add white dimensional paint to the tops of all windows and shutters. Add white dimensional paint to the spaces between the roof shingles and between the peppermint candies on chimney.
15. Add alternating dots of red and white dimensional paint around the window on the dormer.
16. Use white dimensional paint to add icicles to the edges of roof and dormer. Let dry. Fill box with recipe cards.

General Recipe Index

This index lists every recipe in the book by food category, major ingredient and/or cooking method, so you can easily locate recipes to suit your needs.

APPETIZERS & SNACKS

COLD APPETIZERS
Avocado Goat Cheese Truffles, 14
Bacon, Cheddar and Swiss
    Cheese Ball, 11
Brie Appetizers with Bacon-Plum
    Jam, 17
Buffalo Chicken Cheese Ball, 7
Maryland Deviled Eggs, 12
Pacific Northwest Pickled
    Shrimp, 15
Veggie Ranch Tortilla Pinwheels, 96

DIPS
Bacon-Ranch Spinach Dip, 15
Baked Onion Cheese Dip, 106
Broccoli-Carrot Vegetable Dip, 12
Cranberry Salsa with Cream
    Cheese, 18
Creamy Hazelnut Dip, 106
Seven-Layer Mediterranean Dip, 17
Tomato-Bacon Dip with
    Focaccia, 55
Turkey Nacho Dip, 177
Zesty Pepperoni Dip, 10

HOT APPETIZERS
After-Christmas Empanadas, 163
Candied Bacon-Wrapped Figs, 92
Cocktail Mushroom Meatballs, 10
Crab Crescent Triangles, 6
Cranberry Bacon Galette, 12

Holiday Chicken and Sausage
    Wreath, 8
Reuben Rounds, 20
Seasoned Spinach Balls, 20
Shrimp-Stuffed Mushrooms, 9
Sweet Potato Tartlets, 102
Teriyaki Salmon Bundles, 19
Thanksgiving Wontons, 165
Turkey Croquettes with Cranberry
    Salsa, 172
Tuscan Chicken Tenders with Pesto
    Sauce, 13

SNACKS
Buffalo Wing Munch Mix, 156
Chili Spiced Pecans, 149
Cranberry-Nut Granola, 159
Homemade Crisp Crackers, 159
Roasted Cheddar Herb
    Almonds, 7
Sweet & Salty Popcorn, 149

SPREADS
Brandied Blue Cheese
    Spread, 18
Cherry Cheese Logs, 86
Cinnamon-Sugar Spread, 37
Peanut Butter Spread, 151

APPLES
Apple Crumb Tart with Cinnamon
    Cream, 68
Apple-Pecan Gingerbread
    Cobbler, 67
Apple-Topped Ham Steak, 101
Browned Butter Apple Pie with
    Cheddar Crust, 131
Butternut Apple Casserole, 63
Crisp Waldorf Salad, 98
Puffed Apple Pastries, 103
Roasted Apple Salad with Spicy
    Maple-Cider Vinaigrette, 48
Tangy Apple-Ginger Chutney, 50

BACON
Bacon & Eggs Pizza, 22
Bacon, Cheddar and Swiss Cheese
    Ball, 11

Bacon-Ranch Spinach Dip, 15
Bacon Swiss Squares, 109
Brie Appetizers with Bacon-Plum
    Jam, 17
Candied Bacon-Wrapped Figs, 92
Cranberry Bacon Galette, 12
Favorite Loaded Breakfast
    Potatoes, 23
Holiday Hot Browns, 115
Pecan Bacon, 28
Potato Bacon Chowder, 105
Shirred Egg Corn Muffins, 27
Tomato-Bacon Dip with Focaccia, 55

BANANAS
Bananas Foster French Toast, 38
Cranberry-Banana Smoothies, 16

BEANS
Greens and Beans Turkey
    Soup, 171
Hungarian-Style Green Beans, 53
Microwave Corn 'n' Bean Bake, 96

BEEF & CORNED BEEF
(also see Ground Beef)
Beef Tenderloin with Mushroom
    Sauce, 97
Beef Tenderloin with Sauteed
    Vegetables, 91
Meat Lover's Bread Salad, 173
Prime Rib with Fresh Herb
    Sauce, 59
Reuben Rounds, 20

BEVERAGES
Blueberry Lime Slush, 24
Caramel-Chai Tea Latte, 83
Comforting Coffee Milk, 79
Cranberry-Banana Smoothies, 163
Cranberry Orange Mimosas, 37
Cranberry-Orange Sangria, 106
Festive Holiday Punch, 88
Frothy Cafe Bombon, 80
Hot Apple Pie Sipper, 105
Mint Cocoa Mix, 153
Sparkling Celebration Punch, 44
Tiny Bubbles, 36
Winter Herb Tea Mix, 150

BISCUITS & SCONES
Cranberry-Gingerbread Scones, 71
Cranberry Scones with Orange
    Butter, 35
Feather-Light Biscuits, 111
Monkey Bread Biscuits, 87

p. 7

p. 25

BREAD PUDDING
Eggnog Bread Pudding with
  Cranberries, 178
White Chocolate Macadamia Bread
  Pudding, 146

BREADS
(also see Biscuits & Scones;
  Coffee Cakes; Corn Bread &
  Cornmeal; Rolls & Muffins)
Pumpkin Bread with Gingerbread
  Topping, 76
Roasted Butternut Squash
  Bread, 32

BREAKFAST & BRUNCH
Bacon & Eggs Pizza, 22
Bacon Swiss Squares, 109
Baked Egg & Stuffing Cups, 171
Bananas Foster French Toast, 38
Brunch Puff with Sausage Gravy, 36
Caramel-Pecan Pumpkin
  Pull-Aparts, 25
Carolina Shrimp & Cheddar
  Grits, 34
Chocolate Chunk Pancakes with
  Raspberry Sauce, 32
Cinnamon-Sugar Spread, 37
Coconut Granola Parfaits, 35
Cranberry Scones with Orange
  Butter, 35
Favorite Loaded Breakfast
  Potatoes, 23
Gingerbread Belgian Waffles, 75
Hot Spiced Fruit, 24
Monte Cristo Casserole with
  Raspberry Sauce, 177
Orange Ricotta Pancakes, 110
Pecan Bacon, 28
Pineapple Upside-Down Muffins, 31

Pumpkin Crepes with Mascarpone
  Custard, 27
Pumpkin Spice Overnight
  Oatmeal, 30
Raspberry-Almond Coffee Cake, 83
Roasted Butternut Squash Bread, 32
Sausage Mac & Cheese in a
  Pumpkin, 29
Sweet Potato & Andouille Hash, 34
Sweet Potato Dumplings with
  Caramel Sauce, 176
Walnut Butter Spread, 28
Western Omelet Casserole, 23

BROCCOLI
Broccoli-Carrot Vegetable Dip, 12
Roasted Broccoli & Cauliflower, 41

BUTTERNUT SQUASH
Butternut Apple Casserole, 63
Cream of Butternut Squash Soup, 47
Roasted Butternut Squash Bread, 32

CABBAGE & SAUERKRAUT
Creamy Mashed Potatoes with
  Cabbage, 60
Reuben Rounds, 20

CAKES & CUPCAKES
Carrot-Cranberry Spice Cake, 167
Cherrimisu, 138
Chocolate & Peppermint Ice Cream
  Roll, 139
Chocolate Ginger Cake, 132
Chocolate Gingerbread Cupcakes, 69
Coconut-Layered Pound Cake, 99
Cranberry Eggnog Cake, 51
Festive Nut Cake, 145
Fudge-Filled Vanilla Cake, 56
Gingerbread with Lime Cream Cheese
  Icing, 74
Glazed Spiced Rum Pound Cakes, 133
Winter Spice Bundt Cake, 75

CANDIES
Beer and Pretzel Caramels, 154
Bugle Cones, 128
Cherry Mice, 114
Chocolate, Peanut & Pretzel
  Toffee Crisps, 88
Coconut Yule Trees, 125
Holly Butter Mints, 123
Homemade Candy Canes, 157
Melting Snowmen, 126
Neapolitan Fudge, 116
Peanutty Candy Bars, 158

Rudolph Treats, 126
S'mores Candy, 155
Soft Peppermint Candy, 157
Sweet & Salty Snowmen, 119

CARAMEL
Beer and Pretzel Caramels, 154
Caramel-Chai Tea Latte, 83
Caramel-Pecan Pumpkin Pull-Aparts, 25
Fudgy Turtle Pie, 79
Sweet Potato Dumplings with Caramel
  Sauce, 176

CARROTS
Broccoli-Carrot Vegetable Dip, 12
Carrot Cake Jam, 160
Carrot-Cranberry Spice Cake, 167

CASSEROLES
Bacon Swiss Squares, 109
Butternut Apple Casserole, 63
Fettuccine Shrimp Casserole, 60
Microwave Corn 'n' Bean Bake, 96
Monte Cristo Casserole with
  Raspberry Sauce, 177
Potluck Sausage Casserole, 85
Stuffing & Sausage Strata, 164

CHEESE
(also see Cheesecakes; Cream
  Cheese)
Avocado Goat Cheese Truffles, 14
Bacon, Cheddar and Swiss Cheese
  Ball, 11
Bacon Swiss Squares, 109
Baked Onion Cheese Dip, 106
Brandied Blue Cheese Spread, 18
Brie Appetizers with Bacon-Plum
  Jam, 17

p. 11

p. 94

CHEESE (continued)
Browned Butter Apple Pie with
 Cheddar Crust, 131
Buffalo Chicken Cheese Ball, 7
Carolina Shrimp & Cheddar
 Grits, 34
Homemade Crisp Crackers, 159
Monte Cristo Casserole with
 Raspberry Sauce, 177
Orange Ricotta Pancakes, 110
Parmesan-Herb Dinner Rolls, 50
Pumpkin Crepes with Mascarpone
 Custard, 27
Roasted Cheddar Herb Almonds, 7
Sausage Mac & Cheese in a
 Pumpkin, 29
Turkey Nacho Dip, 177

CHEESECAKES
Lovely Lemon Cheesecake, 94
Pumpkin Cranberry Cheesecake, 142

CHERRIES
Cherrimisu, 138
Cherry Cheese Logs, 86
Cherry Cream Cheese Dessert, 98
Cherry Mice, 114
Lime Shortbread with Dried
 Cherries, 153
Pineapple Upside-Down Muffins, 31
Quick Cherry Turnovers, 101

CHICKEN
Buffalo Chicken Cheese Ball, 7
Holiday Chicken and Sausage
 Wreath, 8
Roast Chicken with Vegetables, 53
Tuscan Chicken Tenders with Pesto
 Sauce, 13

CHOCOLATE
(also see White Chocolate)
Cherry Mice, 114
Chocolate & Peppermint Ice Cream
 Roll, 139
Chocolate Chai Snickerdoodles, 153
Chocolate Chunk Pancakes with
 Raspberry Sauce, 32
Chocolate Coconut Pie with Coconut
 Crust, 137
Chocolate Ginger Cake, 132
Chocolate-Ginger Pumpkin
 Muffins, 68
Chocolate Gingerbread Cupcakes, 69
Chocolate Lover's Mousse Torte, 143
Chocolate, Peanut & Pretzel Toffee
 Crisps, 88
Chocolate Reindeer, 115
Coconut Yule Trees, 125
Fudge-Filled Vanilla Cake, 56
Fudgy Turtle Pie, 79
Mint-Chocolate Bombe, 137
Mint Cocoa Mix, 153
Mint Creme Cookies, 81
Mocha Cookie Pretzels, 148
Neapolitan Fudge, 116
Nutella-Stuffed Strawberries, 93
Peanutty Candy Bars, 158
Rudolph Treats, 126
S'mores Candy, 155
Tangerine Chocolate Semifreddo, 140

CINNAMON
Apple Crumb Tart with Cinnamon
 Cream, 68
Cinnamon Candy Cane Cookies, 120
Cinnamon-Spiced Pumpkin Flan, 135
Cinnamon-Sugar Spread, 37

COCONUT
Chocolate Coconut Pie with Coconut
 Crust, 137
Coconut Granola Parfaits, 35
Coconut-Layered Pound Cake, 99
Coconut Yule Trees, 125
Sweetheart Coconut Cookies, 122

COFFEE
Comforting Coffee Milk, 79
Favorite Hazelnut-Mocha Torte, 130
Frothy Cafe Bombon, 80
Mocha Cookie Pretzels, 148

COFFEE CAKES
Gingerbread Coffee Cake, 66
Raspberry-Almond Coffee Cake, 83

CONDIMENTS
Carrot Cake Jam, 160
Hot Spiced Fruit, 24
Peachy Cranberry Sauce, 60
Tangy Apple-Ginger Chutney, 50
Texas-Style BBQ Sauce, 151
Turkey Croquettes with Cranberry
 Salsa, 172

COOKIES & BARS
Beary Cute Cookies, 124
Chocolate Chai Snickerdoodles, 153
Chocolate Reindeer, 115
Cinnamon Candy Cane Cookies, 120
Crisp Button Cookies, 115
Day-After-Thanksgiving Cookies, 166
Elf Cookies, 122
Ginger & Maple Macadamia Nut
 Cookies, 150
Gingerbread Cookie Bites, 72
Gingerbread Peppermint
 Pinwheels, 73
Gingerbread-Pumpkin Cheesecake
 Bars, 74
Holiday Ginger Cookies, 71
Holiday Rum Balls, 102
Lime Shortbread with Dried
 Cherries, 153
Meringue Santa Hats, 117
Mint Creme Cookies, 81
Mocha Cookie Pretzels, 148
Peppermint Candy Cookies, 116
Pinwheels and Checkerboards, 119
Santa Claus Sugar Cookies, 120
Sugar Doves, 121
Sweetheart Coconut Cookies, 122

CORN BREAD & CORNMEAL
Shirred Egg Corn Muffins, 27
Sweet & Moist Corn Bread, 54

CRANBERRIES
Carrot-Cranberry Spice Cake, 167
Cranberry & Walnut Pie, 64
Cranberry Bacon Galette, 12
Cranberry-Banana Smoothies, 163
Cranberry Eggnog Cake, 51
Cranberry Eggnog Muffins, 175
Cranberry-Gingerbread Scones, 71
Cranberry-Nut Granola, 159
Cranberry Orange Mimosas, 37
Cranberry-Orange Sangria, 106
Cranberry Salsa with Cream
 Cheese, 18
Cranberry Scones with Orange
 Butter, 35

Day-After-Thanksgiving Cookies, 166
Eggnog Bread Pudding with
    Cranberries, 178
Great Gramma's Steamed
    Pudding, 134
Holiday Stromboli, 168
Peachy Cranberry Sauce, 60
Pumpkin Cranberry Cheesecake, 142
Thanksgiving Wontons, 165
Turkey Croquettes with Cranberry
    Salsa, 172

CREAM CHEESE
Cherry Cheese Logs, 86
Cherry Cream Cheese Dessert, 98
Cranberry Salsa with Cream
    Cheese, 18
Creamy Hazelnut Dip, 106
Gingerbread-Pumpkin Cheesecake
    Bars, 74
Gingerbread with Lime Cream Cheese
    Icing, 74
Lovely Lemon Cheesecake, 94
Neapolitan Fudge, 116
Pumpkin Cranberry Cheesecake, 142
Veggie Ranch Tortilla Pinwheels, 96

DESSERTS
(also see Bread Pudding; Cakes &
    Cupcakes; Candies; Cheesecakes;
    Cookies & Bars; Pastries; Pies &
    Tarts; Tortes)
Apple-Pecan Gingerbread Cobbler, 67
Cherry Cream Cheese Dessert, 98
Cinnamon-Spiced Pumpkin Flan, 135
French Noisette Cups, 82
Ginger-Poached Pears, 144
Great Gramma's Steamed
    Pudding, 134
Meringue Shells with Lemon Curd, 44

p. 144

Mint-Chocolate Bombe, 137
Nutella-Stuffed Strawberries, 93
Pumpkin Toffee Trifle, 67
Sweet Potato, Pear and Fig Crisp, 63
Tangerine Chocolate Semifreddo, 140

EGGNOG
Cranberry Eggnog Cake, 51
Cranberry Eggnog Muffins, 175
Eggnog Bread Pudding with
    Cranberries, 178
Eggnog Eclairs, 140

EGGS
Bacon & Eggs Pizza, 22
Baked Egg & Stuffing Cups, 171
Brunch Puff with Sausage
    Gravy, 36
Maryland Deviled Eggs, 12
Shirred Egg Corn Muffins, 27
Stuffing & Sausage Strata, 164
Western Omelet Casserole, 23

FIGS
Candied Bacon-Wrapped Figs, 92
Sweet Potato, Pear and Fig Crisp, 63

FISH *(also see Seafood)*
Seafood-Stuffed Salmon Fillets, 92
Teriyaki Salmon Bundles, 19

FRUIT *(also see specific kinds)*
Blueberry Lime Slush, 24
Brie Appetizers with Bacon-Plum
    Jam, 17
Hot Spiced Fruit, 24
Mango Gelatin Salad, 56
Nutella-Stuffed Strawberries, 93
Peachy Cranberry Sauce, 60
Tangerine Chocolate Semifreddo, 140

GARLIC
Onion & Garlic Rolls, 42
Roasted Broccoli & Cauliflower, 41

GINGER
Apple Crumb Tart with Cinnamon
    Cream, 68
Apple-Pecan Gingerbread Cobbler, 67
Chocolate Ginger Cake, 132
Chocolate-Ginger Pumpkin
    Muffins, 68
Chocolate Gingerbread Cupcakes, 69
Cranberry-Gingerbread Scones, 71
Ginger & Maple Macadamia Nut
    Cookies, 150

p. 93

Ginger-Poached Pears, 144
Gingerbread Belgian Waffles, 75
Gingerbread Coffee Cake, 66
Gingerbread Cookie Bites, 72
Gingerbread Peppermint
    Pinwheels, 73
Gingerbread-Pumpkin Cheesecake
    Bars, 74
Gingerbread with Lime Cream Cheese
    Icing, 74
Holiday Ginger Cookies, 71
Pumpkin Bread with Gingerbread
    Topping, 76
Pumpkin Toffee Trifle, 67
Tangy Apple-Ginger Chutney, 50
Winter Spice Bundt Cake, 75

GROUND BEEF
Chili with Barley, 99
Cocktail Mushroom Meatballs, 10
Meatball & Pasta Soup, 85

HAM
Apple-Topped Ham Steak, 101
Brown Sugar Pineapple Ham, 59
Brunch Puff with Sausage Gravy, 36
Fiesta Ham Soup, 162
Meat Lover's Bread Salad, 173
Monte Cristo Casserole with
    Raspberry Sauce, 177
Western Omelet Casserole, 23

HERBS
Lemon-Basil Roasted Potatoes, 93
Parmesan-Herb Dinner Rolls, 50
Prime Rib with Fresh Herb Sauce, 59
Roasted Cheddar Herb Almonds, 7
Tuscan Chicken Tenders with Pesto
    Sauce, 13

ICE CREAM
Chocolate & Peppermint Ice Cream
    Roll, 139
Limoncello Cream Pie, 134
Mint-Chocolate Bombe, 137

LEMON
Festive Holiday Punch, 88
Lemon-Basil Roasted Potatoes, 93
Limoncello Cream Pie, 134
Lovely Lemon Cheesecake, 94
Meringue Shells with Lemon Curd, 44

LIME
Blueberry Lime Slush, 24
Gingerbread with Lime Cream Cheese
    Icing, 74
Lime Shortbread with Dried
    Cherries, 153

MAIN DISHES
Apple-Topped Ham Steak, 101
Bacon & Eggs Pizza, 22
Bacon Swiss Squares, 109
Beef Tenderloin with Mushroom
    Sauce, 97
Beef Tenderloin with Sauteed
    Vegetables, 91
Brown Sugar Pineapple Ham, 59
Caramelized Pork Tenderloin, 110
Carolina Shrimp & Cheddar Grits, 34
Confetti Pasta, 109
Fettuccine Shrimp Casserole, 60
Gobbler Cakes, 165
Holiday Crown Pork Roast, 47
Holiday Rum Balls, 102
Lobster alla Diavola, 41
Monte Cristo Casserole with
    Raspberry Sauce, 177
Orange Roasted Turkey, 61

Potluck Sausage Casserole, 85
Prime Rib with Fresh Herb Sauce, 59
Roast Chicken with Vegetables, 53
Sausage Mac & Cheese in a
    Pumpkin, 29
Seafood-Stuffed Salmon Fillets, 92
Spinach & Turkey Turnovers, 168
Thanksgiving Stuffed Shells, 175
Turkey-Stuffed Acorn Squash, 170

MAPLE
Ginger & Maple Macadamia Nut
    Cookies, 150
Maple-Pecan Cream Pie, 132
Roasted Apple Salad with Spicy
    Maple-Cider Vinaigrette, 48

MARSHMALLOWS
Fluffy Pumpkin Pie, 104
Peanut Butter Spread, 151
S'mores Candy, 155
Sweet Potato Tartlets, 102

MEATBALLS
Cocktail Mushroom Meatballs, 10
Meatball & Pasta Soup, 85

MINT
Chocolate & Peppermint Ice Cream
    Roll, 139
Gingerbread Peppermint
    Pinwheels, 73
Holly Butter Mints, 123
Homemade Candy Canes, 157
Mint-Chocolate Bombe, 137
Mint Cocoa Mix, 153
Mint Creme Cookies, 81
Peppermint Candy Cookies, 116
Soft Peppermint Candy, 157

MIXES
Mint Cocoa Mix, 153
Winter Herb Tea Mix, 150

MUSHROOMS
Beef Tenderloin with Mushroom
    Sauce, 97
Cocktail Mushroom Meatballs, 10
Sherried Mushroom Baked
    Potatoes, 49
Shrimp-Stuffed Mushrooms, 9

NUTS & PEANUT BUTTER
Apple-Pecan Gingerbread Cobbler, 67
Caramel-Pecan Pumpkin
    Pull-Aparts, 25

Cherry Cheese Logs, 86
Chili Spiced Pecans, 149
Chocolate, Peanut & Pretzel Toffee
    Crisps, 88
Cranberry & Walnut Pie, 64
Cranberry-Nut Granola, 159
Creamy Hazelnut Dip, 106
Favorite Hazelnut-Mocha Torte, 130
Festive Nut Cake, 145
French Noisette Cups, 82
Ginger & Maple Macadamia Nut
    Cookies, 150
Maple-Pecan Cream Pie, 132
Nutella-Stuffed Strawberries, 93
Peanut Butter Spread, 151
Peanutty Candy Bars, 158
Pecan Bacon, 28
Raspberry-Almond Coffee Cake, 83
Roasted Cheddar Herb Almonds, 7
Sugar Doves, 121
Sweet Almond Twists, 81
Walnut Butter Spread, 28
White Chocolate Macadamia Bread
    Pudding, 146

OATS & GRANOLA
Coconut Granola Parfaits, 35
Cranberry-Nut Granola, 159
Day-After-Thanksgiving Cookies, 166
Peanutty Candy Bars, 158
Pumpkin Spice Overnight
    Oatmeal, 30
Sweet Potato, Pear and Fig Crisp, 63

ONIONS
Baked Onion Cheese Dip, 106
Onion & Garlic Rolls, 42

ORANGE
Cranberry Orange Mimosas, 37
Cranberry-Orange Sangria, 106
Cranberry Scones with Orange
    Butter, 35
Orange and Beet Salad, 62
Orange Ricotta Pancakes, 110
Orange Roasted Turkey, 61

PASTA & NOODLES
Confetti Pasta, 109
Fettuccine Shrimp Casserole, 60
Lobster alla Diavola, 41
Meatball & Pasta Soup, 85
Potluck Sausage Casserole, 85
Sausage Mac & Cheese in a
    Pumpkin, 29
Thanksgiving Stuffed Shells, 175

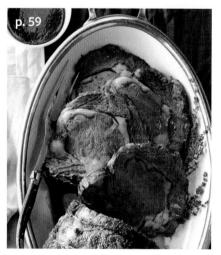

p. 59

p. 48

PASTRIES
Eggnog Eclairs, 140
Puffed Apple Pastries, 103
Quick Cherry Turnovers, 101
Sweet Almond Twists, 81

PEARS
Ginger-Poached Pears, 144
Sweet Potato, Pear and Fig Crisp, 63

PEPPERONI & SALAMI
Meat Lover's Bread Salad, 173
Zesty Pepperoni Dip, 10

PEPPERS
Confetti Pasta, 109
Seven-Layer Mediterranean Dip, 17

PIES & TARTS
Apple Crumb Tart with Cinnamon
    Cream, 68
Browned Butter Apple Pie with
    Cheddar Crust, 131
Chocolate Coconut Pie with Coconut
    Crust, 137
Cranberry & Walnut Pie, 64
Fluffy Pumpkin Pie, 104
Fudgy Turtle Pie, 79
Limoncello Cream Pie, 134
Maple-Pecan Cream Pie, 132

PINEAPPLE
Brown Sugar Pineapple Ham, 59
Pineapple Upside-Down Muffins, 31

PORK
(also see Bacon; Ham; Pepperoni &
    Salami; Sausage)
Caramelized Pork Tenderloin, 110
Holiday Crown Pork Roast, 47

POTATOES
(also see Sweet Potatoes)
Cream of Butternut Squash
    Soup, 47
Creamy Mashed Potatoes with
    Cabbage, 60
Creamy Microwave Scalloped
    Potatoes, 96
Crispy Mashed Potato Cakes, 166
Favorite Loaded Breakfast
    Potatoes, 23
Fiesta Ham Soup, 162
Holiday Stromboli, 168
Lemon-Basil Roasted Potatoes, 93
Potato Bacon Chowder, 105
Sherried Mushroom Baked
    Potatoes, 49
Western Omelet Casserole, 23

PRETZELS
Beer and Pretzel Caramels, 154
Chocolate, Peanut & Pretzel Toffee
    Crisps, 88
Rudolph Treats, 126
Sweet & Salty Snowmen, 119

PUMPKIN
Caramel-Pecan Pumpkin
    Pull-Aparts, 25
Chocolate-Ginger Pumpkin
    Muffins, 68
Cinnamon-Spiced Pumpkin Flan, 135
Day-After-Thanksgiving Cookies, 166
Fluffy Pumpkin Pie, 104
Gingerbread-Pumpkin Cheesecake
    Bars, 74
Pumpkin Bread with Gingerbread
    Topping, 76
Pumpkin Cranberry Cheesecake, 142
Pumpkin Crepes with Mascarpone
    Custard, 27
Pumpkin Spice Overnight
    Oatmeal, 30
Pumpkin Toffee Trifle, 67

RASPBERRIES
Chocolate Chunk Pancakes with
    Raspberry Sauce, 32
Festive Holiday Punch, 88
Monte Cristo Casserole with
    Raspberry Sauce, 177
Neapolitan Fudge, 116
Raspberry-Almond Coffee Cake, 83
Special Raspberry Torte, 145
Sweetheart Coconut Cookies, 122
Tiny Bubbles, 36

ROLLS & MUFFINS
Chocolate-Ginger Pumpkin
    Muffins, 68
Cranberry Eggnog Muffins, 175
Onion & Garlic Rolls, 42
Parmesan-Herb Dinner Rolls, 50
Pineapple Upside-Down Muffins, 31
Shirred Egg Corn Muffins, 27

SALADS
Crisp Waldorf Salad, 98
Hot Spiced Fruit, 24
Jeweled Endive Salad, 43
Mango Gelatin Salad, 56
Meat Lover's Bread Salad, 173
Orange and Beet Salad, 62
Roasted Apple Salad with Spicy
    Maple-Cider Vinaigrette, 48
Romaine & Cherry Tomato Salad, 86
Tequila Vinaigrette with Greens, 91

SANDWICHES
Holiday Hot Browns, 112
Holiday Stromboli, 168

SAUSAGE
(also see Pepperoni & Salami;
    Turkey & Turkey Sausage)
Brunch Puff with Sausage Gravy, 36
Cocktail Mushroom Meatballs, 10
Holiday Chicken and Sausage
    Wreath, 8
Potluck Sausage Casserole, 85
Sausage Mac & Cheese in a
    Pumpkin, 29
Skillet Sausage Stuffing, 103
Sweet Potato & Andouille Hash, 34

p. 42

p. 41

SEAFOOD
Carolina Shrimp & Cheddar Grits, 34
Confetti Pasta, 109
Crab Crescent Triangles, 6
Fettuccine Shrimp Casserole, 60
Lobster alla Diavola, 41
Pacific Northwest Pickled Shrimp, 15
Seafood-Stuffed Salmon Fillets, 92
Shrimp-Stuffed Mushrooms, 9

SIDE DISHES
Creamy Mashed Potatoes with
    Cabbage, 60
Creamy Microwave Scalloped
    Potatoes, 96
Crispy Mashed Potato Cakes, 166
Hungarian-Style Green Beans, 53
Lemon-Basil Roasted Potatoes, 93
Microwave Corn 'n' Bean Bake, 96
Roasted Broccoli & Cauliflower, 41
Sherried Mushroom Baked
    Potatoes, 49
Skillet Sausage Stuffing, 103
Turkey-Stuffed Acorn Squash, 170

SLOW COOKER RECIPES
Bacon-Ranch Spinach Dip, 15
Carolina Shrimp & Cheddar Grits, 34
Pumpkin Spice Overnight Oatmeal, 30
Western Omelet Casserole, 23

SOUPS & CHILI
Chili with Barley, 99
Cream of Butternut Squash Soup, 47
Fiesta Ham Soup, 162
Greens and Beans Turkey Soup, 171
Meatball & Pasta Soup, 85
Potato Bacon Chowder, 105

SPICES
Carrot-Cranberry Spice Cake, 167
Chili Spiced Pecans, 149
Chocolate Chai Snickerdoodles, 153
Glazed Spiced Rum Pound Cakes, 133
Pumpkin Spice Overnight Oatmeal, 30
Winter Spice Bundt Cake, 75

SPINACH
Bacon-Ranch Spinach Dip, 15
Greens and Beans Turkey Soup, 171
Seasoned Spinach Balls, 20
Spinach & Turkey Turnovers, 168

STUFFING
Baked Egg & Stuffing Cups, 171
Gobbler Cakes, 165
Holiday Stromboli, 168
Skillet Sausage Stuffing, 103
Stuffing & Sausage Strata, 164
Thanksgiving Stuffed Shells, 175
Turkey-Stuffed Acorn Squash, 170

SWEET POTATOES
Sweet Potato & Andouille Hash, 34
Sweet Potato Dumplings with Caramel
    Sauce, 176
Sweet Potato, Pear and Fig Crisp, 63
Sweet Potato Tartlets, 102
Turkey Croquettes with Cranberry
    Salsa, 172

TEA
Caramel-Chai Tea Latte, 83
Winter Herb Tea Mix, 150

TOFFEE
Chocolate, Peanut & Pretzel Toffee
    Crisps, 88
Pumpkin Toffee Trifle, 67

TOMATOES
Holiday Hot Browns, 114
Romaine & Cherry Tomato Salad, 86
Tomato-Bacon Dip with Focaccia, 55

TORTES
Chocolate Lover's Mousse Torte, 143
Favorite Hazelnut-Mocha Torte, 130
Special Raspberry Torte, 144

TURKEY & TURKEY
SAUSAGE
After-Christmas Empanadas, 163
Gobbler Cakes, 165
Greens and Beans Turkey Soup, 171
Holiday Hot Browns, 113
Holiday Stromboli, 168
Meat Lover's Bread Salad, 173
Monte Cristo Casserole with
    Raspberry Sauce, 177
Orange Roasted Turkey, 61
Spinach & Turkey Turnovers, 168
Stuffing & Sausage Strata, 164
Thanksgiving Stuffed Shells, 175
Thanksgiving Wontons, 165
Turkey Croquettes with Cranberry
    Salsa, 172
Turkey Nacho Dip, 177
Turkey-Stuffed Acorn Squash, 170

VEGETABLES
(also see specific kinds)
Beef Tenderloin with Sauteed
    Vegetables, 91
Broccoli-Carrot Vegetable Dip, 12
Jeweled Endive Salad, 43
Microwave Corn 'n' Bean Bake, 96
Orange and Beet Salad, 62
Roast Chicken with Vegetables, 53
Roasted Broccoli & Cauliflower, 41
Romaine & Cherry Tomato Salad, 86
Turkey-Stuffed Acorn Squash, 170
Veggie Ranch Tortilla Pinwheels, 96

WHITE CHOCOLATE
Neapolitan Fudge, 116
Sweet & Salty Snowmen, 119
White Chocolate Macadamia Bread
    Pudding, 146

p. 119

Alphabetical Recipe Index

This index lists every recipe in the book in alphabetical order. Just search for the recipe titles you want to easily find your favorites.

A

After-Christmas Empanadas, 163
Apple Crumb Tart with Cinnamon Cream, 68
Apple-Pecan Gingerbread Cobbler, 67
Apple-Topped Ham Steak, 101
Avocado Goat Cheese Truffles, 14

B

Bacon & Eggs Pizza, 22
Bacon, Cheddar and Swiss Cheese Ball, 11
Bacon-Ranch Spinach Dip, 15
Bacon Swiss Squares, 109
Baked Egg & Stuffing Cups, 171
Baked Onion Cheese Dip, 106
Bananas Foster French Toast, 38
Beary Cute Cookies, 124
Beef Tenderloin with Mushroom Sauce, 97
Beef Tenderloin with Sauteed Vegetables, 91
Beer and Pretzel Caramels, 154
Blueberry Lime Slush, 24
Brandied Blue Cheese Spread, 18
Brie Appetizers with Bacon-Plum Jam, 17
Broccoli-Carrot Vegetable Dip, 12
Brown Sugar Pineapple Ham, 59
Browned Butter Apple Pie with Cheddar Crust, 131
Brunch Puff with Sausage Gravy, 36
Buffalo Chicken Cheese Ball, 7
Buffalo Wing Munch Mix, 156
Bugle Cones, 128
Butternut Apple Casserole, 63

C

Candied Bacon-Wrapped Figs, 92
Caramel-Chai Tea Latte, 83
Caramel-Pecan Pumpkin Pull-Aparts, 25
Caramelized Pork Tenderloin, 110
Carolina Shrimp & Cheddar Grits, 34
Carrot Cake Jam, 160
Carrot-Cranberry Spice Cake, 167
Cherrimisu, 138
Cherry Cheese Logs, 86
Cherry Cream Cheese Dessert, 98
Cherry Mice, 114
Chili Spiced Pecans, 149
Chili with Barley, 99
Chocolate & Peppermint Ice Cream Roll, 139
Chocolate Chai Snickerdoodles, 153
Chocolate Chunk Pancakes with Raspberry Sauce, 32
Chocolate Coconut Pie with Coconut Crust, 137
Chocolate Ginger Cake, 132
Chocolate-Ginger Pumpkin Muffins, 68
Chocolate Gingerbread Cupcakes, 69
Chocolate Lover's Mousse Torte, 143
Chocolate, Peanut & Pretzel Toffee Crisps, 88
Chocolate Reindeer, 115
Cinnamon Candy Cane Cookies, 120
Cinnamon-Spiced Pumpkin Flan, 135
Cinnamon-Sugar Spread, 37
Cocktail Mushroom Meatballs, 10
Coconut Granola Parfaits, 35
Coconut-Layered Pound Cake, 99
Coconut Yule Trees, 125
Comforting Coffee Milk, 79
Confetti Pasta, 109
Crab Crescent Triangles, 6
Cranberry & Walnut Pie, 64
Cranberry Bacon Galette, 12
Cranberry-Banana Smoothies, 163
Cranberry Eggnog Cake, 51
Cranberry Eggnog Muffins, 175
Cranberry-Gingerbread Scones, 71
Cranberry-Nut Granola, 159
Cranberry Orange Mimosas, 37
Cranberry-Orange Sangria, 106
Cranberry Salsa with Cream Cheese, 18
Cranberry Scones with Orange Butter, 35
Cream of Butternut Squash Soup, 47
Creamy Hazelnut Dip, 106
Creamy Mashed Potatoes with Cabbage, 60
Creamy Microwave Scalloped Potatoes, 96
Crisp Button Cookies, 115
Crisp Waldorf Salad, 98
Crispy Mashed Potato Cakes, 166

D

Day-After-Thanksgiving Cookies, 166

E

Eggnog Bread Pudding with Cranberries, 178
Eggnog Eclairs, 140
Elf Cookies, 122

F

Favorite Hazelnut-Mocha Torte, 130
Favorite Loaded Breakfast Potatoes, 23
Feather-Light Biscuits, 111
Festive Holiday Punch, 88
Festive Nut Cake, 145
Fettuccine Shrimp Casserole, 60
Fiesta Ham Soup, 162
Fluffy Pumpkin Pie, 104
French Noisette Cups, 82
Frothy Cafe Bombon, 80
Fudge-Filled Vanilla Cake, 56
Fudgy Turtle Pie, 79

G

Ginger & Maple Macadamia Nut Cookies, 150
Ginger-Poached Pears, 144
Gingerbread Belgian Waffles, 75
Gingerbread Coffee Cake, 66
Gingerbread Cookie Bites, 72
Gingerbread Peppermint Pinwheels, 73
Gingerbread-Pumpkin Cheesecake Bars, 74
Gingerbread with Lime Cream Cheese Icing, 74
Glazed Spiced Rum Pound Cakes, 133
Gobbler Cakes, 165
Great Gramma's Steamed Pudding, 134
Greens and Beans Turkey Soup, 171

H

Holiday Chicken and Sausage Wreath, 8
Holiday Crown Pork Roast, 47
Holiday Ginger Cookies, 71

Holiday Hot Browns, 112
Holiday Rum Balls, 102
Holiday Stromboli, 168
Holly Butter Mints, 123
Homemade Candy Canes, 157
Homemade Crisp Crackers, 159
Hot Apple Pie Sipper, 105
Hot Spiced Fruit, 24
Hungarian-Style Green Beans, 53

J
Jeweled Endive Salad, 43

L
Lemon-Basil Roasted Potatoes, 93
Lime Shortbread with Dried
    Cherries, 153
Limoncello Cream Pie, 134
Lobster alla Diavola, 41
Lovely Lemon Cheesecake, 94

M
Mango Gelatin Salad, 56
Maple-Pecan Cream Pie, 132
Maryland Deviled Eggs, 12
Meat Lover's Bread Salad, 173
Meatball & Pasta Soup, 85
Melting Snowmen, 126
Meringue Santa Hats, 117
Meringue Shells with Lemon Curd, 44
Microwave Corn 'n' Bean Bake, 96
Mint-Chocolate Bombe, 137
Mint Cocoa Mix, 153
Mint Creme Cookies, 81
Mocha Cookie Pretzels, 148
Monkey Bread Biscuits, 87
Monte Cristo Casserole with
    Raspberry Sauce, 177

N
Neapolitan Fudge, 116
Nutella-Stuffed Strawberries, 93

O
Onion & Garlic Rolls, 42
Orange and Beet Salad, 62
Orange Ricotta Pancakes, 110
Orange Roasted Turkey, 61

P
Pacific Northwest Pickled Shrimp, 15
Parmesan-Herb Dinner Rolls, 50
Peachy Cranberry Sauce, 60
Peanut Butter Spread, 151
Peanutty Candy Bars, 158
Pecan Bacon, 28

Peppermint Candy Cookies, 116
Pineapple Upside-Down Muffins, 31
Pinwheels and Checkerboards, 119
Potato Bacon Chowder, 105
Potluck Sausage Casserole, 85
Prime Rib with Fresh Herb Sauce, 59
Puffed Apple Pastries, 103
Pumpkin Bread with Gingerbread
    Topping, 76
Pumpkin Cranberry Cheesecake, 142
Pumpkin Crepes with Mascarpone
    Custard, 27
Pumpkin Spice Overnight Oatmeal, 30
Pumpkin Toffee Trifle, 67

Q
Quick Cherry Turnovers, 101

R
Raspberry-Almond Coffee Cake, 83
Reuben Rounds, 20
Roast Chicken with Vegetables, 53
Roasted Apple Salad with Spicy
    Maple-Cider Vinaigrette, 48
Roasted Broccoli & Cauliflower, 41
Roasted Butternut Squash Bread, 32
Roasted Cheddar Herb Almonds, 7
Romaine & Cherry Tomato Salad, 86
Rudolph Treats, 126

S
Santa Claus Sugar Cookies, 120
Sausage Mac & Cheese in a
    Pumpkin, 29
Seafood-Stuffed Salmon Fillets, 92
Seasoned Spinach Balls, 20
Seven-Layer Mediterranean Dip, 17
Sherried Mushroom Baked
    Potatoes, 49
Shirred Egg Corn Muffins, 27
Shrimp-Stuffed Mushrooms, 9
Skillet Sausage Stuffing, 103
S'mores Candy, 155
Soft Peppermint Candy, 157
Sparkling Celebration Punch, 44
Special Raspberry Torte, 144
Spinach & Turkey Turnovers, 168
Stuffing & Sausage Strata, 164
Sugar Doves, 121
Sweet Almond Twists, 81
Sweet & Moist Corn Bread, 54
Sweet & Salty Popcorn, 149
Sweet & Salty Snowmen, 119
Sweet Potato & Andouille Hash, 34
Sweet Potato Dumplings with Caramel
    Sauce, 176

p. 85

Sweet Potato, Pear and Fig Crisp, 63
Sweet Potato Tartlets, 102
Sweetheart Coconut Cookies, 122

T
Tangerine Chocolate Semifreddo, 140
Tangy Apple-Ginger Chutney, 50
Tequila Vinaigrette with Greens, 91
Teriyaki Salmon Bundles, 19
Texas-Style BBQ Sauce, 151
Thanksgiving Stuffed Shells, 175
Thanksgiving Wontons, 165
Tiny Bubbles, 36
Tomato-Bacon Dip with Focaccia, 55
Turkey Croquettes with Cranberry
    Salsa, 172
Turkey Nacho Dip, 177
Turkey-Stuffed Acorn Squash, 170
Tuscan Chicken Tenders with Pesto
    Sauce, 13

V
Veggie Ranch Tortilla Pinwheels, 96

W
Walnut Butter Spread, 28
Western Omelet Casserole, 23
White Chocolate Macadamia Bread
    Pudding, 146
Winter Herb Tea Mix, 150
Winter Spice Bundt Cake, 75

Z
Zesty Pepperoni Dip, 10

Craft Index

This index lists every craft project in the book by craft category, technique and/or main materials, so you can easily locate the types of projects you want.

APPLIQUE
Simple Stocking Pillowcase, 194

BATH AND BODY
Raw Sugar Scrub, 227
Roll-Up Fabric Makeup Organizer, 206
Solid Lotion Jars, 227
Solid Perfume Lockets, 217

BEADING
Beaded Sequin Ornaments, 191
Beaded Snowflakes, 226
Chunky Silver Bracelet, 210

CANDLES & CANDLE HOLDERS
Gold Leaf Glass Vases, 190
Mercury Glass Candle Holders, 187
Musical Candles, 201
Nutshell Candles, 47

CLAY
Gingerbread House Recipe Box, 229
Starry Swirl Bowl, 189

CROCHETING
Baby Stocking Ornaments, 193
Crocheted Toy Balls, 208
Granny Circle Ornaments, 193

EMBROIDERY
Quick Embroidered Ornaments, 199

FABRIC
Burlap Ribbon Wreath, 188
Catnip Mouse Toy, 225
Cozy Sweater Stocking, 185
Hunter's Star Quilt, 197
Pincushion & Notions Jar, 219
Roll-Up Fabric Makeup Organizer, 206
Ruffle Apron, 213
Santa Napkin Holder, 200
Simple Stocking Pillowcase, 194

FASHION & ACCESSORIES
Chunky Basket Weave Cowl, 223

Chunky Silver Bracelet, 210
Ruffle Apron, 213
Silver Chain Earrings, 207
Solid Perfume Lockets, 217

FLORAL/NATURAL CRAFTS
Birdseed Outdoor Ornaments, 216
Magnolia Leaf Wreath, 194
Nutshell Candles, 47
Pinecone Fire Starters, 210

GARLANDS
Holiday Ginger Cookies Garland, 71
Shimmering Paper Party Garland, 94

GENERAL CRAFTS
Button Tree Tags, 215
Cinnamon Applesauce Ornaments, 181
Decoupaged Silhouette Plates, 182
Faux Mosaic Box, 222
Gift-Wrapped Clock, 191
Gift Wrapping Station, 203
Gold Leaf Glass Vases, 190
Holiday Ginger Cookies Garland, 71
Raw Sugar Scrub, 227
Santa Napkin Holder, 200
Solid Lotion Jars, 227
Stamped Metal Pet Tags, 224
Tiered Plate Centerpiece, 204

GIFT PACKAGING
Beaded Snowflakes, 226
Button Tree Tags, 215
DIY Gift Wrap, 211
Faux Mosaic Box, 222
Gift Wrapping Station, 203
Gold Reindeer Trim, 221

GIFTS *(also see Gift Packaging; Greeting Cards)*
Birdseed Outdoor Ornaments, 216
Canning Lid Coasters, 216
Catnip Mouse Toy, 225
Chunky Basket Weave Cowl, 223
Chunky Silver Bracelet, 210

Crocheted Toy Balls, 208
Gingerbread House Recipe Box, 229
Japanese Four-Hole Bound Books, 218
Pincushion & Notions Jar, 219
Pinecone Fire Starters, 210
Raw Sugar Scrub, 227
Roll-Up Fabric Makeup Organizer, 206
Ruffle Apron, 213
Silver Chain Earrings, 207
Solid Lotion Jars, 227
Solid Perfume Lockets, 217
Stamped Metal Pet Tags, 224

GREETING CARDS
Block-Printed Cards, 221
Santa Hat Card, 219

HOME DECOR
Baby Stocking Ornaments, 193
Beaded Sequin Ornaments, 191
Burlap Ribbon Wreath, 188
Canning Lid Coasters, 216
Christmas Stocking Holder, 185
Cinnamon Applesauce Ornaments, 181
Clothespin Card Display, 183
Cozy Sweater Stocking, 185
Decoupaged Silhouette Plates, 182
Gift-Wrapped Clock, 191
Gift Wrapping Station, 203
Gingerbread House Recipe Box, 229
Gold Leaf Glass Vases, 190
Granny Circle Ornaments, 193
Holiday Ginger Cookies Garland, 71
Hunter's Star Quilt, 197

p. 182

p. 195

Magnolia Leaf Wreath, 194
Mercury Glass Candle Holders, 187
Monogrammed Burlap Runner, 180
Musical Candles, 201
Nutshell Candles, 47
Quick Embroidered Ornaments, 199
Retro Paper Ornaments, 87
Santa Napkin Holder, 200
Shimmering Paper Party Garland, 94
Simple Stocking Pillowcase, 194
Snowflake Doormat, 182
Starry Swirl Bowl, 189
Stenciled Peace Sign, 195
Tiered Plate Centerpiece, 204

JEWELRY
Chunky Silver Bracelet, 210
Silver Chain Earrings, 207
Solid Perfume Lockets, 217

KNITTING
Chunky Basket Weave Cowl, 223

PAINTING
Christmas Stocking Holder, 185
Clothespin Card Display, 183
Gingerbread House Recipe Box, 229
Gold Reindeer Trim, 221
Mercury Glass Candle Holders, 187
Snowflake Doormat, 182
Stenciled Peace Sign, 195

PAPER
Block-Printed Cards, 221
DIY Gift Wrap, 211
Japanese Four-Hole Bound Books, 218
Musical Candles, 201
Retro Paper Ornaments, 87
Santa Hat Card, 219
Shimmering Paper Party Garland, 94

PETS/ANIMALS
Birdseed Outdoor Ornaments, 216
Catnip Mouse Toy, 225
Stamped Metal Pet Tags, 224

QUILTING
Hunter's Star Quilt, 197

RECYCLE PROJECTS
Canning Lid Coasters, 216
Cozy Sweater Stocking, 185
Decoupaged Silhouette Plates, 182
Gift Wrapping Station, 203
Pincushion & Notions Jar, 219
Santa Napkin Holder, 200
Tiered Plate Centerpiece, 204

SEWING
Catnip Mouse Toy, 225
Cozy Sweater Stocking, 185
Hunter's Star Quilt, 197
Roll-Up Fabric Makeup Organizer, 206
Ruffle Apron, 213
Santa Napkin Holder, 200
Simple Stocking Pillowcase, 194

STAMPING
Canning Lid Coasters, 216
DIY Gift Wrap, 211

STENCILING
Monogrammed Burlap Runner, 180
Stenciled Peace Sign, 195

TREE ORNAMENTS
Baby Stocking Ornaments, 193
Beaded Sequin Ornaments, 191
Beaded Snowflakes, 226
Birdseed Outdoor Ornaments, 216
Cinnamon Applesauce
    Ornaments, 181
Gold Reindeer Trim, 221
Granny Circle Ornaments, 193
Quick Embroidered Ornaments, 199
Retro Paper Ornaments, 87

WREATHS
Burlap Ribbon Wreath, 188
Magnolia Leaf Wreath, 194

WOOD
Christmas Stocking Holder, 185
Clothespin Card Display, 183
Gift Wrapping Station, 203
Stenciled Peace Sign, 195

p. 216

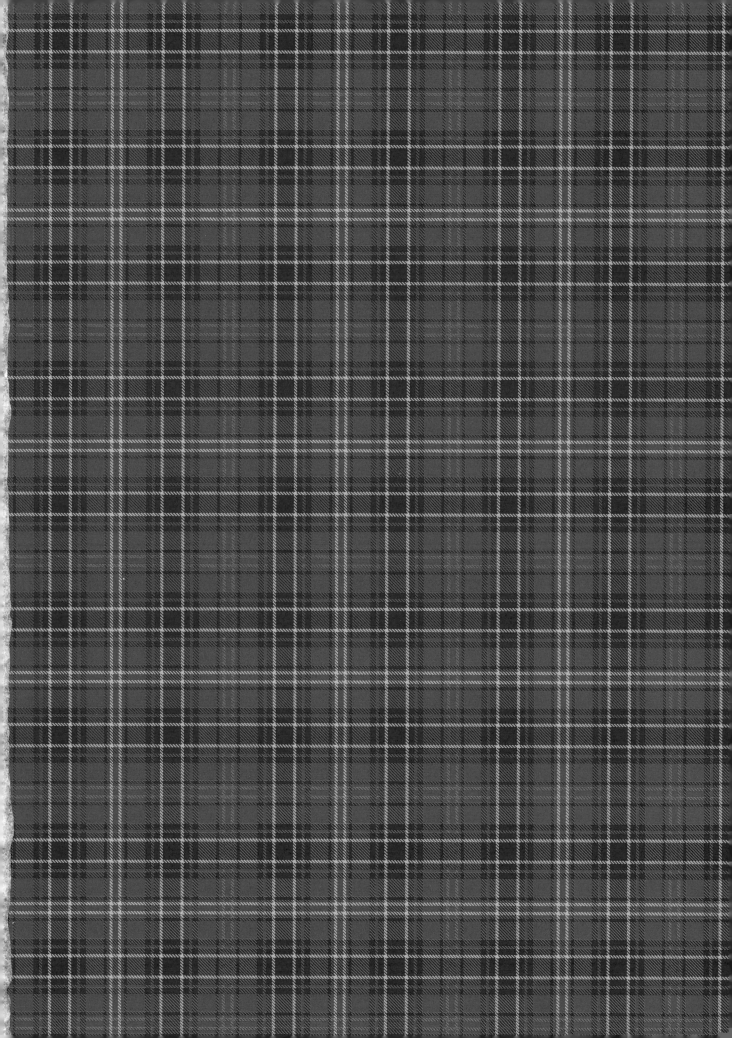